Sara Miller McCune founded SAGE Publishing in 1965 to support the dissemination of usable knowledge and educate a global community. SAGE publishes more than 1000 journals and over 800 new books each year, spanning a wide range of subject areas. Our growing selection of library products includes archives, data, case studies and video. SAGE remains majority owned by our founder and after her lifetime will become owned by a charitable trust that secures the company's continued independence.

Los Angeles | London | New Delhi | Singapore | Washington DC | Melbourne

NQT

WENDY JOLLIFFE & DAVID WAUGH

THE *BEGINNING TEACHER'S GUIDE* TO *OUTSTANDING PRACTICE*

Learning Matters
An imprint of SAGE Publications Ltd
1 Oliver's Yard
55 City Road
London EC1Y 1SP

SAGE Publications Inc.
2455 Teller Road
Thousand Oaks, California 91320

SAGE Publications India Pvt Ltd
B 1/I 1 Mohan Cooperative Industrial Area
Mathura Road
New Delhi 110 044

SAGE Publications Asia-Pacific Pte Ltd
3 Church Street
#10-04 Samsung Hub
Singapore 049483

Editor: Amy Thornton
Production controller: Chris Marke
Project management: Deer Park Productions
Marketing manager: Dilhara Attygalle
Cover design: Wendy Scott
Typeset by: C&M Digitals (P) Ltd, Chennai, India
Printed by CPI Group (UK) Ltd, Croydon, CR0 4YY

Library of Congress Control Number: 2017935030

British Library Cataloguing in Publication Data

A catalogue record for this book is available from the British Library

ISBN 978 1 4739 9912 1 (pbk)
ISBN 978 1 4739 9911 4

At SAGE we take sustainability seriously. Most of our products are printed in the UK using FSC papers and boards. When we print overseas we ensure sustainable papers are used as measured by the PREPS grading system. We undertake an annual audit to monitor our sustainability.

CONTENTS

Contents

ACKNOWLEDGEMENTS

We are grateful to all the teachers and trainee teachers and the organisations who shared case studies and gave us permission to use them.

ABOUT THE EDITORS AND CONTRIBUTORS

Wendy Jolliffe is Professor of Education and was, until recently, Head of Teacher Education at the University of Hull. She has worked as a Regional Adviser for ITT for the National Strategies and advised ITT providers on effective provision for literacy. Wendy is a former deputy head teacher in a primary school in Hull and she has published extensively on teaching English and implementing Cooperative Learning.

David Waugh is subject leader for Primary English at Durham University. He has published extensively in primary English. David is a former deputy head teacher, was Head of the Education Department at the University of Hull, and was Regional Adviser for ITT for the National Strategies from 2008 to 2010. He has written and co-written or edited more than 40 books on primary education. As well as his educational writing, David also writes children's stories and regularly teaches in schools. His most recent novel, *The Wishroom*, was written with 42 children from 16 East Durham Schools.

John Bennett is a lecturer in education at the University of Hull. His main roles are in primary initial teacher education, particularly providing primary English teaching courses for postgraduate and undergraduate trainees. He previously spent twenty-five years working in schools, as a teacher and an advisory teacher, culminating in twelve years as a primary head teacher.

Wendy Delf's experience includes leadership roles in secondary education, working as a senior adviser for Cornwall LA and as an Ofsted inspector. She currently leads on an NQT induction programme for a large Cornish college, oversees primary assessment for her LA, and works extensively with teachers and leaders across the UK as an education trainer and consultant.

Jonathan Doherty lectured in PE at Leeds Met Carnegie for thirteen years before joining the National Strategies as Regional Adviser. He was then co-director of an educational consultancy business and a School Improvement Adviser. Following senior leadership at Manchester Met and Leeds Trinity, he is heavily involved in ITE and CPD work with teachers.

Claire Head is the Associate Principal for the Scarborough Campus, University of Hull. Her main role as a lecturer is in teaching early years and primary English across postgraduate and undergraduate teaching courses. Claire also supports recruitment, development, CPD and teaching activities in the local Teaching School Alliance. Claire is a licensed Talk Boost and Primary Talk trainer and works with students and local teachers to raise awareness of the importance of supporting children's speech, language and communication needs.

Paul Hopkins is a lecturer in education at the University of Hull. He works with teacher trainees and research students in both primary and secondary education, and with both undergraduates and postgraduates. His main areas of research are technology-enhanced learning, where he works nationally and internationally, and evidence-based practice. He has previously worked in all phases of education.

Julia Lawrence is Head of the Teacher Education group at the University of Hull. She specialises in teacher education, professional development and physical education. Julia has also worked in teacher education at Leeds Metropolitan and Brunel Universities. Prior to starting her work within the university sector, Julia taught Physical Education and Science in secondary schools.

Alison McManus is a Teaching Fellow in the Foundation Centre as well as in the School of Education at Durham University. After completing a degree in Psychology, Alison trained as an EFL teacher and worked in a range of contexts before undertaking two further MA degrees, one in Gender Studies and the other in Creative Writing; later, she completed a PhD in English Literature with Creative Writing. She has taught a wide range of subjects to both children and adults. Currently, she teaches both English Literature and Academic Writing to mature learners re-entering higher education, while also leading a Family Learning project in local primary schools.

Hilary Smith is a Programme Leader for the Primary and Early Years PGCE at Bath Spa University. Her teaching career spans more than thirty years, much of this time as a classroom teacher in primary schools and early years settings, and as a behaviour consultant for Bristol Local Authority. She has particular expertise in behaviour and children's social, emotional and mental health. She is a recognised national school leader in behaviour and attendance (NPSLBA) and has a special interest in emotional well-being and resilience, attachment awareness and emotion coaching.

Kamil Trzebiatowski is an EAL Coordinator at a secondary school in Kingston-upon-Hull. He is a frequent EAL trainer and presenter at conferences and teacher events, and has been involved with several universities to train PGCE students. In 2016, he served as a director for Kingston-upon-Hull's first EAL Conference, and organised PedagooHull, a free sharing practice conference for teachers at the University of Hull. He is an associate trainer with EAL Academy, a member of National Association of Language Development in the Curriculum's (NALDIC) executive committee, and one of the Associate Editors of NALDIC's brand-new *EAL Journal*.

Yasmin Valli is a Principal Lecturer and Senior Fellow of HEA at Leeds Beckett University. Based in the Carnegie School of Education and Childhood, she has responsibility for newly qualified teachers (NQTs), CPD and Employability. Her main roles are in initial teacher education, across all phases and widening participation. She is also involved in the MA programme and in-service training courses in the field of Educational and Professional Development. Prior to this she was course leader for the Primary PGCE and OFSTED inspector for the primary and independent sector.

ABOUT THIS BOOK

WENDY JOLLIFFE AND DAVID WAUGH

About this Book

This book focuses on the development of teachers in their early careers, but it may also be helpful for those undertaking their initial teacher training. We have included the Teachers' Standards in full for easy reference. The authors are expert educators, each with many years of experience in the classroom and in teacher education, who are dedicated to the development of high quality, highly effective classroom practitioners.

Chapters provide pedagogical learning features to enhance your learning.

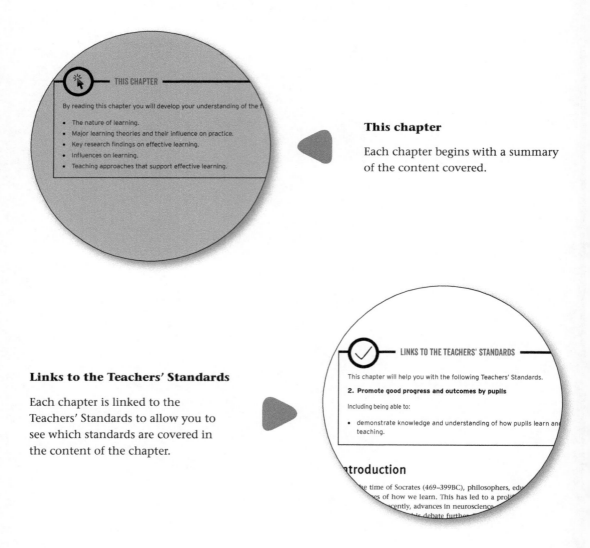

THIS CHAPTER

By reading this chapter you will develop your understanding of the f

- The nature of learning.
- Major learning theories and their influence on practice.
- Key research findings on effective learning.
- Influences on learning.
- Teaching approaches that support effective learning.

This chapter

Each chapter begins with a summary of the content covered.

Links to the Teachers' Standards

Each chapter is linked to the Teachers' Standards to allow you to see which standards are covered in the content of the chapter.

LINKS TO THE TEACHERS' STANDARDS

This chapter will help you with the following Teachers' Standards.

2. Promote good progress and outcomes by pupils

Including being able to:

- demonstrate knowledge and understanding of how pupils learn an teaching.

ntroduction

e time of Socrates (469–399BC), philosophers, edu
es of how we learn. This has led to a proli
cently, advances in neuroscience
tic debate further

RESEARCH/EVIDENCE FOCUS

Learning theories

1. Behaviourism

This theory suggests that humans develop links between their experiences, behaviour. One of the originators of this theory, Edward Thorndike (1874-1949), b incremental and people learn through trial and error. He developed the law of learning ciples. First, the *law of effect* which stated that the *greater the satisfaction or disco strengthening or weakening of the bond* (1911, p244). Second, the *law of readiness* human is in a state of readiness, making a connection will be satisfying and such con tained. Third, the *law of exercise*, which relates to strengthening the connections th frequency of the response. Thorndike's work focused on ways of increasing the occu iours and did not put any emphasis on the role of understanding.

John Watson (1878-1958) was another influential figure in developing the the developed the concept that a change in behaviour results from the conditioning logical process. He believed that humans could be conditioned to react, or fe particular stimulus. His work with a 9-month-old baby is considered today to exposure to a rat, which initially the child showed no fear of, with loud n associate fear and distress with the rat. Watson proposed that huma ional responses to certain animate or inanimate objects and t according to this theory is therefore a consequence of ial figure in the development of the th ng figures of Russian

Research/evidence focus

In all chapters, authors have used this feature to highlight links to relevant research relating to the chapter topic or an exploration of the evidence around the theme.

Questions for reflection and discussion

Throughout the text, the reader is encouraged to actively engage with the learning in chapters by considering questions and scenarios posed to build reflective skills.

around to compensate. He pencil or losing his pen, and then eithe would distract others with noises or off-task ta to complete their work. Miss Evans, his teacher, focused uent praise, but found this had limited effect. She spoke to ening and together they agreed a reward system. Each day the t and efforts to complete work in a report, and in response his parents money to save towards his particular desired goal – a new computer gam

QUESTIONS FOR REFLECTION AND DISCUSSION

1. Consider how effective this strategy might be.
2. Why did the teacher involve parents in this?
3. What are the drawbacks of such rewards for efforts?
4. What other alternatives could the teacher consider?

one-to-one tuition

10. Early years intervention

Classroom focus

Research in your own classroom

This section explores two ways of undertaking implementing some of the practices you have r undertaking research in your own institution o that is taking place via the research schools (se

Practitioner research

As a teacher, you are most likely to w improving your practice and the out you undertake research it wil is that the foc

Classroom focus

In all chapters, content is linked to the classroom and to everyday teaching and learning. These features support you to see how theory translates to your classroom practice.

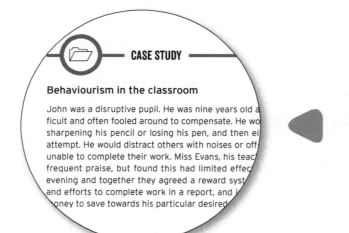

CASE STUDY

Behaviourism in the classroom

John was a disruptive pupil. He was nine years old a
ficult and often fooled around to compensate. He wo
sharpening his pencil or losing his pen, and then ei
attempt. He would distract others with noises or off
unable to complete their work. Miss Evans, his teac
frequent praise, but found this had limited effec
evening and together they agreed a reward syst
and efforts to complete work in a report, and i
oney to save towards his particular desire

Case study

All chapter authors have given examples to illustrate the learning in chapters from classrooms/teachers or through the words of educationalists.

The features are designed to help you navigate the text, to encourage you to consider your own practice in the light of what you have read and to see how your practice links to the Teachers' Standards. Case studies are also included to demonstrate how teachers and trainee teachers have approached a range of challenges.

The chapters also include recommended further reading, to enable you to develop stronger insights into how teachers can become outstanding practitioners.

In Chapter 1, Yasmin Valli looks at the Teachers' Standards and their implications for classroom practice for trainee teachers and NQTs. Yasmin shows how evidence can be provided to show achievement. She goes on to explore continuing professional development and the further study which will support eventual progress into management and leadership roles.

In Chapter 2, Wendy Jolliffe explores key learning theories and their implications for teaching. Findings from recent research, including cognitive neuroscience, demonstrate significant factors in learning, in particular the importance of considering the affective and social dimensions of learning. Wendy focuses on teaching for learning, looking at a range of approaches to support engagement, motivation and inclusion of all children in learning, in particular the use of cooperative learning.

Chapter 3 examines how teachers can have an impact on learning and how planning for learning improves student outcomes. Wendy Delf explains ways in which teachers can best use assessment to support learners, and the importance of effective marking and feedback to support pupil progress.

In Chapter 4, Hilary Smith discusses the challenges newly trained teachers may experience. She looks at the frameworks available to facilitate effective behaviour for learning and to create a positive learning environment. The chapter shows the value of working with colleagues and parents to support positive behaviour and suggests intervention strategies for challenging behaviour.

In Chapter 5, Julia Lawrence shows how the use of video analysis can support teachers to develop as reflective practitioners. Using practical examples, Julia describes how video analysis can be used within the school environment, and the strengths and challenges of using the approach in schools. The chapter emphasises the importance of self-reflection and its value to the developing teacher.

In Chapter 6, Paul Hopkins discusses the development of pedagogical understanding and explores a range of research on teaching and learning. Paul examines the dynamics of 'traditional' and 'progressive' paradigms of education, and looks at how teachers can critically explore the research about teaching and learning. He goes on to suggest ways in which teachers can engage in research in their own classroom as they develop their own practice.

Paul's second chapter describes how new technologies offer a range of opportunities for the new teacher. Chapter 7 explores the way in which technology can support and challenge the new teacher, and how it can be used to create exciting and dynamic resources for teaching and learning. Paul goes on to demonstrate how ongoing professional development can be supported through online communities, and ways in which technology can support assessment and progression.

In Chapter 8, Claire Head examines the impact that speech, language and communication difficulties can have on a child's learning and life skills, and provides examples of effective school-based provision. Claire argues that children need the right environment in order to develop effective communication skills, and to develop their language for thinking, responding and for expressing feelings. She provides further reading and online support that can help teachers access training and guidance throughout their careers.

In Chapter 9, Kamil Trzebiatowski addresses the issue of how mainstream teachers build academic language for English as an Additional Language (EAL) learners by utilising language-appropriate and level-appropriate strategies. Kamil shows how second-language acquisition theories underpin successful strategies, and crucially explains how they can be adapted to meet the needs of individual children.

In Chapter 10, John Bennett looks at an aspect of teaching and learning which has acquired greater significance in the curriculum recently. He explores how new teachers can continue to maintain momentum in developing their knowledge, skills and understanding of aspects of grammar, punctuation and spelling, including approaches to teaching these aspects of the English curriculum. John provides suggestions related to developing personal subject knowledge, teaching activities and methods to support children's effective use of grammar, punctuation and spelling. A key part of the chapter is a focus on understanding the expectations of the end of key stage assessments.

In Chapter 11, Wendy Jolliffe revisits the necessary subject knowledge for teachers to help explain how children learn to read. The chapter discusses the role of phonics in the teaching of reading and emphasises methods of teaching phonics to ensure that this is engaging and interactive. Wendy stresses that teaching phonics alone will not produce good readers – children also need to develop the skills of language comprehension. Early intervention for struggling readers is a key factor and the chapter examines common issues that children may encounter. The chapter will signpost the beginning teacher to appropriate responses to the many challenges teachers face with a summary of a range of intervention programmes.

Chapter 12 focuses on the wider professional responsibilities of teachers. Jonathan Doherty and David Waugh examine what it means to be a 'professional' and show the importance of being proactive in making a positive contribution to the wider life of a school.

About this Book

In Chapter 13, Alison McManus looks at some of the challenges new teachers face. She explores teacher self-efficacy and resilience, and suggests strategies and behaviours teachers can use to combat stress and boost resilience. The chapter focuses on mindfulness and its applications for the classroom as well as for individual teachers.

We hope that you will find this book useful and informative in supporting the beginning of your teaching career.

Wendy Jolliffe
David Waugh
May 2017

THE TEACHERS' STANDARDS

About the standards

These are the Teachers' Standards for use in schools in England from September 2012. The standards define the minimum level of practice expected of trainees and teachers from the point of being awarded qualified teacher status (QTS).

The Teachers' Standards are used to assess all trainees working towards QTS and all those completing their statutory induction period. They are also used to assess the performance of all teachers with QTS who are subject to The Education (School Teachers' Appraisal) (England) Regulations 2012, and may additionally be used to assess the performance of teachers who are subject to these regulations and who hold qualified teacher learning and skills (QTLS) status.

The standards were introduced following the recommendations in the reports of the independent Review of Teachers' Standards, chaired by Sally Coates. These reports are available from GOV.UK.

Preamble

Teachers make the education of their pupils their first concern, and are accountable for achieving the highest possible standards in work and conduct. Teachers act with honesty and integrity; have strong subject knowledge; keep their knowledge and skills as teachers up to date and are self-critical; forge positive professional relationships; and work with parents in the best interests of their pupils.

Part One: Teaching

A teacher must:

1. Set high expectations which inspire, motivate and challenge pupils

- Establish a safe and stimulating environment for pupils, rooted in mutual respect.
- Set goals that stretch and challenge pupils of all backgrounds, abilities and dispositions.
- Demonstrate consistently the positive attitudes, values and behaviour which are expected of pupils.

2. Promote good progress and outcomes by pupils

- Be accountable for pupils' attainment, progress and outcomes.
- Be aware of pupils' capabilities and their prior knowledge, and plan teaching to build on these.
- Guide pupils to reflect on the progress they have made and their emerging needs
- Demonstrate knowledge and understanding of how pupils learn and how this impacts on teaching.
- Encourage pupils to take a responsible and conscientious attitude to their own work and study.

3. Demonstrate good subject and curriculum knowledge

- Have a secure knowledge of the relevant subject(s) and curriculum areas, foster and maintain pupils' interest in the subject, and address misunderstandings.

- Demonstrate a critical understanding of developments in the subject and curriculum areas, and promote the value of scholarship.

- Demonstrate an understanding of and take responsibility for promoting high standards of literacy, articulacy and the correct use of standard English, whatever the teacher's specialist subject.

- If teaching early reading, demonstrate a clear understanding of systematic synthetic phonics.

- If teaching early mathematics, demonstrate a clear understanding of appropriate teaching strategies.

4. Plan and teach well-structured lessons

- Impart knowledge and develop understanding through effective use of lesson time.

- Promote a love of learning and children's intellectual curiosity.

- Set homework and plan other out-of-class activities to consolidate and extend the knowledge and understanding pupils have acquired.

- Reflect systematically on the effectiveness of lessons and approaches to teaching.

- Contribute to the design and provision of an engaging curriculum within the relevant subject area(s).

5. Adapt teaching to respond to the strengths and needs of all pupils

- Know when and how to differentiate appropriately, using approaches which enable pupils to be taught effectively.

- Have a secure understanding of how a range of factors can inhibit pupils' ability to learn, and how best to overcome these.

- Demonstrate an awareness of the physical, social and intellectual development of children, and know how to adapt teaching to support pupils' education at different stages of development.

- Have a clear understanding of the needs of all pupils, including those with special educational needs; those of high ability; those with English as an additional language; those with disabilities; and be able to use and evaluate distinctive teaching approaches to engage and support them.

6. Make accurate and productive use of assessment

- Know and understand how to assess the relevant subject and curriculum areas, including statutory assessment requirements.

- Make use of formative and summative assessment to secure pupils' progress.

- Use relevant data to monitor progress, set targets, and plan subsequent lessons.

- Give pupils regular feedback, both orally and through accurate marking, and encourage pupils to respond to the feedback.

7. Manage behaviour effectively to ensure a good and safe learning environment

- Have clear rules and routines for behaviour in classrooms, and take responsibility for promoting good and courteous behaviour both in classrooms and around the school, in accordance with the school's behaviour policy.

- Have high expectations of behaviour, and establish a framework for discipline with a range of strategies, using praise, sanctions and rewards consistently and fairly.

- Manage classes effectively, using approaches which are appropriate to pupils' needs in order to involve and motivate them.

- Maintain good relationships with pupils, exercise appropriate authority, and act decisively when necessary.

8. Fulfil wider professional responsibilities

- Make a positive contribution to the wider life and ethos of the school.

- Develop effective professional relationships with colleagues, knowing how and when to draw on advice and specialist support.

- Deploy support staff effectively.

- Take responsibility for improving teaching through appropriate professional development, responding to advice and feedback from colleagues.

- Communicate effectively with parents with regard to pupils' achievements and well-being.

Part Two: Personal and Professional Conduct

A teacher is expected to demonstrate consistently high standards of personal and professional conduct. The following statements define the behaviour and attitudes which set the required standard for conduct throughout a teacher's career.

- Teachers uphold public trust in the profession and maintain high standards of ethics and behaviour, within and outside school, by:

  - treating pupils with dignity, building relationships rooted in mutual respect, and at all times observing proper boundaries appropriate to a teacher's professional position

  - having regard for the need to safeguard pupils' well-being, in accordance with statutory provisions

  - showing tolerance of and respect for the rights of others

  - not undermining fundamental British values, including democracy, the rule of law, individual liberty and mutual respect, and tolerance of those with different faiths and beliefs

  - ensuring that personal beliefs are not expressed in ways that exploit pupils' vulnerability or might lead them to break the law.

- Teachers must have proper and professional regard for the ethos, policies and practices of the school in which they teach, and maintain high standards in their own attendance and punctuality.

- Teachers must have an understanding of, and always act within, the statutory frameworks which set out their professional duties and responsibilities.

1
THE TEACHERS' STANDARDS
YASMIN VALLI

THIS CHAPTER

By reading this chapter you will develop your understanding of the following.

- The implementation of the Teachers' Standards and implications for classroom practice for trainees and NQTs.
- Providing evidence against the Teachers' Standards, for trainees and NQTs.
- Continuing professional development and further study.
- Moving into management and leadership roles.

Introduction

Significant changes in education took place after the formation of the new Coalition Government in the UK in May 2010. *The first report of the independent review of teachers' standards: QTS and core standards* (DfE, 2011b) was followed by the publication of the White Paper *The importance of teaching* (DfE, 2010). All teachers completing their training on or after 1 September 2012 should be assessed against the Teachers' Standards. The revised standards, which replaced the former Core Standards, also apply to newly qualified teachers (NQTs). Therefore, these standards apply to teachers at the point of entry to the profession and also to experienced practitioners, providing consistency in the approach taken to judge teacher performance at various levels. These standards offer an overarching platform for the coherent approach to Initial Teacher Education (ITE), induction and continuing professional development (CPD) that the profession aspires to.

The Standards Review Group, who were tasked with formulating the standards, were careful not to place unreasonable expectations on teachers who may have been qualified for a significant period of time, and aimed to reflect the 'timeless' values of teaching (DfE, 2011a, para 3.26).

Mindful of the trust and professionalism of teachers demanded by society, in its preamble the standards state the following.

> *Teachers make the education of their pupils their first concern, and are accountable for achieving the highest possible standards in work and conduct. Teachers act with honesty and integrity; have strong subject knowledge, keep their knowledge and skills as teachers up-to-date and are self-critical; forge positive professional relationships; and work with parents in the best interests of their pupils.*
>
> (DfE, 2012, p7)

Ofsted (2012) considers the extent to which the Teachers' Standards are being met when assessing the quality of teaching in schools. The Education Act 2011 claimed to help teachers raise standards to improve underperformance and strengthen the ways teachers are held accountable for their actions (Department for Education, 2011a, b). There is a clear expectation in both the National Curriculum (DfE, 2013) and in the Teachers' Standards (DfE, 2012) that teachers should have the highest expectations of all learners. This involves setting children challenging ambitious targets that take account of prior assessment.

The Teachers' Standards were intended to raise the bar for effective learning and teaching, and provide a benchmark of the minimum requirement for assessing trainees and teachers. However, the standards also stipulate the expected progress to be demonstrated by teachers relating to the depth and breadth of knowledge required during the various stages of their careers. Informed by the evidence gathered in the Carter Review (DfE, 2015), in July 2016 the DfE produced the Framework of Core Content for initial teacher training (ITT), a document that is applicable to all types of ITT providers (schools and universities), regardless of the nature of their courses and their delivery method. The fundamental aim of the framework of core content is to ensure that ITE programmes enable trainees to meet the Teachers' Standards in full at the level appropriate to the end of a period of initial teacher training (DfE, 2016c, para 1.3).

An introduction to key statements from the Teachers' Standards document

Below are some key statements from the Teachers' Standards document (DfE, 2012) that set out clearly the requirements that are needed from teacher trainees, NQTs and experienced teachers.

The standards apply to the vast majority of teachers regardless of their career stage

The Teachers' Standards apply to: trainees working towards QTS; all teachers completing their statutory induction period; and those covered by the new performance appraisal arrangements (para 3, p2).

The standards need to be applied as appropriate to the role and context within which a trainee or teacher is practising

Providers of initial teacher training (ITT) should assess trainees against the standards in a way that is consistent with what could reasonably be expected of a trainee teacher prior to the award of QTS (para 6, p3).

The standards are presented as separate headings, numbered from 1 to 8 in Part One, each of which is accompanied by a number of bulleted subheadings

The bullets, which are an integral part of the standards, are designed to amplify the scope of each heading.

The bulleted subheadings should not be interpreted as separate standards in their own right, but should be used by those assessing trainees and teachers to track progress against the standard, to determine areas where additional development might need to be observed, or to identify areas where a trainee or teacher is already demonstrating excellent practice relevant to that standard (para 13, p4).

The standards define the minimum level of practice expected of trainees and teachers from the point of being awarded QTS (para 5, p2).

Following the period of induction, the standards continue to define the level of practice at which all qualified teachers are expected to perform (para 9, p3).

The standards have been designed to set out a basic framework within which all teachers should operate from the point of initial qualification. Appropriate self-evaluation, reflection and professional development activity is critical to improving teachers' practice at all career stages. The standards set out clearly the key areas in which a teacher should be able to assess his or her own practice, and receive feedback from colleagues. As their careers progress, teachers will be expected to extend the depth and breadth of knowledge, skill and understanding that they demonstrate in meeting the standards, as is judged to be appropriate to the role they are fulfilling and the context in which they are working (para 14, p4).

The key statements above are geared towards tracking progress against the standards, identifying best practice and areas for further development. Research by Goodwyn (2012) has shown that the standards are complex and interrelated. From a positive perspective, the standards enable teachers to demonstrate their capabilities and values. However, a more negative perspective might focus on performativity and surveillance.

Classroom focus

The implementation of the Teachers' Standards and implications for classroom practice for trainees and NQTs

Published in May 2012, the Teachers' Standards came into effect from September 2012 for all trainees and teachers. Accredited providers of ITE are accountable and responsible for making the professional judgement as to whether each trainee or student has demonstrated the range of skills, knowledge and understanding required to be recommended for Qualified Teacher Status (QTS) at the end of the programme.

Exploring the standards

The table below explores the standards in depth, looking at what each one of them means in a class-room setting for trainees and NQTs, and provides possible evidence.

Continuing professional development (CPD) and further study

Keeping up to date with developments in teaching will require engagement with CPD. However, CPD is more than 'keeping up to date' as it contributes to school improvement, morale, job sat-isfaction and status, and also guides you towards next steps into management and leadership roles. According to Barber and Mourshed (2007), it was very important to get the right teachers into the profession and to develop them as it was the teachers who made the difference to pupils' progress. As reflective practitioners, they recognise what best practice is and identify their develop-mental needs that are informed through the reflection process (p27). Teachers continually evolve. Huberman (1993, 1995) identifies five stages for teacher development: launching one's career, sta-bilising, facing new challenges, 'plateauing', a final phase during which teachers engage in CPD to address developmental needs. A high level of self-awareness is needed from the individual teachers in order for them to make the correct choice of CPD. Field (2011) presents a taxonomy of CPD con-sisting of four forms as dimensions of CPD as follows.

Individual led:	Takes into account observation of good practice and building on existing strengths, it caters for individual needs in line with the stages of develop-ment of individual teachers.
Systems led:	Facilitated by coaching and mentoring, this form of CPD includes a pro-cess of reflection.
Professional led:	This can involve outside agencies and is concerned mainly with improv-ing the learning of pupils in order to drive improvement.
Institutional led:	Concerned with pupil learning outcomes. CPD takes place in collabo-ration between schools and it relies on teamwork, often leading to the sharing of expertise, and values external links to the outside world.

Teachers' Standards – Possible evidence for trainees and NQTs

Teachers' Standards	Possible evidence	Examples
1. Set high expectations which inspire, motivate and challenge pupils • Establish a safe and stimulating environment for pupils, rooted in mutual respect. • Set goals that stretch and challenge pupils of all backgrounds, abilities and dispositions. • Demonstrate consistently the positive attitudes, values and behaviour which are expected of pupils.	**Examples of evidence to demonstrate progress meeting standard** • Lesson plans demonstrate differentiation. • Lesson delivery and outcomes reflect the lesson plan. • In the classroom pupils/students are engaged in lesson, showing curiosity, asking questions, excited about the task. • Objectives are clearly explained to pupils/students and inform teaching the task. • Planning for other adults is in evidence. • Lesson delivery and outcomes reflect the health and safety briefs given to pupils/students at the start of practical lessons. • Appropriate clothing for session – e.g. PE clothing, footwear, aprons – is in evidence. • Pupils/students are able to work in an environment that fosters mutual respect, and are encouraged to support and help each other. • A stimulating environment – examples of display resources and use of other resources – pupils engage with the tasks set. **To meet the standard the NQT may demonstrate:** • Consistently high expectations of pupil attainment and behavior. • An atmosphere which is highly conducive to learning by encouraging pupils to participate and contribute to the learning environment. • High levels of enthusiasm, participation and commitment to learning in their pupils. • They portray high levels of mutual respect between the teacher and the pupils.	**Sources for evidence** • Portfolio of evidence, including scrutiny of lesson plans. • Observation of lessons and feedback record sheet. • Displays and physical environment of classroom. • Observation in the wider school environment – e.g. learning walks. • Professional conversations and interviews with pupils. **Links to other standards** 2, 4, 5, 8: Part 2 personal and professional conduct

Teachers' Standards – Possible evidence for trainees and NQTs

Teachers' Standards	Possible evidence	Examples
	• Show resilience, confidence and independence when tackling challenging activities.	
	• NQT demonstrates the ability to improve a lesson plan when delivering in the classroom to secure better learning outcomes (reflection-in-action).	
	• Tasks set are appropriate for pupils/students – differentiation is evident.	
	• NQT demonstrates an enthusiasm for learning.	
	• Effective use of other adults as part of teaching team – they are well informed of the objectives.	
	• NQT receives consistently positive feedback from induction tutor through observation, one-to-one sessions and in other relevant meetings – targets are achieved with many that exceed expectations.	
2. Promote good progress and outcomes by pupils Scope of standard:	**Examples of evidence to demonstrate progress meeting standard**	**Sources for evidence**
• be accountable for pupils' attainment, progress and outcomes;	• Prior learning is in use and informs lesson planning – recapping of previous work is evident.	• Schemes of work and lesson plans.
• be aware of pupils' capabilities and their prior knowledge, and plan teaching to build on these;	• Different learning styles are applied, including making use of learning outside the classroom to maximise learning opportunities.	• Classroom observations. • Portfolio/assessment file.
• guide pupils to reflect on the progress they have made and their emerging needs;	• The physical arrangement of the classroom is conducive to learning.	• Marking, including sample of student books.
	• Homework is completed in time as per agreed deadlines.	• Lesson observations and induction tutor feedback.
• demonstrate knowledge and understanding of how pupils learn and how this impacts on teaching;	• Sample of students' books are available showing use of marking criteria and targets set for individuals.	**Links to other standards**
	• Promotes behaviour strategies for learning.	4, 5, 6, 7
• encourage pupils to take a responsible and conscientious attitude to their own work and study.	• Pupils engage in peer and self-assessment, and understand the criteria for evaluating their own work and progress.	
	• Success criteria are used effectively – reflect the needs of pupils with SEND and EAL.	
	• Good relationships established with pupils are shown.	

(Continued)

Teachers' Standards	Teachers' Standards – Possible evidence for trainees and NQTs	
	Possible evidence	Examples
	To meet the standard an NQT may demonstrate:	
	• They are informed by data analysis and shows awareness of school's tracking system.	
	• September baseline data are used to inform assessments and target setting for pupils.	
	• They are confident in using the marking system, which makes effective use of feedback with set targets, and the majority of pupils make expected progress.	
	• Pupils are confident to engage in peer and self-assessment in the classroom, and understand the criteria for evaluating their own work and progress.	
	• They use a range of questioning to elicit pupil knowledge and understanding to include all learners and maximise learning opportunities.	
	• They are engaged in research-informed teaching and use theoretical knowledge to support pupils to achieve targets and seek support from more knowledgeable others if insufficient progress is made.	
	• They assume a high level of responsibility for the attainment, progress and outcomes of the pupils they teach, including pupils with SEND and EAL.	
	• Consistently high use of behaviour strategies for learning.	
	• They are willing to take appropriate risks and try new ways to enhance the learning experience – e.g. using ICT or opportunities for outdoor learning.	
	• Pupils show confidence in using self- and peer assessment to support one another in the learning process; they take pride in their work. Effective links with parents inform pupil learning.	
	• They use effective methods that support pupils in reflecting on their learning.	
	• They create opportunities for independent learning.	

Teachers' Standards for trainees and NQTs

Teachers' Standards	Possible evidence	Examples
3. Demonstrate good subject and curriculum knowledge • Have a secure knowledge of the relevant subject(s) and curriculum areas, foster and maintain pupils' interest in the subject, and address misunderstandings. • Demonstrate a critical understanding of developments in the subject and curriculum areas, and promote the value of scholarship. • Demonstrate an understanding of and take responsibility for promoting high standards of literacy, articulacy and the correct use of standard English, whatever the teacher's specialist subject. • If teaching early reading, demonstrate a clear understanding of systematic synthetic phonics. • If teaching early mathematics, demonstrate a clear understanding of appropriate teaching strategies.	• Lesson observations, short- and medium-term planning show secure curriculum and subject knowledge. • Promotes high expectations and stimulates pupil interest in learning. • Addresses misconceptions and sets high expectations of all pupils. • Makes effective use of feedback to enhance learning. • Pupils gain inspiration for learning through the classroom environment. • Updates their own knowledge and understanding of the subject through research, school visits and accessing CPD opportunities. • Takes responsibility to promote high standards of literacy among pupils which can be observed through their effort and attainment. • Oracy and literacy are promoted across the curriculum along with the correct use of standard English. • Takes an active part in phonics training. • For Primary, early reading and mathematics, deploys appropriate teaching strategies, makes appropriate use of equipment and props **To meet the standard the NQT may demonstrate:** • Confidence in subject and curriculum knowledge to plan for progression, and to stimulate and capture pupils' interest. • A critical and very well-developed pedagogical subject knowledge; anticipate common errors and misconceptions in their planning. • Classroom surroundings project a stimulating culture of scholarship shown through displays and learning walls. • They are continuously extending and updating their subject, curriculum and pedagogical knowledge to promote research-informed teaching.	**Sources for evidence** • Lesson plans and classroom. • Observations. • Record of appropriate professional development. **Links to other standards** 1, 2, 4, 6

(Continued)

(Continued)

Teachers' Standards for trainees and NQTs

Teachers' Standards	Possible evidence	Examples
	• Modelling high standards of written and spoken communication in all professional activities to promote articulacy and standard English. • A high learning culture that fosters a strong work ethic and respect for all. • Well-chosen resources contribute significantly to progress in literacy and numeracy. • NQTs display a relentless drive for continuous improvement to gain mastery of subject through CPD opportunities. • NQTs draw on their understanding of synthetic systematic phonics and its role in teaching, and assessing reading and writing to teach literacy very effectively. • Through a high level of confidence and a very strong knowledge and understanding of the principles and practices of teaching early mathematics, NQTs deploy very effective teaching strategies.	
4. Plan and teach well-structured lessons • Impart knowledge and develop understanding through effective use of lesson time. • Promote a love of learning and children's intellectual curiosity. • Set homework and plan other out-of-class activities to consolidate and extend the knowledge and understanding pupils have acquired.	• Schemes of work, samples of lesson plans and evaluations show effective use of lesson time. • Lessons engage pupils and lesson pace is brisk. • Lessons promote intellectual curiosity. • Talk partners are used effectively to engage and stimulate pupils. • Homework is appropriately set, marked with clear feedback given to pupils. • Out-of-class activities are planned with imagination to enhance understanding of new concepts and extend pupils' knowledge.	**Sources for evidence** • Lesson plans. • Observation in the classroom. • Scrutiny of pupils' books. • Conduct learning walks. • Interview focus group of pupils.

Teachers' Standards for trainees and NQTs

Teachers' Standards	Possible evidence	Examples
• Reflect systematically on the effectiveness of lessons and approaches to teaching. • Contribute to the design and provision of an engaging curriculum within the relevant subject area(s).	• Engages in reflection by making systematic use of lesson evaluations and assessment to inform planning and teaching, which may result in changed approaches in lesson delivery. • Plenaries are used effectively. • Pupils take ownership of their own learning. • Sets open-ended tasks to promote pupil participation. • Attends planning and participation in meetings to contribute to curriculum design.	• Contact parents regarding homework/activity. • Record of reflective log. • Record of professional development. • Assessment records (formative and summative). • Discussions with induction tutor/mentor **Links to other standards** 1, 2, 3, 5, 6, 7
	To meet the standard the NQT may demonstrate:	
	• Lessons are highly stimulating and engaging; they consistently promote a love of learning among pupils. • They are imaginative and highly creative in using strategies for planning lessons that match individuals' needs and interests. • Reflective practice through critical evaluation of their practice. • Ability to judge the impact of their practice on individual and groups of learners, making effective use of their evaluation to inform future planning, teaching and learning. • They are a 'team player' showing initiative in contributing to curriculum planning and design. • They are pro-active in developing and producing effective learning resources that will promote the delivery of an effective curriculum within relevant subject areas.	

(Continued)

(Continued)

Teachers' Standards for trainees and NQTs

Teachers' Standards	Possible evidence	Examples
5. Adapt teaching to respond to the strengths and needs of all pupils • Know when and how to differentiate appropriately, using approaches which enable pupils to be taught effectively. • Have a secure understanding of how a range of factors can inhibit pupils' ability to learn and how best to overcome these. • Demonstrate an awareness of the physical, social and intellectual development of children, and know how to adapt teaching to support pupils' education at different stages of development. • Have a clear understanding of the needs of all pupils, including those with special educational needs; those of high ability; those with English as an additional language; those with disabilities; and be able to use and evaluate distinctive teaching approaches to engage and support them.	• Uses prior knowledge of pupils to inform planning and differentiation; appropriate modifications are made to cater for learner needs. • Peer group support is used for stretching pupils and offering additional support. • Is mindful during planning for different learning styles. • Schemes of work contain additional information for implementing differentiation. • Lesson plans show differentiation, demonstrating the different learning needs of pupils and including the intervention strategies used for SEND and EAL pupils. • Participation in team meetings to update information on individual pupil needs. • Lesson observation includes comments on differentiation and care taken to address factors inhibiting learner needs. • Through effective use of marking and targets setting, engages individual learners in taking ownership of their learning. • Is knowledgeable about the different stages of child development. • Makes effective use of questioning, and effective use of other adults and resources to support SEND and EAL pupils. • Is aware of and uses school systems and policies to support learners.	• Pupil interviews and learning walks. • Discussions with staff and parents. • Book scrutiny. • Lesson plans. • Observation in the classroom. • Review sessions with the induction tutor. • Observation in the wider school environment. • Feedback from other teachers. **Links to other standards** 1, 2, 4, 6, 7

Teachers' Standards for trainees and NQTs		
Teachers' Standards	**Possible evidence**	**Examples**
	To meet the standard the NQT may demonstrate:	
	• They consistently build on pupil prior knowledge to inform planning and differentiation.	
	• They show ability to make appropriate modifications (in-action) to cater for learner needs.	
	• Through reflection and critical evaluations (on-action) they make adjustments to support learners.	
	• They draw on a range of factors that can inhibit pupils' ability to learn in order to respond to pupils with different needs.	
	• They make effective use of questioning to target learner strength, understanding and need.	
	• They make continuous use of CPD opportunities to update knowledge about specific issues affecting pupils and how they learn (including SEND and EAL pupils).	
	• They have an excellent rapport with pupils and can work with difficult pupils.	
	• They seek appropriate expert knowledge when required (including information from parents).	
	• They use a range of effective intervention strategies to secure progression for individuals and groups.	
	• They make effective use of different teaching approaches that impact on learning and make lessons engaging.	
	• They understand the different stages of child development, and incorporate theoretical knowledge about the physical, social and intellectual development of children to inform planning, differentiation and delivery of lessons.	

(Continued)

Teachers' Standards for trainees and NQTs

Teachers' Standards	Possible evidence	Examples
6. Make accurate and productive use of assessment • Know and understand how to assess the relevant subject and curriculum areas, including statutory assessment requirements. • Make use of formative and summative assessment to secure pupils' progress. • Use relevant data to monitor progress, set targets and plan subsequent lessons. • Give pupils regular feedback, both orally and through accurate marking, and encourage pupils to respond to the feedback	• Evidence of tracking data assessments both formative and summative used to measure pupil progress and assessment. • Makes use of national benchmarks to gauge level of pupil performance and shows awareness about statutory assessment. • Makes notes during the lessons, including critical incidents. • Targets are set for individuals – promotes personalised learning. • Evaluations lead to alterations on planning and assessment • Uses marking systems and gives clear feedback to pupils. • Formative and summative assessment is evident during lesson delivery through setting-focused group activities. • Strategies for assessment for learning are used to mark books to show progress. • Makes effective use of marking and gives constructive feedback. **To meet the standard the NQT may demonstrate:** • They are assessing work accurately and demonstrate ability to assess pupils' attainment against national benchmarks; they seek moderation. • They are confident in analysing information gathered by data-tracking systems including pupil premium, PLASC and raise-on-line data, and use information for forward planning. • They are consistent in using formative and summative assessment during lesson delivery using a range of assessment strategies to inform future planning. • Assessment file is a 'working document' used systematically and effectively to check learner progress, anticipating where intervention may be needed through assessment for learning, which impacts positively on the quality of pupils' learning.	**Sources for evidence** • Lesson plans • Observation in the classroom • Observation in the wider school environment Meetings with Subject Coordinators/Heads of Department/Comments from mentors Pupil interviews/discussions • Assessment file (primary) **Links to other standards** 1, 2, 4, 5

Teachers' Standards for trainees and NQTs

Teachers' Standards	Possible evidence	Examples
	• Regularly works with learners to articulate feedback and sets targets to further improvement towards personalised learning plans to promote rapid progress. • Deploys additional strategies to gauge the progress of SEND and EAL pupils. • NQT meets marking deadlines and provides constructive feedback (in line with school marking policy).	
7. Manage behaviour effectively to ensure a good and safe learning environment • Have clear rules and routines for behaviour in classrooms, and take responsibility for promoting good and courteous behaviour both in classrooms and around the school, in accordance with the school's behaviour policy. • Have high expectations of behaviour and establish a framework for discipline with a range of strategies, using praise, sanctions and rewards consistently and fairly. • Manage classes effectively, using approaches which are appropriate to pupils' needs in order to involve and motivate them.	• Working within the school's framework for behaviour, they can apply rules and routines consistently and fairly. • They show understanding about a range of strategies that experienced teachers use to promote positive behaviour and apply these effectively and consistently to promote high expectations regarding behaviour. • They establish good behaviour to create an environment that is conducive to learning and use the school sanctions, rewards and praise appropriately to promote progress in learning. • Behaviour contributes to a smooth transition during lessons and beyond. • They understand that good behaviour is dependent on engaging learners through planning challenging lessons that incorporate strategies for all learners and is linked to assessment. • They are aware of applying appropriate behavior strategies in a range of situations in and out of the classroom, during breaks and lunchtimes, in class time, in assemblies and in extra-curricular activities including during performances and trips. • They know where to seek additional support in order to address the needs of pupils with challenging behaviour.	**Sources for evidence** • Lesson plans. • Observation in the classroom. • Observation in the wider school environment. • Use of resources. • Shows knowledge about pupil groupings. • Good transition during lessons and between tasks. • Evidence that the pupil/ student knows and understands rules and guidelines. • Lesson pace. • Learning walks.

(Continued)

(Continued)

Teachers' Standards	Possible evidence	Examples
	Teachers' Standards for trainees and NQTs	
	To meet the standard the NQT may demonstrate:	
• Maintain good relationships with pupils, exercise appropriate authority and act decisively when necessary.	• They re-enforce school policies and ensure that the pupil/student knows and understands rules and guidelines. • They make effective use of managing pupil behaviour that contributes to learning – learners display high levels of engagement, courtesy, collaboration and cooperation. • They work confidently within the frameworks established for behaviour in different settings, applying rules and routines consistently and fairly. • They swiftly adapt behaviour strategies to the different circumstances in which they train. • They have a consistent approach in applying the school's policy for behaviour and demonstrate consistently high expectations. • They create an environment that is highly supportive of learning by applying a range of strategies that promote positive behaviour effectively, including sanctions, rewards and praise. • They are proactive in seeking additional support in addressing the needs of pupils with challenging behaviour.	• Class displays. • Through interviews with pupils. • Effective use of resources. • Effective use of other adults. **Links to other standards** 1, 2, 4, 5
8. Fulfil wider professional responsibilities • Make a positive contribution to the wider life and ethos of the school. • Develop effective professional relationships with colleagues, knowing how and when to draw on advice and specialist support.	• They support the ethos of the school and are willing to contribute to the wider life of the school in appropriate ways. • They are able to work collaboratively with colleagues on a regular basis and build strong professional relationships. • They collaborate with support staff, understand their roles and deploy them effectively to support learners. • They value the feedback they receive from more experienced colleagues, using it to inform their teaching and further their development.	**Sources of evidence** • Lesson plans. • Observation in the classroom. • Observation in the wider school environment. • Review sessions with mentor/tutor and feedback from teaching assistants.

Teachers' Standards for trainees and NQTs

Teachers' Standards	Possible evidence	Examples
• Deploy support staff effectively. • Take responsibility for improving teaching through appropriate professional development, responding to advice and feedback from colleagues. • Communicate effectively with parents with regard to pupils' achievements and well-being.	• They identify opportunities to develop their own professional learning and respond positively to the feedback they receive. • They take on board the responsibility to communicate, both verbally and in writing, with parents and carers in relation to pupils' achievements and well-being, including parents' evenings and through school reports. **To meet the standard the NQT may demonstrate:** • They actively seek opportunities to promote the wider school life and the ethos of the school. • They are confident and resilient, earning respect and showing high ability to work collaboratively to build strong professional relationships with colleagues. • They are pro-active in updating their knowledge and understanding through continuous engagement with CPD. • They respond positively to all the feedback they receive and develop a critical understanding of their own developmental needs by engaging in reflective practice. • They engage positively with parents/carers at the start and end of the school day (primary) and, when appropriate, makes contact with home. • Very effective communication, both verbal and in writing, with parents and carers for general matters, but also in relation to individual pupils' needs. • They take responsibility for deploying support staff in their lessons, and teaching assistants show good understanding about their roles. • They seek advice from relevant professionals in relation to pupils with individual needs. • They communicate effectively, both verbally and in writing, with parents and carers in relation to pupils' achievements and well-being.	• Feedback from other teachers. • Record of CPD activity. • Record of communications with home. • Responses from parents. **Links to other standards** 1, 7

(Continued)

Teachers' Standards for trainees and NQTs

Teachers' Standards	Possible evidence	Examples
Part Two – Personal and professional conduct A teacher is expected to demonstrate consistently high standards of personal and professional conduct. The following statements define the behaviour and attitudes which set the required standard for conduct throughout a teacher's career. Teachers uphold public trust in the profession and maintain high standards of ethics and behaviour, within and outside school, by: • treating pupils with dignity, building relationships rooted in mutual respect, and at all times observing proper boundaries appropriate to a teacher's professional position; • having regard for the need to safeguard pupils' well-being, in accordance with statutory provisions of showing tolerance of and respect for the rights of others;	• Teachers uphold public trust in the profession and maintain high standards of ethics and behaviour, within and outside school, and collaborate with the wider school community. • They are proud of their work and care about the professionalism – they are confident, well presented (dress code) and show a friendly and courteous approach to pupils. • They build professional relationships, treat pupils with respect and are aware of their boundaries. • They are trained in safeguarding, and health and safety awareness, including prevent duty, safe use of the Internet – e.g. Facebook/social media – and they know who to seek advice from. • There is evidence of promoting British values in their planning and teaching, and extra-curricular activity. They show regard for democracy, mutual respect and the rule of law. • They observe the school policy on punctuality and attendance. • They are familiar with the professional duties of teachers as set out in the school, teachers' pay and conditions document. • They understand their statutory professional responsibilities, including the requirement to promote equal opportunities and to provide reasonable adjustments for pupils with disabilities, in line with the current equalities legislation.	Sources of evidence: • Evidence may be seen from how the NQT evidences the eight teaching standards. • References made to items in Part 2 through addressing Standards in Part 1. • An NQT is critically reflective. • An NQT meets their obligations to undertake statutory duties. • Feedback from a variety of sources including pupils/students, parents and carers, other staff. **Links to other standards** Links to the eight teaching standards

Teachers' Standards for trainees and NQTs		
Teachers' Standards	**Possible evidence**	**Examples**
• not undermining fundamental British values, including democracy, the rule of law, individual liberty and mutual respect, and tolerance of those with different faiths and beliefs; • ensuring that personal beliefs are not expressed in ways that exploit pupils' vulnerability or might lead them to break the law; • having a proper and professional regard for the ethos, policies and practices of the school in which they teach, and maintaining high standards in their own attendance and punctuality; • having an understanding of, and always acting within, the statutory frameworks which set out their professional duties and responsibilities.		

The dimensions demonstrate that CPD is best when it is planned, personalised, sustained, collaborative and evaluated. All the above CPD dimensions are in evidence today and teachers engage with these in line with their stages of development.

The *Teachers' Standards* (DfE, 2012, para 14, p4) state the importance of self-evaluation, reflection and professional development as a critical activity for improving teachers' practice at all career stages. The standards set out a number of expectations about professional development – namely, that teachers should:

- *keep their knowledge and skills as teachers up-to-date and be self-critical;*

- *take responsibility for improving teaching through appropriate professional development, responding to advice and feedback from colleagues;*

- *demonstrate knowledge and understanding of how pupils learn and how this has an impact on teaching;*

- *have a secure knowledge of the relevant subject(s) and curriculum areas;*

- *reflect systematically on the effectiveness of lessons and approaches to teaching; and know and understand how to assess the relevant subject and curriculum areas.*

(DfE, 2016b, p3)

The Government White Paper *Educational Excellence Everywhere* (DfE, 2016a) includes the need to develop high-quality CPD to support teachers by introducing a new Standard for Teachers' Professional Development to help schools improve the quality and availability of CPD (para 2.44). In July 2016, the DfE published the document *Standard for Teachers' Professional Development – Implementation guidance for school leaders, teachers, and organisations that offer professional development for teachers* (DfE, 2016b). In it they state that effective professional development should be seen as a key driver not only of staff development, but also of recruitment, retention, well-being and school improvement. The standard identifies a five- point strand which should be approached together to create effective professional development.

- *Professional development should have a focus on improving and evaluating pupil outcomes.*

- *Professional development should be underpinned by robust evidence and expertise.*

- *Professional development should include collaboration and expert challenge.*

- *Professional development programmes should be sustained over time.*

  And all this is underpinned by, and requires that:

- *Professional development must be prioritised by school leadership.*

(DfE, 2016b, p6)

CPD has been built into the ITT training programme for NQTs for many years and has served to fill the gap in areas of knowledge and skills that needed developing. Providers and local authorities also offer a structured programme to engage trainees and NQTs in CPD activities. Although on the whole such activities have been very well received by trainees, at times CPD has been reactive, serving only the immediate needs that are identified as deficit areas, rather than having a developmental approach. The standard for professional development promotes a programme setting out a case for school leaders, teachers and providers of professional development to work in collaboration to offer effective CPD through addressing the five points above. For NQTs, there are additional ways of engaging in professional development that is offered by some providers – for example, a number of universities offer modules, either by distance learning or by attending taught sessions through an accredited programme allowing NQTs to gain further Master's credits. The case study below offers an example.

 **CASE STUDY**

Engaging in professional development during the NQT year

Ameera had the opportunity of studying modules at Master's level during her PGCE course leading to QTS. This was an exciting prospect as she had always wanted to do a Master's degree. Through the course she had gained 60 credits towards a Master's degree. However, when she was offered the opportunity by Leeds Beckett University to gain further credits towards a Master's degree through studying on a tailor-made distance-learning module for NQTs called Reflecting on Professional Practice, Ameera jumped at the chance. This meant that as she progressed towards completing her Teachers' Standards during her NQT year, she was able to make that experience count through engaging in reflective practice. This was particularly appropriate as her delivery was rooted in reflection and research-informed practice, adding breadth and depth to her knowledge and understanding about the requirements, and at the same time enabling her to deliver outstanding lessons. Ameera particularly enjoyed engaging in discussion forums with fellow NQTs. At the end of the year she gained more credits and moved closer towards gaining her Master's degree. She felt motivated and is currently studying more modules that are immersed in action research, which allow her to continue to excel in her classroom performance (NQT, 2015).

The need for reflective practice is highlighted in the case study and is central to the module. It also expands on Donald Schön's (1983) notion of differentiation between reflection-on-action and reflection-in-action. The former allows NQTs to keep reflective logs and diaries to inform future practice. The latter, reflection-in-action – thinking on your feet – follows the same reflective process but occurs during rather than after the teaching episode where changes are made in the moment.

 QUESTIONS FOR REFLECTION AND DISCUSSION

- How would a structured approach to carrying out reflection help you to promote good teaching?
- What are the benefits of research-informed teaching?
- How would the opportunity to network through this module benefit NQTs in gathering evidence for the Standards?
- What opportunity will the NQT have to disseminate good practice gained through the CPD?

Moving into management and leadership roles

As the teaching profession continues to evolve and new constructs are created, the need to ensure greater professionalism for leadership is paramount. It is not uncommon to hear from NQTs who have successfully progressed towards the end of their induction year that they have been allocated Teaching and Learning Responsibility (TLR) which marks the beginning of their journey into leadership roles; they will work closely with experienced members of staff, often shadowing and modelling best practice. This process is supported by networked relationships and interpersonal exchange (Bourdieu, 1986), where leadership roles contribute to a process of building social capital within an organisation. This approach enables groups of people and teams to work together in a meaningful way and leadership embraces all members of the school community. For the NQTs, the process also contributes to creating a community of practice (Wenger, 1999) whereby NQTs collaborate confidently with school colleagues as they enter a new transitional phase developing leadership skills along the way. According to Fullan (2005), building leadership capacity as a form of investment in social capital in schools is essential. It should emerge into the school daily practice, by sharing, networking, coaching and supporting each other to build a learning community. This approach is in line with the systems-led CPD mentioned above.

Given that many NQTs are handpicked at the ITE stage through 'talent spotting', head teachers identify leadership potential for NQTs and NQTs begin with confidence knowing that they have the potential to lead. Therefore, with support and an organised career structure from the outset, NQTs can move into leadership roles quite rapidly. In such cases, CPD is internally organised, with coaching and mentoring, and there is a leadership development progression structure from the moment an NQT starts in the school.

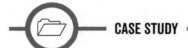 **CASE STUDY**

Journey towards leadership

Richard acquired outstanding grades in his final school placement and he already knew that the school was interested in him applying for a job there as an NQT. The head teacher had spotted leadership skills in Richard that would benefit the school as he had impressed the school by leading a project on promoting fundamental British values (FBV) which had an impact on the local community. Richard was successful in obtaining his first job at the school and as an NQT he was responsible for a Year 5 class. As a self-directed and motivated individual, Richard took on board opportunities for development through CPD and compiled an impressive portfolio of evidence that illustrated his developmental journey through the NQT year. After successful completion of his NQT year, Richard acquired a TLR post for FBV as part of a team led by someone with a teaching and learning responsibility. He kept up his CPD, reflected and acted upon advice and became an outstanding teacher. By the end of his second year of teaching, he gained more responsibility for planning aspects of the year group's work. To progress further, Richard would become part of a curriculum development team before progressing to year group or subject leadership, heading towards a middle leader TLR post and the prospect of an SLT post for the able and ambitious.

This case study highlights a clear progressive route through intermediary roles that allow NQTs to develop and hone their skills in leading learning.

QUESTIONS FOR REFLECTION AND DISCUSSION

Case study questions

1. What barriers might NQTs face as they progress towards leadership roles?

2. How does effective CPD contribute to leadership?

3. How do NQTs understand the concept of teacher leadership, their work and their development as leaders?

Conclusion

The main focus for this chapter was to examine the Teachers' Standards and their implications for classroom practice for trainee teachers and NQTs. As the standards play a pivotal role in the process of progression and transition from trainee teacher to NQT and beyond into leadership roles in school, it is critical that we develop a fuller understanding about achieving these at the various stages of the teaching career. However, this journey can be complex if the appropriate support is not sought, as there are other factors to consider both internally and externally that will impact upon success. For example, the standards carry a strong message about accountability and trust (Goepal, 2012). With parents, governors and the community playing a greater role in schools, teachers need to develop values such as collegiality, negotiations, collaboration and partnership to agree action (Nixon et al., 1997). Such skills to manage 'social accountability' can be developed from appropriate CPD and targets setting to enhance leadership opportunity. As they progress through their career, trainees and NQTs need not only to develop expertise in their subject knowledge, but also to develop skills to address the wider remit of school life. Opportunities to engage with continuing professional development and further study will provide evidence to show achievement, which will support their eventual progress into management and leadership roles.

 CHAPTER SUMMARY

You should now have a greater understanding of the following.

- The implementation of the Teachers' Standards and implications for classroom practice for trainees and NQTs.

- Providing evidence against the Teachers' Standards, for trainees and NQTs.

- Continuing professional development and further study.

- Moving into management and leadership roles.

━━━━ **FURTHER READING** ━━━━━━━━━━━━━━━━━━━━━━━━━━━━━━━━━━━━━━

Becoming a teacher: teachers' experiences of initial teacher training, induction and early professional development: research report. DCSF Research Report No RR115. Available at: http://dera.ioe.ac.uk/11168/1/DCSF-RR115.pdf.

This sets out a six-year research project to explore beginning teachers' experiences of initial teacher training and their induction in schools. A range of case studies provides useful guidance.

Hargreaves, A and Fullan, M (2012) *Professional Capital: Transforming Teaching in Every School.* Abingdon: Routledge.

This provides a depth of understanding of effective ways to ensure effective learning and teaching, and the vital importance of teachers as professionals.

━━━━ **REFERENCES** ━━━

Barber, M and Mourshed, M (2007) How the world's best performing school systems can come out on top. McKinsey & Company. Available at: www.closingtheachievementgap.org/cs/ctag/view/resources/111 (accessed December 2016).

Bourdieu, P (1986) The forms of capital. In Richardson, JG (ed.) *Handbook of Theory and Research for the Sociology of Education.* New York: Greenwood Press, pp241–60.

Department for Education (2010) The importance of teaching – the schools White Paper. Available at: www.education.gov.uk/publications/standard/publicationdetail/page1/CM%207980 (accessed 12 December 2016).

Department for Education (2011a) First report of the independent review of teacher's standards: QTS and core standards. London: DfE. Available at: www.education.gov.uk (accessed 12 December 2016).

Department for Education (2011b) First report of the independent review of Teachers' Standards: QTS and core standards. London: DfE. Available at: www.education.gov.uk/publications/standard/publicationDetail/Page1/DFE-00065-2011 (accessed 12 December 2016).

Department for Education (2012) Teacher's Standards. London: DfE. Available at: www.education.gov.uk (accessed 12 December 2016).

Department for Education (2013) The national curriculum in England: key stages 1 and 2 framework document. Available at: www.gov.uk/government/uploads/system/uploads/attachment_data/file/425601/PRIMARY_national_curriculum.pdf (accessed 5 January 2017).

Department for Education (2015) Carter review of initial teacher training. London: DfE. Available at: www.gov.uk/government/publications/carter-review-of-initial-teacher-training

Department for Education (2016a) Educational excellence everywhere. Government White Paper. London, DfE. Available at: www.gov.uk/government/uploads/system/uploads/attachment_data/file/508447/Educational_Excellence_Everywhere.pdf (accessed 12 December 2016).

Department for Education (2016b) Standard for teachers' professional development. London: DfE. Available at: www.gov.uk/government/uploads/system/uploads/attachment_data/file/537030/ 160712__PD_standard.pdf (accessed 12 December 2016).

Department for Education (2016c) Framework for core content for ITT. London: DfE. Available at: www.gov.uk/government/uploads/system/uploads/attachment_data/file/536890/Framework_Report_ 11_July_2016_Final.pdf (accessed 13.01.17).

Field, K (2011) An audit tool for identifying the most appropriate forms for CPD for staff. CPD update, 6–8.

Fullan, M (2005) *Leadership and Sustainability*. Thousand Oaks, CA: Corwin Press.

Goepel, J (2012) Upholding public trust: an examination of teacher professionalism and the use of Teachers' Standards in England. *Teacher Development*, 16(4): 489–505. DOI:10.1080/13664530.2012.72 9784

Goodwyn, A. (2012) One size fits all: the increasing standardisation of English teachers' work in England. *English Teaching: Practice and Critique*, 11(4): 36–53.

Huberman, M (1993) *The Lives of Teachers*. London: Cassell.

Huberman, M (1995) Professional careers and professional development: some intersections. In Guskey,TR and Huberman, M (eds) *Professional Development in Education: New Paradigms and Practices*. New York: Teachers College Press.

Nixon, J, Martin, J, McKeown, P and Ranson, S (1997) Towards a learning profession: changing codes of occupational practice within the new management of education. *British Journal of Sociology of Education*, 18: 5–18.

Ofsted (2012) Initial teacher education inspection. London: Ofsted. Available at: www.gov.uk/ government/publications/initial-teacher-education-inspection-handbook (accessed 13 January 2017).

Schön, DA (1983) *The Reflective Practitioner: How Professionals Think in Action*. New York: Basic Books.

Wenger, E (1999) *Communities of Practice: Learning, Meaning and Identity*. Cambridge: Cambridge University Press.

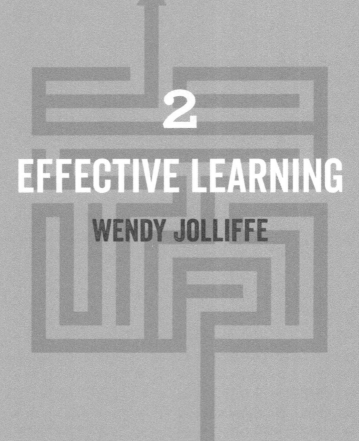

2

EFFECTIVE LEARNING

WENDY JOLLIFFE

THIS CHAPTER

By reading this chapter you will develop your understanding of the following.

- The nature of learning.
- Major learning theories and their influence on practice.
- Key research findings on effective learning.
- Influences on learning.
- Teaching approaches that support effective learning.

This chapter will help you with the following Teachers' Standards.

2. Promote good progress and outcomes by pupils

Including being able to:

- demonstrate knowledge and understanding of how pupils learn and how this impacts on teaching.

Introduction

Since the time of Socrates (469–399BC), philosophers, educators and psychologists have examined the processes of how we learn. This has led to a proliferation of theories and numerous research projects. More recently, advances in neuroscience, with the ability to scan brain activity more accurately, have informed this debate further. For the purposes of this chapter, which aims to provide early career teachers with an overview of these theories and how this impacts on practice, a brief overview of key theories will be discussed which will focus on three main strands:

1. Behaviourism.

2. Cognitivism.

3. Social constructivism (social cognition).

The chapter will review findings from recent major research projects into learning and what they tell us about effective practice. The underlying influences on learning will also be examined, including the work of Carol Dweck (2008) on developing what she calls 'growth mindsets', or developing attitudes of mind that encourage pupils to view their ability as capable of growth and not fixed. There are also clear links with the work of Hart (2004) on *Learning Without Limits* where research has demonstrated the impact of not 'labelling' or ability grouping children.

Having examined key theories and recent research, the chapter will focus on teaching for learning, looking at a range of approaches to support engagement, motivation and inclusion of all children in learning. It will provide examples of learning that is active and social.

What is learning?

Learning is a basic function that has helped humans to adapt and acquire knowledge and skills. It occurs informally, as in the example of young children learning such skills as talking and walking, and it occurs formally in educational contexts where instruction is given to enable us to grasp more complex concepts and skills. Pollard et al. (2014: 34) define learning as: *the process by which people acquire, understand, apply and extend knowledge, concepts, skills and attitudes.* It is also important to understand it is an interaction between different elements – cognitive, social and affective – and a teacher's knowledge and understanding of these is crucial.

More recent developments in research, and particularly through neuroscience, have led to a *science of learning* (Bransford et al., 2000). This has resulted in five areas that have had a fundamental impact on our understanding of learning:

1. Memory and the structure of knowledge, which relates to the importance of how knowledge is organised and how learners develop coherent structures.

2. Problem-solving and reasoning skills, derived from knowledge of how expert learners use strategies effectively to solve problems.

3. Early foundations of learning gleaned from studies of young children which have helped rethink the skills young children bring to school, such as their developing abilities to organise information, infer and develop problem-solving strategies.

4. Metacognitive processes and self-regulation that enable self-monitoring of performance, and are skills that can be taught.

5. Cultural experience and community participation which highlights the importance of social practice as a fundamental form of learning.

The drive to understand the nature of learning has led to numerous research projects, including an OECD study (Dumont et al., 2010) which set out to answer key questions about how we learn and what influences learning, and studied the benefits of different types of learning. The motivation behind such projects often lies in economic reasons to develop what politicians have called 'human capital' and to develop competencies – often termed '21st-century skills'. The issue for schools is translating such research into effective practice, so that the OECD question whether it is possible to construct *bridges ... to inform practice by this growing evidence base* (2010, p13). The conclusions of this study are summarised in seven main principles and that an effective learning environment should:

1. recognise the learners as central and encourage their active involvement and encourage students to become self-regulated learners, developing metacognitive skills;

2. be founded on the social nature of learning and actively encourage well-organised cooperative learning;

3. be highly attuned to the learners' motivations and the key role of emotions in achievement as emotional and cognitive aspects of learning are interlinked;

4. be acutely sensitive to the learners' individual differences and their prior knowledge and build learning from this;

5. devise programmes that demand effort and challenge without excessive overload;

6. demonstrate clarity of expectations and use assessment strategies consistent with these, with a strong emphasis on formative feedback to support learning;

7. promote connections across areas of knowledge and subjects, and to the community and wider world, thereby making learning relevant.

It is important to understand the underlying theories that explain such principles of learning and, while there is a proliferation of such theories, there are three overarching perspectives that have influenced education: behaviourism, constructivism and social constructivism. The following theory section explores each of these and goes on to review their implications for practice in the classroom.

 **RESEARCH/EVIDENCE FOCUS**

Learning theories

1. Behaviourism

This theory suggests that humans develop links between their experiences, their thinking and their behaviour. One of the originators of this theory, Edward Thorndike (1874-1949), believed that learning is incremental and people learn through trial and error. He developed the law of learning involving three principles. First, the *law of effect* which stated that *the greater the satisfaction or discomfort the greater the strengthening or weakening of the bond* (1911, p244). Second, the *law of readiness* where, if an animal or human is in a state of readiness, making a connection will be satisfying and such connections will be maintained. Third, the *law of exercise*, which relates to strengthening the connections through practice and the frequency of the response. Thorndike's work focused on ways of increasing the occurrence of certain behaviours and did not put any emphasis on the role of understanding.

John Watson (1878-1958) was another influential figure in developing the theory of behaviourism. He developed the concept that a change in behaviour results from the conditioning process rather than a biological process. He believed that humans could be conditioned to react, or feel certain emotions, due to a particular stimulus. His work with a 9-month-old baby is considered today to be disturbing, as he combined exposure to a rat, which initially the child showed no fear of, with loud noises. This conditioned the child to associate fear and distress with the rat. Watson proposed that humans could be conditioned to produce emotional responses to certain animate or inanimate objects and that anyone can be trained in this way. Learning according to this theory is therefore a consequence of such conditioning.

Another influential figure in the development of the theory of behaviourism is Ivan Pavlov (1849-1936). He was one of the founding figures of Russian psychology and his studies with animals formed a basis of the development of this theory. Pavlov studied factors that could influence given responses and his most famous experiment involved dogs and the power of association, so that he found when he gave food to a dog and rang a bell, the dog associated the bell with food and would salivate just at the sound of the bell. This is because the response was learned, or conditioned. He referred to this phenomenon as *classical conditioning*.

(Continued)

(Continued)

Burrhus Frederick Skinner (1904–90) developed the ideas of Pavlov and Watson and others to develop what he termed 'radical behaviourism'. He used a number of devices for his experiments with animals, with the Skinner box being the best known. The box was fitted with a lever inside which, when pressed, would produce food or water for rats, which became known as *positive reinforcement*. He also studied the effects of *negative reinforcement* where the removal of an unpleasant reinforcement can strengthen behaviour. He argued that the experiment with rats was not a reflex action (as in the case of Pavlov's dogs), but the rats in a relatively short time learned to press the lever every time they wanted food. This became known as *operant conditioning,* which related to changing behaviour by the use of a reinforcement or stimulus, which results in an increased probability of that behaviour occurring again.

The influence of behaviourism in education has been extensive and formed the foundation for whole-class didactic teaching in which the learners are frequently passive and the teacher imparts knowledge and skills. This is often followed by the use of drill and practice activities, or what Thorndike called the *law of exercise*. In order to explore behaviourism today in the classroom, read the case study below and the questions that follow.

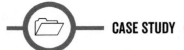 **CASE STUDY**

Behaviourism in the classroom

John was a disruptive pupil. He was nine years old and since formal schooling at five, found learning difficult and often fooled around to compensate. He would use task-avoidance strategies such as frequently sharpening his pencil or losing his pen, and then either refuse to complete a task or make only a poor attempt. He would distract others with noises or off-task talking and be a frequent cause of others being unable to complete their work. Miss Evans, his teacher, focused on positive behaviours he displayed with frequent praise, but found this had limited effect. She spoke to the parents at a parent consultation evening and together they agreed a reward system. Each day the teacher would note John's behaviour and efforts to complete work in a report, and in response his parents would reward him each week with money to save towards his particular desired goal – a new computer game player.

 QUESTIONS FOR REFLECTION AND DISCUSSION

1. Consider how effective this strategy might be.
2. Why did the teacher involve parents in this?
3. What are the drawbacks of such rewards for efforts?
4. What other alternatives could the teacher consider?

 **RESEARCH/EVIDENCE FOCUS**

2. Constructivism

Constructivism is a theory that is fundamentally different from behaviourism. Learners need to be active and learn from an interaction of thinking and experience, and through developing more complex cognitive structures. This theory principally equates learning with creating meaning from experience, rather than acquiring it. Learners do not transfer knowledge from the external world; they build personal interpretations based on individual experiences and interactions.

One of the key theorists behind this perspective on learning is Jean Piaget (1896-1980). Piaget's theory differed from others in several ways:

- It is concerned with children, rather than all learners.
- It focuses on development, rather than learning per se, so it does not address learning of information or specific behaviours.
- It proposes distinct stages of development, rather than a gradual increase in the number and complexity of behaviours, concepts, etc.

Piaget's theory of constructivism has been hugely influential in education and led to child-centred approaches in the 1960s and 1970s, and more recently to the use of cognitive acceleration and the development of thinking skills. He was the first to understand that children create knowledge rather than 'receive' it from the teacher.

There are three main aspects to his theory:

1. Schemas or building blocks of knowledge enable us to form mental representations of the world. Piaget believed that children have a small number of innate schemas, such as the infant sucking reflex for feeding, and that gradually these schemas become more complex and numerous.

2. Explanation of the processes that enable the transition from one stage to another so that when children encounter a new experience they both 'accommodate' their existing thinking to it and 'assimilate' aspects of the experience. This process leads to a state of mental 'equilibrium'.

3. Defined stages of child development, specifically the following:

   - Sensorimotor (birth to 2 years) - where the main milestone is object permanence and knowing that an object exists even if it cannot be seen.

   - Preoperational (2-7 years) - where children are able to think symbolically, although they are still mainly egocentric and have difficulty in seeing the viewpoint of others.

   - Concrete operational (7-11 years) - where a child is able to work things out internally in their head rather than physically enacting it. They are also able to conserve number and weight

(Continued)

(Continued)

> (i.e. understand that something stays the same in quantity even though its appearance changes).

- Formal operational (11 years and over) – where a child is able to think about abstract concepts and logically test hypotheses.

In recent years, there have been major criticisms of Piaget's work and in particular his notion of defined stages. The work of Margaret Donaldson (1978) and Tizard and Hughes (1984) demonstrated that children's intellectual capacities are far greater than Piaget proposed at younger ages, particularly when they are presented with meaningful contexts in which to solve problems. The legacy of Piaget's theory, while diminished in relation to fixed stages of development, still holds sway in relation to explaining the complex mental processes in acquiring new knowledge and structuring such knowledge into coherent schemas.

Read the case study below of the same pupil, John, and the questions that follow to examine how aspects of Piaget's theory could help teachers in planning effective learning experiences for him.

 **CASE STUDY**

Constructivism

John had a particular fascination with computer games and especially one that created imaginary worlds with links to ancient myths and legends. John's teacher, Miss Evans, wanted him to improve his comprehension skills in reading, but he was a reluctant reader. She spent time researching computer games and downloaded reviews of them. She gave John the task of reading these and then to present to his class a comparison of them with stars for the best and clear reasons for these. John immersed himself in this, using a laptop containing a folder of all the material. He created a poster to present a summary of the top games and then presented this to his class with his reasons for selecting them. The class were fascinated by his project and Miss Evans was amazed at his engagement and focus on this task. John was delighted with the reaction of his peers and it proved a turning point in his motivation and engagement in learning.

 QUESTIONS FOR REFLECTION AND DISCUSSION

1. Why do you think this approach proved successful?

2. How do the actions of the teacher link to constructivism?

3. What does this this tell you about how to engage children in learning?

4. How does this approach compare to the previous behaviourist example and which do you think has been more successful and why?

 **RESEARCH/EVIDENCE FOCUS**

3. Social cognition

Social cognition has two main strands. First, it emphasises the importance of language as a tool for learning which is facilitated through social interaction and social practices, or culture. This is termed 'sociocultural'. Second, it views the importance of the more experienced person, or the more knowledgeable other, in supporting another less knowledgeable person. Theorists who focus on the second part highlight the role of 'scaffolding' the learning through providing levels of support that is gradually withdrawn (such as Bruner, 1986 and Wood, 1997). This is termed 'social constructivist'.

One of the most influential psychologists to develop social constructivism is Lev Vygotsky (1896-1934). Vygotsky's theories were regarded as highly controversial during his lifetime in Russia and only became commonly known in the West through the translations of his work (1962 and 1978). They became a central part of the new paradigm of social development theory. The key parts of this theory include the following:

- The effects of cultural influences which influence cognitive development.
- The social factors involved in learning and that cognitive development stems from social interaction.
- The central importance of language as a means of communicating with others, including 'inner speech' which is the process when language and thought unite to create verbal thinking and which enables *thinking in pure meanings* (Vygotsky, 1962, p149).
- The importance of the more knowledgeable other who can guide the learning.
- The concept of the *zone of proximal development*, which is: *the distance between the actual development level (of the child) as determined through problem solving and the level of potential development as determined through problem solving under adult guidance or in collaboration with more capable peers* (Vygotsky, 1978, p86).

Social constructivism has become increasingly influential in education since the early 1980s. A number of psychologists and educationalists have explored this theory and showed its relevance to education, including Tharp and Gallimore (1988), Wells (1999), Rogoff (2003) and Wertsch (2008). The legacy is largely in understanding the importance of talk to support learning through peer and adult interaction, and providing structural support, or scaffolding.

Now read the case study of applying this theory to the classroom.

 **CASE STUDY**

Social constructivism

In order to exploit John's interest and skills with computers and computer games, his teacher, Miss Evans, decided to use this for him to teach others. She had begun to teach coding to the class and

(Continued)

(Continued)

some children really struggled with this. As she had expected, John picked it up quickly and was really engaged. She put the class into groups of three or four and considered the composition of the groups carefully. She gave the children roles in groups of organiser, resource manager, recorder and time-keeper. John was the organiser. She set them a problem-solving task applying basic coding skills, and they had to share their solution to the rest of class through use of a strategy whereby one or two children stayed in the group and the others visited other groups to observe each other's work. They then returned to their group to report back. John thrived in this situation, really enjoying the fact that he was able to share his rapidly growing understanding with others. He tuned into the difficulties others were having and patiently explained aspects to them. Above all, he enjoyed the respect he gained from his peers for this and there was a marked improvement in his general behaviour in class.

 QUESTIONS FOR REFLECTION AND DISCUSSION

1. Why do you think this approach proved successful?

2. How do the actions of the teacher link to social-constructivism?

3. What does this this tell you about how to engage children in learning?

4. How does this approach compare to the previous examples and which do you think has been more successful and why?

 # Classroom focus

The three main strands of learning theories are all applicable today in the classroom in differing degrees and different ways. It is important to have a clear understanding of these, as they help inform the decisions and actions teachers take in the classroom. Now look at the grid below and consider the application of all three further. You will find suggested answers on p53.

 QUESTIONS FOR REFLECTION AND DISCUSSION

Activity 1: Implications of theories in practice

Questions	Behaviourism	Constructivism	Social constructivism
How does learning occur?			
What factors influence learning?			
What is the role of memory?			
What kinds of learning are best explained by this theory?			

It is important to note that the theories discussed are not mutually exclusive. In most classrooms, a mixture of approaches underpinned by different theories can be used. Now look at the scenarios that follow and consider which approach would be best suited to each. You will find answers on p53.

Activity 2: Scenarios

1. Learning a specific skill in gymnastics, such as forward roll.

2. Exploring cause and effect in electricity using a range of resources such as batteries, wires and bulbs.

3. Responding to a specific request, such as being silent when asked.

4. Being able to explain a concept to a peer.

5. Providing step-by-step guidance to complete a mathematics problem.

6. Providing a diagram or model to help explain a process in science.

 RESEARCH/EVIDENCE FOCUS

Cognitive neuroscience: what it tells us about learning

Cognitive neuroscience is an area of science that combines psychology and neuroscience, and it is growing at a rapid rate with numerous academic papers being published each year. The growth is aided by the development of new techniques to study the brain's functions, in particular Functioning Magnetic Resonance Imaging (fMRI) and Positron Emission Tomography (PET). This area of study has provoked strong interest from the public generally and from educationalists in particular. This led to what Geake (2008) calls *neuromyths*, such as the widely held belief in different learning styles (see also Weisberg et al., 2008) that we only use 10 per cent of our brains, and that the difference that can be linked to the right and left brain explains differences among learners. All of these neuromyths lack credible evidence.

The Royal Society has published a series of modules to help teachers understand recent developments in neuroscience (see: https://royalsociety.org/topics-policy/projects/brain-waves/education-lifelong-learning/) and their possible implications. Some of the key aspects of what is being called educational neuroscience that are helpful to those in education include understanding that:

- the brain is capable of constant change as a result of learning and is described as being 'plastic'. Neuroscience has shown that learning literally changes the brain, but that these changes do not last if the activity ceases – thus the often used expression 'use it or lose it';

- learning is the result of both biological and environmental factors – i.e. the previously held 'nature or nurture' debate is invalid – learning is a combination of both factors;

- education can help develop our responses to stress and adversity, and support resilience, which can have lasting effects;

(Continued)

(Continued)

- the brain has mechanisms for self-regulation and this ability to inhibit inappropriate behaviour continues to develop into adolescence and early adult life. This is linked to large differences in young children's abilities to delay gratification or reward for an action, and these have been associated with higher educational attainment later (Mischel et al., 1989).

While there are major challenges for educationalists in understanding the complex world of neuroscience, ensuring an ongoing dialogue between the two areas will help reduce possible misconceptions. It would also help ensure a more holistic view of the interaction of culture, experience and biological influences in development.

Teaching for learning

As noted earlier in the chapter, large-scale international studies have explored the factors in effective learning and the development of what are often described as twenty-first century learning skills. The OECD study (Groff, 2012, p12) cites specific building blocks for innovative learning environments which are as follows:

- Service/community learning – education engages students in community service that is integrated with the objectives of the curriculum.

- Cooperative learning – where pupils support each other in learning.

- Home school partnerships – the importance of building connections between home and school as home is a highly influential learning environment.

- Learning with technology to provide tools for effective learning.

- Formative assessment that provides feedback to continually inform the learner.

- Enquiry-based approaches with meaningful projects that support sustained engagement.

The majority of these building blocks are based on social-constructivism and it is one of these, cooperative learning, that the next section will explore in more detail.

Cooperative learning

Terms such as collaborative groupwork, peer learning, teamwork and cooperative learning are often used interchangeably when referring to practices in classrooms. Genuine cooperative learning between pupils requires certain conditions to be in place, particularly interdependence, usually termed 'positive interdependence'. This exists when pupils know they can only succeed in a task if they work together with each pupil required to fulfil their part. Merely placing pupils in pairs or small groups, and expecting them to work together without consideration of the key ingredients necessary for this to thrive, largely leads to failure. Because of this, large-scale studies in England show that within the majority of primary classrooms children sit *in* groups but rarely work together *as* groups (Galton et al., 1980, 1999; Baines et al., 2009).

Research demonstrates that when this is implemented properly, cooperative learning presents an ideal method of supporting not only children's learning, but also the effective use of talk (Johnson and Johnson, 1989; Slavin, 1995, 1996; Sharan, 1990; Jenkins et al., 2003, Kyndt et al., 2013). The first step is to ensure that pupils are supported to develop the necessary interpersonal and small-group skills to cooperate. The second step is to structure the tasks to maximise the potential to cooperate. This process needs to be developed in a staged way and teachers require ongoing support to become confident and competent in its use. For comprehensive details of how to implement cooperative learning, see Jolliffe (2007).

A range of structures, principally derived from Spencer Kagan (1994), to facilitate paired and/ or group work can be applied to various activities across the curriculum. Some of these are 'think–pair–share', 'rally table', 'line up', 'three-step interview', 'two stay and two stray' and 'jigsaw groups'. For further guidance on these structures, see Kagan (1994) and www.kaganon line.com. You will also find many ideas for cooperative learning structures on Pinterest: https:// uk.pinterest.com.

Using cooperative learning or other strategies such as enquiry-based learning helps pupils to gain many essential skills of cooperating and working in a team. Research also shows that it supports academic attainment and engagement with learning (Johnson and Johnson, 1975, 1989; Slavin, 1995; Sharan, 1990; Jenkins et al., 2003). Cooperative learning also improves attitudes to learning, and the research-focus below discusses the work of Carol Dweck (2008) on such attitudes and developing what she calls *growth mindsets*.

 RESEARCH/EVIDENCE FOCUS

Developing 'growth mindsets' and 'learning without limits'

Increasingly, psychologists have questioned concepts about intelligence. These originated from the work of Alfred Binet, the inventor of the IQ test (1916), and the practice of labelling a person as 'intelligent' or having a 'high IQ' persists. In contrast, the work of Gardner (1983) and his concept of 'multiple intelligences' helped value the many different strengths that individuals have, and has fuelled the debate over what is 'intelligence'. While there has been much critical debate about the categorisation of intelligences used by Gardner, it has served a powerful function to fuel the debate and led to further work in this area, including a focus on 'emotional intelligence', through the work of Daniel Goleman (1996). Emotional intelligence is the capacity to recognise emotions in oneself and in others, to manage emotions and to use emotional information to guide thinking and behaviour, and to understand others' behaviour.

The work of psychologist Carol Dweck has developed the theory that our thinking and beliefs can have a fundamental impact on learning. With the right mindset or belief - a growth mindset - we can achieve our goals, and it is important that early influences from home or school do not lead us to develop fixed ideas on what we can or cannot do. A lack of belief can lead children in school to give up, instead of developing resilience and a love of learning. Dweck et al. (2014, p. 13) noted:

(Continued)

(Continued)

> *In our pursuit of educational reform, something essential has been missing: the psychology of the student. Psychological factors—often called motivational or non-cognitive factors—can matter even more than cognitive factors for students' academic performance.*

The psychology of the student refers to students' beliefs about themselves and how they view school and learning so that they develop a desire to learn and are able to regulate themselves to promote learning. This develops the intrinsic motivation for learning. What is required, argue Dweck et al. (2014), is a *tenacity for learning* which involves the following pupil characteristics:

- Belonging academically and socially.
- Viewing school as relevant to their future.
- Working hard and postponing immediate pleasures.
- Refusing to be derailed by intellectual or social difficulties.
- Seeking challenges.
- Remaining engaged for a sustained time.

Strategies for encouraging a growth mindset in schools include the following:

1. Setting achievable micro-goals to encourage incremental progress.
2. Praising pupils' efforts and strategies when they succeed, rather than their ability or intelligence.
3. Helping pupils to focus on and value the process of learning.
4. Designing classroom activities that involve cooperative rather than competitive or individualistic work.

Applying research to practice

Schools have become increasingly interested in developing growth mindsets in pupils and have found links to the work of Guy Claxton (2002, p17) on the 4Rs necessary to develop positive attitudes to learning. These are as follows:

1. Resilience – being ready, willing and able to lock on to learning. This includes the capacity to be absorbed in learning, being able to manage distractions, noticing significant factors and persevering with a task.
2. Resourcefulness – being ready, willing and able to learn in different ways. This includes skills of questioning, making links, imagining, reasoning and capitalising on resources.
3. Reflectiveness – being ready, willing and able to become more strategic about learning. This includes the skills of planning, revising, distilling and meta-learning (understanding about one's own learning).
4. Reciprocity – being ready, willing and able to learn alone and with others. This includes the skills of interdependence, collaboration, empathy and listening and imitation.

These represent a shift to a focus by educationalists on the affective and social dimensions of learning.

A number of major national projects have looked at how such findings can be applied to practice. Most notable of these is the Teaching and Learning Research Programme (TLRP) (James and Pollard, 2011) and the Learning to Learn project (Wall et al., 2010). The Learning to Learn project (www.campaign-for-learning.org.uk) focused very specifically on the relationship between assessment and learning, and how a beneficial synergy might be established. The TLRP project lasted over ten years, with an aim to improve outcomes for learning and to explore effective pedagogy. A number of reports and academic papers resulted, but one of the objectives was to communicate the findings broadly, and accordingly a synthesis of ten evidence-based principles was produced and distributed to schools nationally in 2007. The principles are summarised below (for further information see Pollard, 2014 and the accompanying website (www.reflectiveteaching.co.uk) and resources).

1. Effective pedagogy equips learners for life in its broadest sense.

2. Effective pedagogy engages with valued forms of knowledge.

3. Effective pedagogy recognises the importance of prior experience and learning.

4. Effective pedagogy requires learning to be scaffolded.

5. Effective pedagogy needs assessment to be congruent with learning.

6. Effective pedagogy promotes the active engagement of the learner.

7. Effective pedagogy fosters both individual and social processes and outcomes.

8. Effective pedagogy recognises the significance of informal learning.

9. Effective pedagogy depends on the learning of all those who support the learning of others.

10. Effective pedagogy demands consistent policy frameworks with support for learning as their primary focus.

The same period has also seen the publication of meta-analyses of the measured effects of different teaching strategies (Hattie, 2009) and a programme of randomised control trials in England funded by the Educational Endowment Trust, the results of which have been provided for schools in the Sutton Trust-EEF Teaching and Learning Toolkit (www.educationendowmentfoundation.org.uk/toolkit). The Toolkit ranks strategies as most effective in relation to demonstrating the impact on pupils' attainment, cost and strength of evidence. These studies demonstrate many similarities and in particular the value of feedback – i.e. information given to the learner about the learner's performance related to specific learning goals, which can then redirect the learner to focus on specific aspects to achieve the goal. Other approaches that are rated highly in these meta-analyses are meta-cognitive and self-regulation strategies, and collaborative learning approaches.

Conclusion

This chapter began by exploring what learning is and provided summaries of three main categories of theories of learning. It has presented case studies showing how such theories relate to practice, to enable teachers to reflect on the relevance of these for the classroom. The rapid developments in cognitive neuroscience and the need for a continuing dialogue between these disciplines have also been discussed.

Numerous large-scale research projects seek to explore effective learning and supporting teaching approaches. Key findings such as the OECD (Groff, 2012) building blocks for effective learning and meta-analyses such as that produced by the Sutton Trust have been examined. The aim of such resources is to provide teachers with succinct and accessible summaries of research.

The chapter has emphasised the importance of the affective dimension to learning and the works of Dweck and Claxton highlight the need for teachers to support 'growth mindsets' which are helped by attitudes of resilience, resourcefulness, reflectiveness and reciprocity. The social dimension to learning has been a strong theme in the chapter, linked to social constructivism, and this is embodied in cooperative learning.

 QUESTIONS FOR DISCUSSION AND REFLECTION

1. Discuss with colleagues the non-cognitive factors to consider in planning for effective learning.
2. What skills should be developed to encourage positive attitudes to learning?
3. Why is the social dimension to learning so important and how can it be encouraged?

 CHAPTER SUMMARY

You should now understand the following.

- The nature of learning.
- Major learning theories and their influence on practice.
- Key research findings on effective learning.
- Influences on learning.
- Teaching approaches that support effective learning.

FURTHER READING

Jolliffe, W (2007) *Cooperative Learning in the Classroom*. London: Sage.

This provides an introduction to cooperative learning and step-by-step implementation.

Pollard, A (2014) *Reflective Teaching in Schools* (4th edn). London: Bloomsbury.

Chapter 2 on learning provides an excellent summary of learning theories with links to associated reading.

REFERENCES

Baines, E, Rubie-Davies, C and Blatchford, P (2009) Improving pupil group work interaction and dialogue in primary classrooms: results from a year long intervention study. *Cambridge Journal of Education,* 39(1): 95–117.

Binet, A and Simon, T (1916) *The Development of Intelligence in Children.* Baltimore, Williams & Wilkins (reprinted 1973). New York: Arno Press.

Bransford, JD, Brown, AL and Cocking, RR (2000) *How People Learn: Brain, Mind, Experience, and School.* Washington, DC: National Academy Press.

Bruner, J (1986) *Actual Minds, Possible Worlds.* Cambridge, MA: Harvard University Press.

Claxton, G (2002) *Building Learning Power.* Bristol: TLO.

Donaldson, M (1978) *Children's Minds.* London: Fontana.

Dumont, H, Istance, D and Benavides, F (2010) The nature of learning: using research to inspire practice. Paris: OECD.

Dweck, C (2008) *Mindset: How you can Fulfil your Potential.* New York: Ballantine Books.

Dweck, C, Walton, G and Cohen, G (2014) Academic tenacity: mindsets and skills that promote long-term learning. Available at: https://ed.stanford.edu/sites/default/files/manual/dweck-walton-cohen-2014.pdf *(accessed 21 September 2016).*

Galton, M, Hargreaves, L, Comber, C, Wall, D and Pell, A (1999) *Inside the Primary Classroom: 20 Years On.* London: Routledge.

Galton, M, Simon, B and Croll, E (1980) *Inside the Primary Classroom.* London: Routledge & Kegan Paul.

Gardner, H (1983) *Frames of Mind: The Theory of Multiple Intelligences.* London: Heinemann.

Geake, J (2008) Neuromyths in education. *Educational Research,* 50(2): 123–33.

Goleman, D (1996) *Emotional Intelligence: Why it Can Matter More than IQ.* London: Bloomsbury.

Groff, J (2012) The practitioner guide. The nature of learning: using research to inspire practice. Paris: OECD. Available at: www.oecd.org/edu/ceri/thenatureoflearningusingresearchtoinspirepractice.htm (accessed 10.10.16).

Hart, S (2004) *Learning Without Limits.* Maidenhead: Open University Press.

Hattie, J (2009) *Visible Learning: A Synthesis of Over 800 Meta-analyses Relating to Achievement.* London: Routledge.

James, M and Pollard, A (2011) TLRP's ten principles for effective pedagogy: rationale, development, evidence, argument and impact. *Research Papers in Education,* 26(3): 275–328.

Jenkins, J, Antil, L, Wayne, S, and Vadasy, P (2003) How cooperative learning works for special education and remedial students. *Exceptional Children,* 69, 279–92.

Johnson, DW and Johnson, R (1989) *Cooperation and Competition: Theory and Research.* Edina, MN: Interaction Book Company.

Jolliffe, W (2007) *Cooperative Learning in the Classroom: Putting it into Practice*. London: Paul Chapman Publishing.

Kagan, S (1994) *Cooperative Learning*. San Clemente, CA: Kagan.

Kyndt, E, Raes, E, Lismont, B, Timmers, F, Cascallar, E and Dochy, F (2013) A meta-analysis of the effects of face-to-face cooperative learning: Do recent studies falsify or verify earlier findings? *Educational Research Review*, 10, 133–49.

Mischel, W, Shoda, Y and Rodriguez, ML (1989) Delay of gratification in children. *Science*, 244(4907): 933–38.

Pollard, A (2014) *Reflective Teaching in Schools*. London: Bloomsbury.

Rogoff, B (2003) *Apprenticeship in Thinking: Cognitive Development in Social Contexts*. Oxford: Oxford University Press.

Sharan, S (1990) *Cooperative Learning: Theory and Research*. Westport, CN: Praeger.

Slavin, RE (1995) *Cooperative Learning: Theory, Research, and Practice*. Boston, MA: Allyn & Bacon.

Slavin, RE (1996) *Education for All*. Lisse: Swets & Zeitlinger.

Tharp, R and Gallimore, R (1988). *Rousing Minds to Life: Teaching, Learning and Schooling in Social Context*. New York: Cambridge University Press.

Thorndike, E (1911) *Human Learning*. New York: Prentice Hall.

Tizard, B and Hughes, M (1984) *Young Children Learning: Talking and Learning at Home and School*. London: Fontana.

Vygotsky, LS (1962) *Thought and Language*. Cambridge, MA: MIT Press.

Vygotsky, LS (1978) *Mind in Society: The Development of Higher Psychological Processes*. Cambridge, MA: Harvard University Press.

Vygotsky, LS (1986 [1934]) *Thought and Language*. Cambridge, MA: MIT Press.

Wall, K, Hall, E, Baumfield, V, Higgins, S, Rafferty, V, Remedios, R, Thomas, U, Tiplady, L, Towler, C and Woolner, P (2010) Learning to learn in schools and learning to learn in further education. Campaign for Learning. Available at: www.campaign-for-learning.org.uk *(accessed 17.10.16)*.

Weisberg, DS, Keil, FC, Goodstein, J, Rawson, E and Gray, JR (2008) The seductive allure of neuroscience explanations. *Journal of Cognitive Neuroscience*, 20(3): 470–77.

Wells, G (1999) *Dialogic Inquiry: Towards a Socio-cultural Practice and Theory of Education*. New York: Cambridge University Press.

Wertsch, JV (1985) *Vygotsky and the Social Formation of Mind*. Cambridge, MA: Harvard University Press.

Wood, D (1997) *How Children Think and Learn: The Social Contexts of Cognitive Development*. London: Wiley-Blackwell.

Suggested answers to activities

Activity 1: Implications of theories of practice

Questions	Behaviourism	Constructivism	Social constructivism
How does learning occur?	Learning is observable through behaviour	Through personal experiences and interactions with outside world	Learning is constructed jointly with others
What factors influence learning?	The nature of the stimulus, rewards and punishments	Providing the environment for learning to explore	Through engagement, participation, social interaction
What is the role of memory?	Memory is the hardwiring of repeated experiences, where rewards and punishments are most influential	Making connections to existing schemas	Prior knowledge related to current context
What kinds of learning are best explained by this theory?	Task-based learning	First-hand experiences	Social, collaborative and open-ended tasks

Activity 2: Scenarios

1. Learning a specific skill in gymnastics such as forward roll (use of scaffolding – social constructivism).

2. Exploring cause and effect in electricity using a range of resources such as batteries, wires and bulbs (constructivism).

3. Responding to a specific request, such as being silent when asked (use of praise and rewards – behaviourism).

4. Being able to explain a concept to a peer (use of language and social interaction – social constructivism).

5. Providing step-by-step guidance to complete a mathematics problem (use of scaffolding – social constructivism).

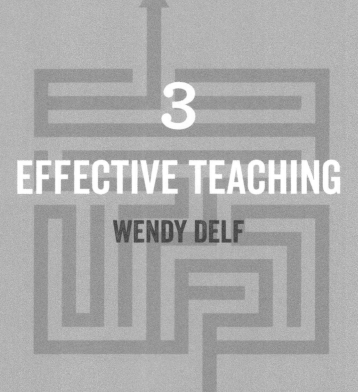

3

EFFECTIVE TEACHING

WENDY DELF

THIS CHAPTER

By reading this chapter you will develop your understanding of the following.

- How the role of the teacher impacts on learning.
- How planning for learning improves student outcomes.
- How teachers can best use assessment to support their learners.
- How to use effective marking and feedback to support student progress.

LINKS TO THE TEACHERS' STANDARDS

This chapter will help you with the following Teachers' Standards.

1. **Set high expectations which inspire, motivate and challenge pupils**

2. **Promote good progress and outcomes by pupils**

4. **Plan and teach well-structured lessons**

5. **Adapt teaching to respond to the strengths and needs of all pupils**

6. **Make accurate and productive use of assessment**

Introduction

Albert Einstein said that 'education is what remains after one has forgotten everything one learned at school'

(Albert Einstein, in Claxton, 2008, p88)

One of the most daunting tasks for newly qualified teachers is to develop an effective practice which ensures that their pupils are not only provided with the skills and knowledge required to engage in a school's curriculum or examination specification, but also that the individual needs of young people are met so that they are able to be successful in the next phase of their education and beyond. Providing this as well as meeting the demands of a changing curriculum and exam specifications, assessment results, national and international league tables can leave newly qualified teachers with feelings of anxiety and uncertainty as to their role in the classroom. This can be further compounded as teachers who are new to the profession attempt to combine what they might consider to be the traditional role of a teacher: one who will provide all the skills, being a fount of all knowledge, and one who ultimately controls the classroom learning, compared with that of a teacher working in a technologically-driven twenty-first century classroom. Teachers need to recognise that this traditional approach can no longer be the case and that the locus of control needs to shift from teacher to pupil as they become increasingly aware of their own learning needs. In order that pupils can develop these skills of life-long learning, they need to develop their self-efficacy, to understand more of the learning process for themselves and to be provided with the clarity needed to understand how they are making progress over time.

This chapter will explore the role of teachers in a twenty-first century classroom; the relationship that they foster with their pupils and how this environment can support pupils in the learning process. It will also consider what teachers should focus on to enable pupils to understand more of their own learning and progress, and how the pupil/teacher relationship, through their assessment of pupils' learning and subsequent feedback, can increase the rate at which pupils learn.

Through references to research, the chapter will also consider what teachers need to do to ensure that the time they give to planning, assessment and feedback supports better outcomes for pupils and ultimately contributes to the raising of standards over time.

Focus on theory: the work of John Hattie

Regardless of a teacher's passion or skill, it is clear that learning is not always easy, not always fun and, sadly, for some of our learners, can feel pointless. Therefore, teachers need to reflect on not only the knowledge to provide coverage in lessons, but also the skills that are required to develop successful learners in our schools. Claxton suggests that the dispositions of curiosity and resilience along with a thirst for feedback from others are traits that need to be taught explicitly to our pupils, arguing that it is these habits of mind that provide the basis of real-life learning (Claxton, 2008). This further links to the work of Carol Dweck (2006) on fixed and growth mindsets and Angela Duckworth (2016) who identifies the role of 'grit' in the learning process. The ability of the teacher to encourage pupils to engage in this learning process is further discussed in Chapter 2.

All practising teachers, and certainly teachers who have taught for many years, will be able to articulate the features of what, in their opinion, makes a great teacher. For many, it is the case that if their approach was successful, it should be replicated without thought or evaluation of that practice. However, for teachers who have just embarked on their teaching career, this sometimes confusing and contradictory advice makes it difficult for them to focus on the pedagogical approaches that will make the difference to their pupils' achievement. This chapter will provide the opportunity to reflect on what teachers should see as key to being successful in their classrooms and the dispositions and skills needed for all their pupils to make progress.

Hattie's (2009) meta-analysis provides a detailed insight into what actually works in the classroom. He suggests in his introduction that *what works best for students is similar to what works best for teachers* (2009, pi) so that pupils and teachers create a symbiotic and congruent relationship that enables learning to happen: *It is what teachers get the students to do in the class that emerged as the strongest component of the accomplished teacher's repertoire, rather than what the teacher specifically does* (2009, p35).

So what do great teachers get pupils to do? What does this repertoire look like and how do newly qualified teachers engage with these approaches? Hattie's research suggests that teachers need to be able to evaluate the impact they are having on their pupils, whether this is through their interactions with them in the classroom or through formative and summative assessments which can identify and then close pupils' learning gaps.

Hattie's research confirms that nearly everything a teacher brings to a lesson can affect pupil achievement to some degree. For example, direct instruction, problem solving, worked examples and homework all have a positive effect on pupil achievement. However, teachers need to focus on not what works but what has the most impact on pupils' outcomes and how teachers can express this. Hattie's research suggests that this can be expressed through the use of *effect sizes* where an *effect size* of 0.40 describes a year's input from the teacher, equating to one year of progress from the pupil (Hattie, 2012, p14).

Hattie's research identifies a number of approaches that can support positive outcomes for pupils (see the table below). Some of these may already be part of a teacher's repertoire to support pupils' learning.

Effect sizes from teaching	Effect size
Quality of teaching	0.77
Reciprocal teaching	0.74
Teacher–student relationships	0.72
Providing feedback	0.72
Teaching student self-verbalisation	0.67
Metacognitive strategies	0.67
Direct instruction	0.59
Mastery learning	0.57

Source: Hattie (2009, p244)

However, just as we are able to use these approaches to support pupil progress – and there are many that newly qualified teachers can explore – our own values and beliefs as teachers can also either destroy or support our understanding of our pupils' learning journeys. Hattie states that *teachers' beliefs and commitments are the greatest influence on student achievement* (Hattie, 2012, p25). Therefore, teachers need to reflect on the way they perceive their pupils' ability to learn; how they can provide a classroom climate so that making mistakes is part of the learning process; where clarity around learning intentions and success criteria provide the motivation for pupils to want to succeed, and where effective feedback provides an understanding of what pupils are able to do and what they need to do next.

The Education Endowment Foundation (EEF), which analyses a substantial body of research, continues to evaluate the approaches taken by schools and teachers to impact on their learners. The EEF's (2016) *Teaching and Learning Toolkit*, originally published through the Sutton Trust, suggests that to embed approaches such as those in Figure 3.1 will take time, that there is no silver bullet to improve pupil outcomes, and certainly any new, high-quality pedagogical interventions will be lengthy to embed. However, the research acknowledges that high-quality teaching and learning is crucial in supporting the educational outcomes of pupils. The toolkit covers a range of projects and research projects that have been evaluated and are ongoing. Teachers and leaders are able to use the interactive toolkit to identify approaches that have a positive effect size – for example, collaborative learning, feedback, metacognition and self-regulation – as well as providing information on ongoing research projects such as the testing of a two-year professional development programme on embedding formative assessment.

Coe et al. (2014) suggest six components of great teaching: subject knowledge; the quality of instruction including questioning and use of assessment; the classroom climate, including the interactions of the teachers and their students; the management of the classroom by the teacher; teacher beliefs and the impact they have on pupil outcomes; and the ability of teachers to reflect on their practice and teachers' ongoing professional development. Teachers are therefore learners themselves and continue to learn throughout their careers. These are all reflected in other research noted in this chapter and suggest that there are a number of key areas on which newly qualified teachers should focus as part of their ongoing professional development.

The role of formative assessment, which involves the planning, teaching and assessment of pupils' progress, is also seen to be an integral element of an effective teacher's repertoire. The Assessment Reform Group (2002) identifies specifically how the list below improved the quality of the teacher's impact on pupil outcomes.

- Active involvement of pupils in their own learning.

- Sharing learning goals with pupils.

- Involving pupils in self-assessment.

- Effective questioning.

- Providing feedback which leads to pupils recognising their own learning.

- Adjusting teaching to take account of the results of assessment.

- Confidence that every pupil can improve (untapped potential rather then 'fixed IQ' belief).

The Assessment Reform Group's main findings included how, for example, teacher questioning can support pupil progress. Their findings suggested that many teachers do not always plan for pupil questioning and that the *wait time* between asking a question and responding could be as short as one second (Assessment Reform Group, 2002). This approach to questioning also led to a 'ping-pong' version of classroom dialogue, whereby the teacher focused on superficial questioning and rapid responses, often from a limited number of pupils. By increasing the wait time and moving to a 'volley-ball' approach to questioning, classroom discussion moved to a more dialogic approach, engaging more pupils in the discussion and providing more opportunities for teachers to assess the understanding or misconceptions of their pupils.

Clarke's (2003) research also focused specifically on the impact of formative assessment where pupils are able to take on the role of assessment–capable-learners through *a gradual power shift, through modelling and training, enabling children to gradually take more and more control over their learning and the decisions they make to enhance their learning* (2003, p2). For this to be effective, teachers need to consider *what* pupils will learn; *how* they will learn so that learning becomes a highly motivating activity in the classroom, as pupils have clarity over what they are learning through the explicit understanding of learning intentions and success criteria; *how* they will learn through ongoing self-assessment of the learning process and understand *when* the learning gap is closing so that they can articulate their their next steps. This also links closely to Hattie's view of assessment of capable visible learners who continually ask the questions *Where am I going? How am I going* and *Where to next?*

Clarke, through the Gillingham study, focused on the use of 'product' success criteria in the classroom. Many teachers had used this strategy to support 'product' success criteria rather than 'process' success criteria, the former leading to pupils engaging in end-point products – e.g. something they had made or answering correctly rather than how the learning would be completed; this shift of emphasis to the process of learning led to pupils becoming more motivated in their learning rather than just producing work for assessment (Clarke, 2003, p33).

It therefore appears that, through their planning, effective teachers are able to identify where pupils are in their learning, know what their pupils should be aiming for that is neither too challenging nor too easy, and are able to plan how the teaching will support this learning so that pupils are on track or that the learning process needs to be amended. This use of day-to-day formative assessment, collected through discussions with pupils, questioning and observation, and the more formal summative assessment of pupils' learning through written work or end of unit tests, provides teachers with a wide range of evidence to track pupils' progress over time.

Another longitudinal study involving over 3,000 teachers over a three-year period was the Measures of Effective Teaching (MET) project, which set out to test new approaches to effective teaching. Their findings link closely to the work of Black et al. (2002) and Coe et al. (2014) who have attempted to identify the components of great teaching. The findings of the MET project included teachers becoming students of their own learning, using student voice and observations, and also linked to Fullan's idea of a new pedagogy where students and teachers work as learning partners, with Fullan (2013) and Hattie's (2012) teacher as 'activator' involving reciprocal teaching, feedback, meta-cognition and evaluating the effect of teaching on learning.

 RESEARCH/EVIDENCE FOCUS

Assessment Reform Group (2002)

Testing has always been used by teachers to assess what pupils know and to provide feedback to pupils on how they are progressing in their learning. The research undertaken by the Assessment Reform Group in 2002 focused not on whether teachers and schools should assess, but rather on how they should assess and how they can do this so that pupils are motivated in their learning. The research highlighted what teachers should do more and less of to counteract the negative impact of testing and increase pupil motivation for learning (Assessment Reform Group, 2002). These suggestions included the following.

Teachers should do more ...	Teachers should do less ...
Provide choice and help pupils to take responsibility for their learning.	Give frequent drill and practice test taking.
Help pupils to understand the criteria by which their learning is assessed and to assess their own work.	Allow pupils to judge their work in terms of scores and grades.
Help pupils in relation to their learning goals and how to make further progress.	Use tests and assessments to tell students where they are in relation to others.
Give feedback that enables pupils to know the next steps and how to succeed in taking them.	Give feedback relating to pupils' capabilities, implying a fixed view of each pupil's potential.

The Learning Pit

Nottingham's (2015) Learning Pit is used in some schools to enable pupils to find a shared language, develop metacognitive strategies for learning and to develop pupils' growth mindset so that they see their learning as a process that can be discussed and shared with their peers and their teacher, and to promote high levels of challenge in classrooms. Nottingham's Learning Challenge reflects Edwards' (2006) model of transformational learning. Nottingham's model provides pupils with four stages during the learning process: *concept, conflict, construct, consider.* Pupils can become highly motivated when they recognise that their learning has a process that can be articulated, and that emotions that previously may have led to a negative view of learning can be reassessed as stages of learning, where learning is seen as a model for enquiry, discussion and, at the same time, challenging and rewarding. The Learning Pit uses metacognitive skills that pupils can recognise and then articulate in their learning through these four stages.

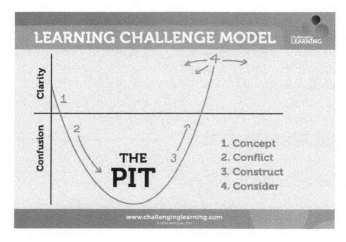

Figure 3.1   Effect sizes from teaching

Available at: www.jamesnottingham.co.uk/learning-pit/

 # Formative assessment

It has already been noted in the chapter that the role of the teacher and their impact on pupil progress has been explored by numerous researchers and academics. The role of formative assessment has been increasingly linked with the constructivist model (Clarke, 2003) whereby learners become increasingly responsible for their own learning through a better understanding of what they are learning, working effectively with others and making clear connections with previous learning. The use of formative assessment has also become an increasingly important aspect of a teacher's practice with the removal of levels across the primary phases and in Key Stage 3 at secondary school. With the removal of these levels and a focus on in-school formative assessment linking the key milestones of the end of KS1, KS2 and KS4, it has become imperative for teachers to explore their own understanding of what progress looks like for their learners and for learners across the school.

Since the publication of Black and Wiliam's *Inside the Black Box* (1998), teachers have been encouraged to use 'learning intentions' and 'success criteria' as part of their planning. However, the understanding and effectiveness of this practice are inconsistent. Some schools adopted the use of WALT (we are learning to ...) and WILF (what I'm looking for ...) as a short cut to communicating this in their classrooms. Sadly, for some, these two phrases took on a life of their own (sometimes with the use of puppets called Walt and Wilf). This has led to some teachers and pupils having a limited understanding of the function of these terms, resulting in pupils being clear about the task they are required to do but having little understanding of the learning involved in this process or how this could be transferred to other areas of the curriculum.

The 8 schools project (Department for Education and Skills, 2007) was an action research project (July 2005–October 2006) which looked to identify the key factors in developing independent learning and whether formative assessment could impact on pupil progress and standards over time. Through working with eight different schools that were all engaged in the use of formative assessment, the key message from the project was that if all pupils have a clear understanding of what they are trying to learn (learning objectives), how they can recognise achievement (learning outcomes), what 'good' looks like (success criteria), and why they are learning this in the first place (that is, the big picture, sometimes linked to personal curricular targets), they will develop independent learning habits. Hattie (2009) also acknowledges the importance of learning intentions and states that:

> *Learning intentions describe what it is we want students to learn in terms of the skills, knowledge, attitudes and values within any particular unit or lesson. Learning intentions should be clear, provide guidance to the teacher about what to teach, help learners be aware of what they should learn from the lesson and form the basis for assessing what the students have learnt and for assessing what the teachers have taught well to each student.*

> (Hattie, 2009, p162)

However, this needs to be linked to the success criteria to provide a clear picture of success for pupils and help them to identify the gaps and subsequently the next steps in their own learning.

Hattie links this to direct instruction (not to be confused with didactic teaching) which provides clarity on what the teacher has planned for pupils to learn and opportunities for them to engage in their learning. It enables the teacher to regularly check that pupils are on track with that learning, and it provides clear success criteria by which teacher and pupil can assess the progress made. Teachers need to *invite the students to learn, provide much deliberate practice and modelling, and provide appropriate feedback and multiple opportunities to learn.* (2009, p73)

In many ways, this clarity of teaching can result in pupils being exposed in terms of not only their successes but also their failures, and for this reason the learning environment needs to be one where teacher-to-pupil and pupil-to-teacher feedback can be given and received. Classrooms, where errors are part and parcel of the learning process, need to be planned and nurtured over time. Dweck's *Mindset* (2006), which encourages pupils to develop *growth mindsets*, can only be developed through a safe learning environment with the development of resilience and the motivation to see learning as a process. However, this should not just be seen as teachers developing the mindsets of their pupils, but also as teachers engaging in the evaluation of their own approach to learning situations and their belief in their own pupils' successes.

The work of Bishop (2011), whose research has focused on the educational experiences of Mauri pupils in New Zealand, created what he termed a *culturally responsive pedagogy of relations* where the beliefs of teachers and their mindsets needed to be explored first so that, regardless of class, race, gender or ethnicity, teachers have to create a classroom

> *that is responsive to the culture of the child ... based upon the notion of relationships being paramount to educational performance ... It's a serious business, education. It's about caring for people, caring that they learn, and it's about creating learning relationships so that you ensure they are able to learn, and we term it a culturally responsive pedagogy of relations.*
>
> (Bishop, 2011)

This *culturally responsive pedagogy* where teachers are aware of how they create a learning relationship with their pupils is also reflected in Hattie's teacher mind frames. These mind frames, which include teachers acting as *change agents* or *activators ... deliberate change agents and directors of learning* (Hattie, 2009, p25), suggest that teachers not only need to provide clarity of the learning experience, but also have the belief themselves that all pupils are able to learn, achieve and make progress regardless of their starting points or backgrounds.

The following case studies, taken from both a primary and secondary setting, illustrate the importance of teacher clarity. Through teachers recognising what they are attempting to teach and, consequently, how pupils will learn, pupils were seen to become more motivated in their learning, which in turn enabled teachers to take more risks in their teaching.

 **CASE STUDY**

The role of teacher clarity in the primary classroom

An NQT was failing to meet the standards, particularly Standard 7. Through observation, it was noted that the relationship that the teacher had with his pupils (Y3) was deteriorating. Pupils were unclear about their learning, the expectations of their teacher and how they would be successful learners in his classroom. They could articulate what the task of the lesson was about, but were unsure how this linked to prior learning or how the task of the lesson would help them to become better learners. Pupils were therefore becoming quickly disengaged, repeatedly off task, and therefore the teacher was focusing on pupil behaviour. The relationship between teacher and pupil was declining rapidly with the teacher losing confidence in his ability to engage with and teach his class.

Through discussion with the teacher, it became clear that he was unsure of how his planning supported the progress of his learners. Much of it was focused on a range of activities to keep the pupils occupied around the given subject area. The teacher was then reintroduced to learning intentions and success criteria, supported by his reading of Shirley Clarke's (2003) *Unlocking Formative Assessment and Enriching Feedback in the Primary Classroom*. This led to the teacher planning for learning (rather than doing) and identifying what pupils would achieve by the end of the lesson, the week and the unit of work. Through a clear focus on planning the intention of learning and the resultant success criteria for all learners, pupils became more confident in their ability to make progress during the lesson, were motivated to work on their next steps and became more engaged in their learning. The teacher–pupil relationship within the class improved dramatically as the teacher could see the pupils engaging in learning. This led to fewer incidents of off-task behaviour and the climate for learning in the classroom improved. The NQT realised that Standard 7 should not have been the standard to focus on, but Standards 2 and 4.

 **CASE STUDY**

The use of teacher clarity to support independent learning in the secondary classroom

A Food Technology teacher in a large secondary school taught pupils in a Y10 GCSE Food Technology class with a wide range of abilities. Through observation, it was noted that pupils were unclear about the learning in the lesson, which was often focused on activities – for example, 'we are making scones …, we are making pizza', which was linked to the practical element of their GCSE exam. After the teacher demonstrated the practical element of the lesson, students were unable to work independently and lower achieving students, in particular, were demanding her attention and relying on her for their next steps. In a large group of 20, this was not sustainable.

Through discussion, it became clear that the teacher was unsure what a learning intention for her lessons should be and had resorted to tasks – for example, 'we are learning to make pizza'. The teacher then evaluated what skills and processes the pupils needed to know in order to be successful learners in their Food Technology class. For example, they were learning a 'rubbing in' method which would allow them to create a number of dishes. She also evaluated how her students could become more independent during practical sessions. This led her to produce simple photos of the key steps in the learning process, taken at each stage of the modelling, so that pupils were able to check their own progress against the photos.

Through discussion with her group, the teacher was also able to make links for her pupils so they could see that the 'rubbing in method' would allow them to choose the outcome of their skill – for example, to use the dough to make pizza, scones or pastry and to take a photo of their finished task. This was then compared with the success criteria for the task. The teacher noted that pupils were gaining more confidence in their own learning and understanding of the skills required for their practical exam. They also became more motivated to understand what progress looked like and how it related to the exam criteria. This approach also led to more detailed and effective peer assessment as pupils were able to articulate what had gone well and what should be improved the next time.

Conclusion

This chapter has provided an opportunity for teachers to consider the approaches to teaching and learning that can make a difference. It has reflected on the function of learning intentions and success criteria, and how a better understanding of how these can enable pupils to better understand the learning process and be motivated to engage more in their learning. Through the focus on the work of the Assessment Reform Group and the work of Shirley Clarke, teachers have been introduced to the complex interaction of planning for assessment and feedback so that they can plan for pupils' next steps and the pupils themselves become independent learners within the classroom.

QUESTIONS FOR DISCUSSION AND REFLECTION

If we are going to be effective in the classroom we must evaluate the impact we are having on our pupils' learning. There are a number of questions we can ask our pupils which will provide an insight into the learning process and how they view you as their teacher and your role in their learning.

- *What are you learning today?* If they can discuss their learning, rather than the task, the learning intention is clear.

- *What will you do if you are stuck during the learning?* Pupils are able to use a range of strategies and language to describe the learning process and the metacognitive approaches to support this.

- *How will you know if you have been successful today?* The success criteria are clear – co-constructed success criteria are more highly motivating.

- *What are your next steps in this learning?* Pupils understand what progress looks like for them and, through your feedback, they are able to articulate what their next steps will be.

- *How does feedback help you? Written feedback? Oral feedback?* The pupils are using feedback to understand their learning needs, misconceptions and gaps in their learning. By providing opportunities to address this, they will close the learning gap more effectively.

- *What makes a good learning? Do they see themselves as responsible for their own learning? Do they rely on you and other adults? Do they incorporate behaviours – e.g. sitting straight on the mat, doing well in tests – as qualities of being a good learner?*

 CHAPTER SUMMARY

You should now know the following.

- How your role as a teacher can impact on pupil progress.

- How we can better plan for positive pupil outcomes.

- Where to find further information to support your understanding of teaching approaches that support pupil progress.

FURTHER READING

Black, P, Harrison, C, Lee, C, Marshall, B and Wiliam, D (2002) *Working Inside the Black Box.* London: Department of Education and Professional Studies.

This research still resonates in classrooms today. It provides a context of why the research was carried out and how the findings link closely to many of the key messages around formative assessment.

Clarke, C (2003) *Unlocking Formative Assessment and Enriching Feedback in the Primary Classroom.* Abingdon: Hodder & Stoughton.

Along with other books published by Clarke on this area, this book provides practical guidance on how to improve the planning of the learning process and effective feedback strategies.

Hattie, J (2012) *Visible Learning for Teachers.* Abingdon: Routledge.

Chapter 7 in particular provides very practical advice on the power of feedback and a model of feedback developed by Hattie and Timperley.

▬▬ REFERENCES ▬▬

Assessment Reform Group (2002) *Testing, Motivation and Learning.* Cambridge: Cambridge University Faculty of Education.

Bishop, R (2011) Effective teaching is culturally responsive, seniorsecondary.tki.org.nz (accessed 21 November 2016).

Black, P, Harrison, C, Lee, C, Marshall, B and Wiliam, D (2002) *Working Inside the Black Box.* London: Department of Education and Professional Studies.

Black, P and Wiliam, D (1998) *Inside the Black Box: Raising Standards through Classroom Assessment.* London: GL Assessment.

Clarke, C (2003) *Unlocking Formative Assessment and Enriching Feedback in the Primary Classroom.* Abingdon: Hodder & Stoughton.

Claxton, G (2008) *What's the Point of School?* Oxford: Oneworld Publications.

Coe, R, Aloisi, C, Higgins, S and Major, LE (2014) *What Makes Great Teaching? Review of the Underpinning Research Durham?* Centre for Evaluation and Monitoring.

Department for Education and Skills (2007) *Assessment for Learning 8 Schools Project Report.* London: Department for Education and Skills.

Dweck, C (2006) *Mindset: The New Psychology of Success.* New York: Ballantine.

Duckworth, A (2016) *Grit: The Power of Passion and Perseverance.* New York: Scribner.

Education Endowment Foundation (2016) Teaching and learning toolkit. Available at: https://educationendowmentfoundation.org.uk/resources/teaching-learning-toolkit (accessed 9 September 2016).

Edwards, J (2006) Magnificent classrooms – if you want your classroom to change, you have to change. Available at: www.learningnetwork.ac.nz/shared/professional/Reading/MAGSCHOOLS.ppt (accessed 26.09.16).

Fullan, M (2013) The new pedagogy: students and teachers as learning partners, *LEARNing Landscapes,* 6(2): 23–9.

Griffith, A and Burns, M (2012) *Outstanding Teaching Engaging Learners.* Bancyfelin: Crown House Publishing.

Hattie, J (2009) *Visible Learning: A Synthesis of Over 800 Meta-analyses Relating to Achievement.* Abingdon: Routledge.

Hattie, J (2012) *Visible Learning for Teachers.* Abindgon: Routledge.

Nottingham, J (2015) The learning challenge. Available at: www.jamesnottingham.co.uk/learning-pit/ (accessed 14 October 2016).

4

BEHAVIOUR FOR LEARNING

HILARY SMITH

THIS CHAPTER

By reading this chapter you will develop your understanding of the following.

- The context and concept of Behaviour for Learning (B4L).
- The practical application of an intervention for children in a highly charged emotional state.
- Whole-class systems for establishing a positive learning environment.

Introduction

The behaviour of children in schools or, rather, their *mis*behaviour, is frequently cited as one of the main reasons for teachers leaving the profession early in their careers. Persistent disruption by one or more children in the classroom, if it continues unabated, can lead to feelings of frustration and inadequacy, and become a source of considerable anxiety and stress, especially for NQTs.

Advice and support on behaviour issues can come in many guises and it can be challenging for any teachers, not just NQTs, to navigate the plethora of government documents, academic research, advice from so-called 'experts' and various 'top-tips for teachers' to find what is statutory, what is useful and what will most effectively support their classroom practice.

It would be impossible in one short chapter to provide definitive advice on such a broad and amorphous aspect of teaching as behaviour, so the focus here is to address the key concerns frequently raised by new teachers who have developed ideas during their initial training on how they would like to manage their own class (and how they would *not* like to) and who now have the opportunity to build on those ideas and put them into practice.

The themes explored here focus on how to establish and maintain a positive learning environment based on building meaningful relationships with children rather than depending on traditional behaviourist methods to 'manage' them. It recognises the aspirations of those new to the profession who wish be transformative in their teaching without controlling or suppressing children's natural curiosity and enthusiasm, but who also want robust, tried and tested, methods for providing order and safety in their classroom, and effective systems that promote self-efficacy and self-regulation in their young learners.

The chapter is divided into three parts. The first part sets the scene by providing the background to the concept of Behaviour for Learning (B4L), explains how the conceptual framework works and provides a case study to illustrate its practical application. The second part considers the issue of attachment needs, an aspect of behaviour which teachers are increasingly concerned with, and focuses on a particular intervention, emotion coaching, which has shown to be very effective in calming down children who are in a highly charged emotional state. The third and final part reflects on classroom codes and describes the use of class charters as a positive alternative to the traditional practice of using 'top-down' rules.

 RESEARCH/EVIDENCE FOCUS

Behaviourism v. Behaviour for Learning

In 2004, Powell and Tod published *A Systematic Review of how Learning Theories Explain Learning Behaviour in School Contexts*, which resulted in the development of a conceptual framework for behaviour in schools with the term 'learning behaviour' being coined and the phrase 'Behaviour for Learning' (B4L) becoming widely used by teachers and academics (Ellis and Tod, 2009). It also spawned a government-funded website Behaviour4learning (now archived) which provided a comprehensive platform for research and evidence-based advice and guidance for teachers on all aspects of behaviour in schools. It coincided with the Steer Report (DfES, 2005a), which made extensive recommendations to support teachers in establishing and maintaining positive learning behaviour in their classrooms. The focus of advice for teachers at that time recognised research into children's motivation, self-esteem and self-regulation, and promoted approaches in schools that took account of social and emotional aspects of learning and emotional literacy (DfES, 2005b). Since then, successive governments have disregarded the B4L approach; it is not evident in the current Teachers' Standards (DfE, 2012a) or reflected in any recent government documents on behaviour (DfE, 2011, 2012b, 2016a). The return to the rhetoric of discipline, designed to regenerate teachers as figures of authority, was based on the popular notion that teachers were no longer being treated with respect and that behaviour in schools had become a source of serious concern with many children's behaviour out of control (Paton, 2014). Rooted in a behaviourist approach, official guidance on behaviour management techniques since 2010 has relied on controlling children's behaviour through rules, rewards and sanctions. Critics comment that reverting to the language of 'misbehaviour' and 'punishment' espouses a deficit model of behaviour, which implies that children have to be controlled and 'managed' by adults before any learning can take place and ignores the significant psychological evidence to the contrary (Adams, 2009; Rose et al., 2013; Ellis and Tod, 2015).

The Behaviour for Learning Conceptual framework

Ellis and Tod's guiding framework for B4L (see Figure 4.1) emphasises the importance of relationships with self, others and the curriculum, to encourage positive learning behaviour and a classroom ethos where self-efficacy and agency can flourish.

The framework places learning behaviour at its centre, recognising that the shared aim is to promote behaviour that enables effective learning. It is placed within a triangle that represents the social, emotional and cognitive factors which are addressed through the three relationships with self (engagement), others (participation) and the curriculum (access). The arrows surrounding the triangle indicate that the development of learning behaviour is a dynamic process and the three

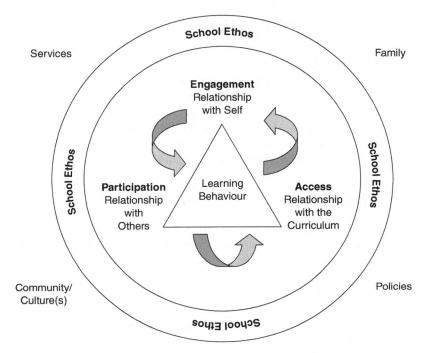

Figure 4.1   The Behaviour for Learning conceptual framework

Source: Ellis, S and Tod, J (2015) *Promoting Behaviour for Learning in the Classroom.* Abingdon: Routledge, p11.

relationships are interrelated. School ethos encompasses the triangle, and acknowledges the context within which learning behaviour exists, and the terms outside of this boundary are a reminder that learning does not take place in a vacuum and there are external influences which impact on pupils' dispositions to learning.

In order to use the B4L framework as an effective tool, teachers need to give attention to each of the three relationships which are summarised below.

Engagement (relationship with self)

Engagement refers to the internal thoughts, perceptions and feelings that learners hold about themselves. Resistance to learning and challenging behaviour can occur when learners lack self-awareness, have low self-esteem or have an impaired or inflated view of themselves and how others see them. An inability to recognise their own emotional state or the feelings of others can also be a significant barrier to positive learning behaviour. Teachers can address these issues at a classroom level by using methods which encourage self-efficacy (helping children to have achievable goals), metacognition (helping children to understand and reflect on how they know what they know) and emotional literacy (helping children to recognise their emotions and respond appropriately to the feelings of others).

Participation (relationship with others)

Participation refers to the interactions that take place between peers, and between children and adults. Its theoretical origins can be found in social learning theory (Bandura, 1971) and included in the pathology of human behaviour (Maslow, 1976) as well as ecological systems theory (Bronfenbrenner, 1979). More recent neuroscientific research highlights social relationships, particularly with early attachment figures, as being an essential component for developing neural pathways and crucial in having the ability to engage in learning at all (Gerhardt, 2014; Music, 2016). To support this aspect of B4L, teachers need to be proactive in creating an ethos where social engagement, cooperation and collaboration are encouraged, and a sense of belonging and group cohesion are supported.

Access (relationship with the curriculum)

Access refers to the way in which learners access, process and respond to the information imparted to them. It requires teachers to consider how to transmit learning through active, dynamic interactions that engage and challenge all children. It addresses the need to navigate through a largely subject-based curriculum with prescribed age-related outcomes in a way that captures the interest and absorption of self-initiated exploration. Revisiting the play-based principles of early years education can provide a useful and significant direction here (Bennett and Henderson, 2013), as can the suggestions for active learning (Vickery, 2014). When teachers encounter children who persistently fail to be engaged with school work, they can support them through a range of strategies, including openly exploring the child's perspective with them, being more explicit about the purpose and meaning of tasks, building in mechanisms that enable dialogue and negotiation of how goals can be met, and establishing feedback systems that support self-worth (Higgins et al., 2007).

The three relationships outlined above, which comprise the B4L model, provide a structure for teachers to use as a basis for establishing positive learning behaviours in their classroom and to troubleshoot any challenging behaviour they may encounter.

The following case study illustrates an example of its use in solving a common classroom problem.

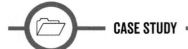 CASE STUDY

Using the B4L framework to manage a boisterous reception class

Sarah is an NQT in a reception class in a one-form entry urban primary school. She successfully completed her final placement at the school while on her PGCE and was thrilled to have gained a post there.

Sarah's first term went well and by November she felt confident that she had established positive relationships with the children in her class and set clear rules and routines. However, as the winter months approached, she noticed that the atmosphere in the classroom had become quite boisterous. Each day began calmly enough, but by mid-morning noise levels had risen considerably and by lunchtime there was normally at least one incident of a child complaining of being shouted at or hurt by another child. Sarah's usual system of praising positive behaviour and disapproving of inappropriate behaviour was becoming increasingly ineffective and she was feeling anxious about losing control of the class. She began to increase the amount of sanctions she used – e.g. individual children lost their playtime if they had hurt others – and she found herself raising her voice to counteract the loudness of the children. However, this did little to improve the situation.

Sarah was advised by her induction mentor to step back and review what was happening, so she systematically made a series of focused observations of the class at particular times. She also asked her class TA as well as her mentor to do some observations as well.

What emerged was that it was not the whole class causing the disruptive atmosphere, but a small group of individual children who were independently becoming restless and off-task within a short time of going to their table-top activities. These particular children were often fidgety and distracted each other by getting out of their seats, chatting to others, calling out across the classroom and getting into minor conflicts.

Having identified the issues, Sarah used the B4L framework to try to problem-solve them. She addressed each of the relationships in the framework – participation, engagement and access – and set up the following action plan.

Participation (relationship with others) To enable this group of children to interact with others more positively, Sarah directed each of them to activities that required them to work in pairs or take turns and interact in mutually supportive ways rather than to work individually on parallel tasks – e.g. setting up a shopping role-play for counting money. She also introduced regular circle-time sessions for the whole class, initially focusing on talking and listening, and being kind to each other.

Engagement (relationship with self) To encourage those children who were calling out and becoming increasingly loud to understand and value quietness, Sarah introduced individual 'quiet voice' targets as well as using the Too Noisy app (an application for electronic devices which monitors noise levels and sets off a visual and audible alarm). She practised and modelled different noise levels with the children in a fun way to help them recognise and control the volume of their voices, and gave particular attention and praise to those who were the quietest.

Access (relationship with the curriculum) To increase the children's motivation and interest in the tasks set, Sarah made sure that each task had a physically active, multi-sensory element. Having previously limited the children's access to the outside area because of the colder weather, she reinstated more activities in the covered outdoor play space and made sure that every child had warm, waterproof clothing.

Within a couple of weeks, there was a marked change in the atmosphere in Sarah's classroom; it was calmer and quieter, and the children who had previously been rowdy and loud, were increasingly on-task and more cooperative. The most successful strategies seemed to be using the Too Noisy app and increasing the amount of opportunities to be active and outside.

 QUESTIONS FOR DISCUSSION/REFLECTION

1. What tensions might there be in using the B4L concept alongside traditional behaviourist methods?

2. What other ways can the B4L framework be used to support positive learning behaviour?

3. How might the framework be shared with parents/carers?

4. How could the B4L framework be used to support individual children with challenging behaviour?

Attachment awareness

Children are not slates from which the past can be rubbed by a duster or a sponge, but human beings who carry their previous experiences with them and whose behaviour in the present is profoundly affected by what has gone before.

(Bowlby, 1951, p. 114)

The theory of attachment was first proposed by John Bowlby who believed that children need to develop a secure attachment to their main care-giver during their early years in order to thrive emotionally, physically and cognitively (Bowlby, 1951). Subsequent research, and in particular recent advances in neuroscience, have confirmed and extended Bowlby's theory such that it is now well understood that not only do a child's primary attachments lay the foundations for their capacity to learn, but also that a child with secure attachment relationships will achieve higher academic attainment, have better self-regulation and be more socially competent than their insecurely attached counterparts (Rose et al., 2013).

Now that it is widely recognised that a child with an attachment disorder is highly likely to struggle with all aspects of school life, some of the most challenging behaviours that teachers encounter in classrooms today can be explained by children displaying the effects of insecure attachment (Cozolino, 2013). Nevertheless, there is increasing evidence to suggest that teachers can make a difference in ameliorating some of the impact of disordered attachment while at the same time enhancing the learning experiences of all pupils (Tucker et al., 2002; Davis, 2003). This is partly based on the suggestion that children can form multiple attachments (Sroufe, 1995; Robson, 2011) and that an attuned, empathetic and responsive teacher can enable children to self-regulate their behaviour through forming positive and secure relationships with them (Bergin and Bergin, 2009).

One method that has been shown to be effective in helping adults in school to build strong, supportive relationships with children whose behaviour is challenging, and who struggle to focus on learning or calm down when they are in a highly charged emotional state, is the use of emotion coaching (Rose et al., 2015). It is an intervention that has had significantly positive results for children with a range of behavioural disorders, but in particular for children with attachment issues.

Emotion coaching

The emotion coaching approach (or meta-emotion philosophy) was developed by John Gottman (Gottman and DeClaire, 1997) and is based on the development of self-regulation through recognition of the emotions that are driving behaviour rather than the behaviour itself. It enables children to understand and express their feelings in appropriate and more socially acceptable ways, supports their capacity to refocus on learning when overwhelmed with strong feelings, and helps them to become more emotionally resilient. The practice requires adults to 'empathise and guide' through a series of suggested interactions. These have been broken down into three key steps by Rose et al. (2015) who conducted a two-year pilot project on emotion coaching in schools in Wiltshire. The steps include validating the child's feelings in the first instance through an empathetic and sensitive acknowledgement of their emotional state, without focusing on their behaviour. This has been shown to have a powerful effect in calming children down and in physiological terms suggests that simply recognising and engaging with the emotions being experienced can trigger the parasympathetic system (Immordino-Yang and Damasio, 2007). Guidance comes in the form of the next step, which may not always be necessary but which requires the establishment of boundaries, making it clear that while accepting the emotions being felt, there are limits to what is acceptable behaviour. This provides the child with direction and safety, supporting them in their understanding of what is socially appropriate and the consequences of anti-social or harmful behaviour. The final step occurs later, when the child has fully calmed down, and involves adult and child revisiting the incident and problem-solving together how to avoid a recurrence. This engagement is designed to further develop a trusting and nurturing relationship between the adult and child as well as give the child the opportunities to 'own' their behaviour and better learn emotional self-regulation.

The following case study illustrates how emotion coaching made a significant difference to the relationship between a troubled boy and his teacher.

 **CASE STUDY**

Using emotion coaching to help a child with anger issues

Gemma is a Yr3 teacher in a large primary school with a mixed demographic. She has been teaching for five years and was recently trained in emotion coaching techniques as part of a cluster-wide training and found it particularly helpful when working with one child in her class, Tristan, whose angry outbursts would often disrupt her teaching and create an atmosphere of fear and anxiety among the other children.

Tristan is the eldest of a family of four children and lives with his mum and stepdad. He has a different father from his three siblings and although he has some contact with his own dad, it is intermittent and unreliable. He has struggled with behaviour problems throughout his school career and while he does not have a diagnosis of an attachment disorder, his mum has been very open about her difficulties in bonding with him as a baby and her continued concern about his behaviour.

Knowing Tristan's history, Gemma tried to establish a positive relationship with him from the outset and the first term went quite well with only a few minor incidents, but soon Tristan's old behaviour patterns began to re-emerge. He started having outbursts of frustration, such as tearing up his work or throwing equipment on the floor or shouting at other children, and when asked the reason for his outbursts, would claim that the work he had been set was too hard or someone in the class had insulted him or got in his way. Gemma's response was to try to control the situation by using the class sanctions – for example, telling Tristan that he had lost minutes from his Golden Time or would be staying in at playtime, but this often escalated into an angrier and occasionally aggressive response from him, in one instance resulting in him ripping a whole classroom display from the wall and throwing a chair across the room. This was considered sufficiently dangerous for the head teacher to be called. She sent Tristan home and imposed a one-day fixed term exclusion, which had happened on a number of occasions the previous year.

On Tristan's return it was agreed that sanctions seemed to be ineffective and a different approach was needed. Gemma was keen to try emotion coaching instead and planned the three-step method learned on her training: recognising and validating feelings and showing empathy; setting limits on behaviour; problem-solving with the child.

(Continued)

(Continued)

Gemma began by watching for early signs of Tristan becoming frustrated and would try to intervene quickly by naming his emotions verbally and offering to talk them through by saying 'I can see you're getting very frustrated and upset right now. That must be hard for you. Shall we talk about how you're feeling?' When empathising with Tristan's feelings, Gemma noticed that he began to calm down almost immediately and, once calm, he was able to talk about his frustration and anger with her and they worked together to think of some ways by which they could prevent his feelings from leading to damaging behaviours.

When Gemma was unable to identify the signs of Tristan's frustration early enough and he had an outburst and behaved inappropriately, instead of using a sanction Gemma would include limit-setting statements in her response, such as 'I can see you are angry now but it's not OK to rip up your work or shout at people. I need to help you to feel calm so that you don't break anything or hurt anyone', and encourage Tristan to use some of the calming down techniques they had discussed and been practising. One of these was to sit in the classroom's 'Peaceful Place' which was screened off from the rest of the class and had tactile and sensory objects such as glass beads, colouring-in sheets, soft fabrics, gentle music (to listen to through headphones) and cognitive prompts such as a display, photos and books about feelings and problem-solving.

Emotion coaching did not eliminate Tristan's problems completely, but Gemma noticed that the approach did have a significant effect on the frequency of his outbursts and that he was able to calm down much more quickly, usually without causing any damage. Over time, Tristan learnt to recognise for himself when his feelings were getting the better of him and would seek out Gemma or another adult to talk things through or would implement one of his calming down techniques.

QUESTIONS FOR DISCUSSION/REFLECTION

1. What are the barriers to learning for children with attachment difficulties?
2. How can emotion coaching be included in everyday interactions?
3. What challenges are there in using emotion coaching for an individual while expecting other children to follow the usual classroom rules?
4. How might emotion coaching be shared with parents/carers?
5. In what other ways can emotional literacy be developed in the classroom?

RESEARCH/EVIDENCE FOCUS

Classroom codes

Creating a classroom code that reflects the school behaviour policy but is personalised for each class of children can be a really effective way to establish and maintain positive learning behaviour. The current view in positive psychology is that when classroom rules are made explicit, children experience a sense of safety and well-being which enhances their capacity to learn (Swinson and Harrop, 2012). Porter (2014) claims that 89 per cent of disruptive behaviours can be prevented when teachers consistently provide clear behaviour expectations. Articulating desired behaviours in an accessible and positive way removes uncertainty for children who feel anxious or vulnerable about what is expected of them (and what might get them into trouble). It also enables teachers to feel more confident that their behaviour expectations will be met (Holmes, 2009). Government guidance is unequivocal that school behaviour policies need to include a set of rules and Charlie Taylor's guidance (DfE, 2011) exhorts teachers to *Display school rules clearly in classes and around the building*. However, government advice on how to develop these rules is minimal and mostly set within the context of rewards and sanctions (DfE, 2016a), rules, rewards and sanctions being referred to by Ellis and Tod as *the behavioural trinity* (2009, p151). More recent advice offered to trainee teachers from the 'Behaviour Guru' Tom Bennett does not refer to classroom rules as such, but in his *3 Rs of the Behaviour Curriculum* (DfE, 2016b) he recommends that teachers communicate shared values and behaviours openly, and regularly model and reinforce expectations and boundaries.

Rights respecting schools and classroom charters

Most authors who provide advice on how to create an effective classroom code agree on similar principles – namely, that the expectations should be inclusive, explicit, few in number and phrased positively (Dix, 2007; Holmes, 2009; Chaplain, 2014; Robinson et al., 2016). They also suggest that when children have some involvement in the design of their classroom code, they feel a sense of ownership and are more likely to be motivated not only to cooperate fully themselves, but also to encourage their peers to as well. Rogers (2012) goes further and promotes the use of a framework of rights, responsibilities and rules based on an agreed set of values shared by the whole school community. He believes that behaving well is the joint responsibility of all class members and that *the most fundamental rights of a classroom member are those of respect and fair treatment ... they relate to due responsibility and fair and agreed rules* (2012, p15).

The theme of rights and responsibilities as a basis for respectful behaviour in schools has been established in England by UNICEF (United Nations International Children's Emergency Fund) through an award known as the Rights Respecting Schools (RRS) Award (UNICEF(a)) which promotes the UN Convention on the Rights of the Child (1989). The award was the result of an initiative introduced in Hampshire in 2002 to encourage human rights education and develop dispositions and behaviours that support social justice within the school community (Covell et al., 2010). Results from this initiative showed that in participating schools, children demonstrated higher levels of engagement in learning, more respectful behaviour and greater participation in school life than children in non-participating schools (Covell and Howe, 2008).

One of the key features of schools that follow the RRS agenda is that, consistent with children's rights to participation in matters that affect them (Article 12 of the Convention), school rules and behaviour codes are decided democratically, giving children opportunities to have a voice in decisions that affect them, and although the remit for the RRS award goes considerably beyond setting up classroom codes of behaviour, it does provide guidance and support on how to create and use a classroom charter (UNICEF(b)). In 'rights-respecting' schools, at the beginning of each year, children and teachers work together in each class to create an agreement of everyone's rights and their corresponding responsibilities. These may include such statements as *we have the right to be treated fairly and the responsibility to treat each other fairly; we have the right to be heard and the responsibility to listen to and respect other people's ideas; we all have the right to learn, so we will help each other* (Covell, 2013, p42).

The following case study illustrates how the use of a class charter helped a teacher establish positive learning behaviour in his classroom.

 **CASE STUDY**

Setting up a class charter to establish behaviour expectations

Craig's first career was as a graphic designer. He is now into his second year of teaching and takes every opportunity to bring his creative skills into the classroom. He has an energetic, positive approach and his lessons are often lively and engaging, but during his NQT year he struggled to maintain positive behaviour and cooperation in his class and often felt that he was not fully in control of what was happening. He began his second year in a Year 5 class in a different school and was keen to establish clear behaviour expectations from the outset.

The school that Craig moved to is a 'Rights Respecting School' (RRS) and he was advised to follow the UNICEF guidance on how to establish a class charter in the first week after the summer holidays. Using the school's RRS resources, he planned a series of lessons designed around the UN Convention of the Rights of the Child (CRC): recapping the articles of the CRC, their importance and why they exist; discussing with the children which articles to base their class charter on; agreeing the wording of the charter and designing it; signing the charter and displaying it in the classroom. The resulting agreement consisted of a list of 'rights' with direct links to articles in the CRC, and a list of 'responsibilities' which every member of the class (including Craig and his teaching assistant, Michelle) signed.

Craig wanted the charter to be meaningful and relevant to all the children in his class, so over the next two weeks he used a carousel of inclusive activities: drama and role-play, creative writing, photography, artwork and game design to bring the charter alive and encourage every child to be involved and to feel a sense of ownership of it. Once the charter was established, he regularly referred to it. For example, acknowledging children for behaviour that specifically related to one of their class articles: 'I can see you two are really listening to each other's ideas. Well done for following Article 13!'; or using it to remind children whose behaviour was disrespectful or inappropriate that they were breaking their agreement: 'I can see that Asif is hurt by what you just said. That is not in keeping with our responsibility to be kind and respectful to everyone.' As well as modelling the language of the charter himself, Craig encouraged the children to use the same words when reflecting on their own behaviour or describing the behaviour of others following an incident. In this way, he was able to reinforce the behaviour expectations by consistently relating children's actions to the agreement they had all made.

Although the UNICEF guidance states that a class charter is not intended to be used as a behaviour management tool, Craig found that by combining it with guidance from the school behaviour policy he was able to use it to generate a menu of rewards for children who followed the class charter and an agreed set of consequences if any of the articles were broken. He had a round of discussions with the children, giving them choices from a range already agreed in the school behaviour policy, until they came to a consensus about the rewards and consequences they thought were fair for their class. These were displayed on a poster alongside the charter and included rewards such as a 'teacher text' to a parent/carer's mobile phone, extra playtime, and an end-of-term class pizza party, as well as the regular whole-school rewards of house points, afternoon tea with the head teacher and the 'Big Yellow Duck Award' (given for particular acts of kindness). Consequences for unkind or uncooperative behaviour were chosen with varying degrees of severity ranging from missing five minutes of playtime or working alone on the 'Thinking Table', to doing 'community service' (which involves doing jobs around the school during a series of lunchtimes) or being placed 'on report'. In the spirit of being a Rights Respecting School, these consequences also include opportunities for reparation and supporting children to make amends for any harm or damage caused.

Craig continued to use the charter, and the rewards and consequences system, on a daily basis and by the end of term 2 he was pleased to notice that he had been able to teach exciting, highly active and creative lessons without being concerned that children would be uncooperative or challenging, as had happened with his previous class. He said 'the class charter has really made a difference to how I think about behaviour … it's based on everyone respecting each other and looking out for each other … the children in my class have ownership of it and are cooperative because they want to be, they make that choice themselves, not because I'm some strict disciplinarian that makes them do what I want. I'm so glad I've found a way to have good behaviour in my classroom without becoming the stereotypical male teacher who is "good with discipline" just because I'm a bloke.'

QUESTIONS FOR DISCUSSION/REFLECTION

1. What are the benefits and disadvantages of using rewards and sanctions?

2. How could the RRS guidance be used in other ways to support positive learning behaviour?

3. What challenges might there be in creating a class charter?

4. What are the rights and responsibilities of the teacher in terms of behaviour in the classroom?

CHAPTER SUMMARY

This chapter has provided a summary of the context for Behaviour for Learning, explained the conceptual framework with suggestions on how it can be applied, and given an illustration of its use as a classroom intervention. By focusing on B4L, it offers a blueprint for creating a positive learning ethos without resorting to traditional methods of discipline and control. The chapter has also considered the importance of attachment issues and proposed emotion coaching as a strategy to support children in a highly charged emotional state, a method that can empower children who are in distress and give teachers greater confidence in using this intervention to support them. The practice of creating a classroom code or charter also offers children greater ownership and opportunities for self-regulating their behaviour. It is a positive and effective alternative to imposing 'top-down' rules and further endorses the message from B4L that behaviour management is 'all about relationships' (Holmes, 2009, p89).

SOME FINAL POINTS

- The strategies suggested here are likely to be more powerful if shared with parents/carers, particularly for those who are coping with challenging behaviour from their children at home. Consider how each method might be used to forge positive links between home and school.

- School behaviour policies frequently focus on rewards and sanctions, do not take account of the importance of relationships and are rarely written in consultation with children. Reflect on the way in which a behaviour policy is translated into practice and how it might be developed and used more positively and effectively.

- Behaviour for Learning, emotion coaching and the Rights Respecting Schools agenda all take a pro-active and positive stance towards children's behaviour. However, the language and practice of behaviourism are still prevalent in schools and even the word 'behaviour' persistently has a negative connotation. Consider how this might be challenged and how teachers might be encouraged to take a more optimistic approach.

FURTHER READING

Ellis, S and Tod, J (2015) *Promoting Behaviour for Learning in the Classroom: Effective Strategies, Personal Style and Professionalism.* Abingdon: Routledge.

This latest book by Ellis and Tod provides further insights into the principles and practice of the B4L conceptual framework. It draws on teachers' everyday experiences of interactions and relationships in the classroom and is designed to appeal to those new to the profession.

Gottman, J and DeClaire, J (1997) *Raising an Emotionally Intelligent Child: The Heart of Parenting.* New York: Prentice-Hall.

Although now nearly 20 years old, and addressed to parents, this is Gottman's seminal work on emotion coaching and a 'must read' for anyone who wants to understand more about this strategy and how to practise it.

Robins, G (2012) *Praise, Motivation and the Child.* Abingdon: Routledge.

This highly accessible book written by a former deputy head teacher brings clarity to the theory and practice of behaviourism, constructivism and positive psychology. It considers the use of extrinsic and intrinsic rewards, and gives children a voice in expressing what their motivations are and how teachers can best support them in developing positive learning behaviours.

Useful websites

Attachment Aware Schools: http://attachmentawareschools.com

This website provides a comprehensive introduction to attachment and the implications for learning and behaviour, as well as links to further resources, including guidance on emotion coaching.

Behaviour4learning: http://webarchive.nationalarchives.gov.uk/20101021152907/http:/www.behaviour4learning.ac.uk

This website provides background research, resources and ideas for teachers in all aspects of the B4L approach. Although now part of the national archive, its content is still highly relevant for today's classrooms. NQTs may find the '26 scenarios' particularly useful.

Behaviour2Learn videos: www.youtube.com/user/Behaviour4Learning

This collection of video clips covers a broad range of behaviour issues from practical classroom tips to debates on how best to respond to challenging behaviour.

Rights Respecting Schools: www.unicef.org.uk/rights-respecting-schools/about-the-award/what-is-the-rights-respecting-schools-award/

This link takes you to the UNICEF site that provides all the information on the RRS award, including how to create a class charter.

▬▬ REFERENCES ▬▬

Adams, K (2009) *Behaviour for Learning in the Primary School*. Exeter: Learning Matters.

Bandura, A (1971) *Social Learning Theory*. New York: General Learning Press.

Bennett, V and Henderson, N (2013) Young children learning: the importance of play. In Ward, S (ed.) *A Student's Guide to Education Studies* (3rd edn). Abingdon: Routledge, pp168–77.

Bergin, C and Bergin, D (2009) Attachment in the classroom. *Educational Psychology Review,* 21: 141–70.

Bowlby, J (1951) Maternal care and mental health. *Bulletin of the World Health Organisation,* 3: 355–534.

Bronfenbrenner, U (1979) *The Ecology of Human Development: Experiments by Nature and Design.* Cambridge, MA: Harvard University Press.

Chaplain, R (2014) Managing classroom behaviour. In Cremin, T and Arthur, J (eds) *Learning to Teach in the Primary School*. London: Routledge, pp181–201.

Covell, K (2013) Children's human rights education as a means to social justice: a case study from England. *International Journal for Social Justice,* 2(1): 35–48.

Covell, K and Howe, RB (2008) Rights, respect and responsibility: final report on the county of Hampshire Rights Education Initiative. Hampshire County Council.

Covell, K, Howe, RB and McNeil, JK (2010) Implementing children's human rights education in schools. *Improving Schools,* 13(2): 1–16.

Cozolino, LJ (2013) *The Social Neuroscience of Education: Optimising Attachment and Learning in the Classroom.* London: WW Norton.

Davis, HA (2003) Conceptualizing the role and influence of student–teacher relationships on children's social and cognitive development. *Educational Psychologist,* 38(4): 207–34.

Department for Education (2011) Getting the simple things right: Charlie Taylor's behaviour checklists. Available at: www.gov.uk/government/uploads/system/uploads/attachment_data/file/571640/Getting_the_simple_things_right_Charlie_Taylor_s_behaviour_checklists.pdf (accessed November 2016).

Department for Education (2012a) Teachers' Standards: guidance for school leaders, school staff and governing bodies. Available at: www.gov.uk/government/uploads/system/uploads/attachment_data/file/301107/Teachers__Standards.pdf (accessed November 2016).

Department for Education (2012b) Ensuring good behaviour in schools. Available at: www.gov.uk/government/uploads/system/uploads/attachment_data/file/239943/Ensuring_Good_Behaviour_in_Schools-summary.pdf (accessed November 2016).

Department for Education (2016a) Behaviour and discipline in schools: advice for *head teachers and school staff*. Available at: www.gov.uk/government/uploads/system/uploads/attachment_data/file/488034/Behaviour_and_Discipline_in_Schools_A_guide_for_headteachers_and_School_Staff.pdf (accessed November 2016).

Department for Education (2016b) Developing behaviour management content for initial teacher. Available at: www.gov.uk/government/uploads/system/uploads/attachment_data/file/536889/Behaviour Management_report_final__11_July_2016.pdf (accessed November 2016).

Department for Education and Skills (2005a) Learning behaviour: the report of the practitioners group on school behaviour and discipline (the Steer Report). Nottingham: DfES. Available at: http://cw.routledge.com/textbooks/9780415485586/data/BehaviourTheSteerReport.pdf (accessed November 2016).

Department for Education and Skills (2005b) Excellence and enjoyment: social and emotional aspects of learning: guidance. Available at: http://webarchive.nationalarchives.gov.uk/20110809101133/nsonline.org.uk/node/87009 (accessed November 2016).

Dix, P (2007) *Taking Care of Behaviour: Practical Skills for Teachers.* Harlow: Pearson Education.

Ellis, S and Tod, J (2009) *Behaviour for Learning: Proactive to Behaviour Management.* London: David Fulton.

Ellis, S and Tod, J (2015) *Promoting Behaviour for Learning in the Classroom.* London: Routledge.

Gerhardt, S (2014) *Why Love Matters: How Affection Shapes a Baby's Brain* (2nd edn). London: Routledge.

Gottman, J and Declaire, J (1997) *Raising an Emotionally Intelligent Child: The Heart of Parenting.* New York: Prentice-Hall.

Higgins, S, Baumfield, V and Hall, E (2007) Learning skills and the development of learning capabilities report. In *Research Evidence in Education Library.* London: EPPI-Centre, Social Science Research Unit, Institute of Education, University of London.

Holmes, E (2009) (2nd edn) *The Newly Qualified Teachers Handbook.* London: Routledge.

Immordino-Yang, M and Damasio, A (2007) We feel, therefore we learn: the relevance of affective and social neuroscience to education. *Mind, Brain and Education Journal,* 1(1): 310.

Maslow, A (1976) *The Farther Reaches of Human Nature.* New York: Penguin Books.

Music, G (2016) *Nurturing Natures: Attachment and Children's Emotional, Sociocultural and Brain Development* (2nd edn). London: Routledge.

Paton, G (2014) Ofsted: an hour of teaching each day lost to bad behaviour. Available at: www.telegraph.co.uk/education/educationnews/11119373/Ofsted-an-hour-of-teaching-each-day-lost-to-bad-behaviour.html (accessed November 2016).

Porter, L (2014) (3rd edn) *Behaviour in Schools: Theory and Practice for Teachers*. Maidenhead: Open University Press.

Powell, S and Tod, J (2004) *A Systematic Review of How Learning Theories Explain Learning Behaviour in School Contexts*. London: EPPI-Centre, Social Science Research Unit, Institute of Education, University of London.

Robinson, C, Bingle, B and Howard, C (2016) *Surviving and Thriving as an NQT*. Northwich: Critical Publishing.

Robson, S (2011) Attachment and relationships. In Moyles, J, Georgeson, J and Payler, J (eds) *Beginning Teaching, Beginning Learning: In Early Years and Primary Education*. Maidenhead: Open University Press.

Rogers, B (2012) (3rd edn) *You Know the Fair Rule*. Harlow: Pearson.

Rose, J, Gilbert, L and Smith, H (2013) Affective teaching and the affective dimensions of learning. In Ward, S (ed.) *A Student's Guide to Education Studies* (3rd edn). Abingdon: Routledge, pp178–88.

Rose, J, McGuire-Snieckus, R and Gilbert, L (2015) Emotion coaching – a strategy for promoting behavioural self-regulation in children/young people in schools: a pilot study. *The European Journal of Social and Behavioural Sciences*, XIII.

Sroufe, A (1995) *Emotional Development*. Cambridge: Cambridge University Press.

Swinson, J and Harrop, A (2012) *Positive Psychology for Teachers*. London: Routledge.

Tucker, CM, Zayco, RA, Herman, KC, Reinke, WM, Trujillo, M and Carraway, K (2002) Teacher and child variables as predictors of academic engagement among low-income African American children. *Psychology in the Schools*, 39: 477–88.

UNICEF (a): Rights Respecting Schools Award. Available at: www.unicef.org.uk/rights-respecting-schools/about-the-award/what-is-the-rights-respecting-schools-award/ (accessed November 2016).

UNICEF (b): Classroom Charters. Available at: www.unicef.ca/sites/default/files/imce_uploads/UTILITY%20NAV/TEACHERS/DOCS/GC/Classroom_Charters_Instructions.pdf (accessed November 2016).

UNICEF (1989) The United Nations Convention on the Rights of the Child. Available at: http://353ld710iigr2n4po7k4kgvv-wpengine.netdna-ssl.com/wp-content/uploads/2010/05/UNCRC_PRESS200910web.pdf (accessed November 2016).

Vickery, A (ed.) (2014) *Developing Active Learning in the Primary Classroom*. London: Sage.

5
REFLECTING ON YOUR TEACHING

JULIA LAWRENCE

THIS CHAPTER

By reading this chapter you will develop your understanding of the following.

- How reflecting on your own practice can support your induction and development as a teacher during your NQT year.
- How different tools can be used to support you to develop as a reflective practitioner.
- How to improve your knowledge of practical examples of tools which can be used within the school environment.
- How to identify strengths and challenges in using this type of approach in schools.

LINKS TO THE TEACHERS' STANDARDS

This chapter will help you with the following Teachers' Standards.

4. Plan and teach well-structured lessons

Including being able to:

- Reflect systematically on the effectiveness of lessons and approaches.

8. Fulfil wider professional responsibilities

Including being able to:

- Develop effective professional relationships with colleagues, knowing how and when to draw on advice and specialist support.
- Take responsibility for improving teaching through appropriate professional development, responding to advice and feedback from colleagues.

Introduction

Reflective practice has an allure that is seductive in nature because it rings true for most people as something useful and informing. However, for reflection to genuinely be a lens into the world of practice, it is important that the nature of the reflection be identified in such a way as to offer ways of questioning taken-for-granted assumptions and encouraging one to see his or her practice through others' eyes. The relationship between, time, experience, and expectations of learning through reflection is an important element of reflection.

(Loughran, 2002, p33)

The adoption of a more school-led approach to initial teacher education and training, and the development of Teaching Schools with their current remit to support research and development activities, have heightened the need for teachers to develop the knowledge, skills and understanding necessary to support high-level reflection (Blandford, 2013). Furthermore, the publication of the Carter Review (2015) places continual knowledge development and enhancement as central to improvements in the training and career development of teachers.

By reading this chapter you should develop a deeper understanding of the reflective process and how it can support you to develop into a reflective practitioner. Focusing on reviewing your own practice and using it as a source of evidence, this chapter will encourage you to consider your own practice with a view to enhancing the quality of your teaching and, as a consequence, improve the progress of pupils both within lessons and over time.

Reflection in education

Education requires individuals to reflect on themselves in respect of their values, practice and understanding. Through such reflection teachers are able to learn from their experiences, raising their personal self-awareness as well as modifying their teaching behaviours.

Reflection in education is not a new concept and is frequently defined using Dewey's definition as *active, persistent, and careful consideration of any belief or supposed form of knowledge* (1933, p9). Loughran argues that effective reflection occurs when *it leads the teacher to make meaning from the situation in ways that enhance understanding so that she or he comes to see and understand the practice setting from a variety of viewpoints* (2002, p36). Rhine and Bryant view it as how the *ability to look back, rethink, and expand one's view of a classroom enables pre-service teachers to examine the effect that their actions and their students actions have on teaching and learning* (2007, p347). More recently, Tripp and Rich define reflection *as a self-critical, investigative process wherein teachers consider the effect of their pedagogical decisions on their situated practice with the aims of improving those practices* (2012, p678).

Reflection activities

What is not disputed is that teachers should reflect on their own teaching and the strategies they employ as a way of supporting pupil progress. Initial teacher training and continuing professional development have for many years required trainees to evaluate lessons (Standal and Moe, 2013; Farrell, 2014), or focus on specific aspects of the Teachers' Standards (DfE, 2011) to identify strengths and areas for development. Models of reflection (Schön, 1933; Gibbs, 1988) provide a framework against which analysis can take place. However, reflection can be time-consuming and it therefore becomes important to look at ways in which reflective activities can be developed in order that they complement day-to-day practice and become accessible to all.

The degree to which we reflect, and the purpose of this reflection, may well differ over time. Research (Loughran, 2002; Kayapinar and Erkus, 2009; Lawrence et al., 2016) suggests that our capacity and ability to engage effectively in the reflective process are progressive in their development. Over time the individual travels along a continuum, moving from basic thinking, through problem analysis, culminating in a well-defined and crafted approach. Thus, movement is seen from a description of the event where initial thoughts start to emerge, to a more detailed analysis where the individual is more constructive in his or her evaluation of impact with a view to make transformative changes to practice.

While we might understand the need to reflect on our practice, it is the value we assign to the process that results in our level of engagement and consequently the potential impact it has on our professional development (Kayapinar and Erkus, 2009; Tondeur et al., 2013). In undervaluing the process, we run the risk of any engagement becoming superficial (such a concept is discussed later in this chapter). Thus, from the start it becomes important to identify the purpose of reflection and how it will be used to improve the performance of both the teacher and the learner.

The use of video to support reflection

Reflection can be undertaken as an individual activity or through the support of others (Tripp and Rich, 2012). Technological advances have resulted in the development of software to support the use of video to record and identify good practice. For example, the use of video stimulated recall (VSR) allows individuals to review experiences by watching specific episodes that have been captured using a camera (this may be free-standing or involve using a tablet or other device). While not a new practice, the software that is now available allows the observer to 'tag' episodes, either during the initial capture of the experience or at a later time, to highlight specific examples of behaviours, enhancing any potential reflection by providing concrete visual examples.

In doing so, the teachers being videoed are able to observe their own teaching, rather than relying on the feedback provided by an observer making notes during an observation. For many, this can be more beneficial than some traditional feedback provided by an external source, as it allows them the opportunity to see what they were doing at any given time, rather than relying on the interpretations of someone else. Thus, we are better able to visualise our reflections, which are based on the observation of our own practice, allowing us to provide a concrete record of our teaching and how our practice evolves over time. We therefore become the core of the reflective cycle and the resulting progression in learning.

The importance of your approach to reflection

Hobson (2016) argues that central to any reflective process is the need to be open, honest and where possible avoid the tendency of many to make judgements. In reviewing the concept of 'judgementor-ing', Hobson identifies that when there is an insistence on making a judgement (in a teaching concept this could be reflected in the awarding of a lesson grade), it may result in a reluctance to become fully involved in the process, reflected in the participant becoming more reluctant to seek support, seek out opportunities for observations and to reflect at the level necessary for future progress to be achieved. This has the potential for individuals to become withdrawn and in extreme cases experience significant negative impacts on them as an individual. While his research focused on the impact of mentors on trainee teachers, there is an argument that suggests that if we are self-reflecting, we ourselves may become too judgmental on our own performance and therefore negatively impact on our self-worth through negative thought processes. However, we must always remember that where reflection is effective, improvements will be seen in the practices of those engaging in the process.

The transition from your training to newly qualified teacher (NQT) year may be stressful as you move from being a trainee or beginner teacher to become more embedded in the profession. Both Shanks (2014) and Hobson (2016) indicate that this period may result in you as a teacher feeling somewhat isolated, powerless and lacking control. Thus, it becomes important to think about how we will engage in the reflective process and, where possible, minimise the risks to ourselves.

So far, we have identified that the reflective cycle is an integral part of the role of the teacher. It allows us to review our progress and impact, but carries with it an element of risk if it is not controlled. The next part of this chapter looks at some approaches that can be adopted to support the process. These are then further developed in a section that looks at the application of practice to the classroom.

Reflective models

Reflective models encourage us to consider what it is we want to achieve, how we reflect and what we reflect on. By using them we are encouraged to think about the processes or practices we use, so we need to have some form of framework against which our reflections can take place. In essence, we need a mirror to look into and see what is reflected back. Common approaches used are those of Schön (1933), who views reflection taking place during (in-action) or after an event (of-action), or Kolb (1984), whose reflective cycle encourages us to plan, experience, reflect, understand and then plan for the next episode, using the experiences we have used to reflect on.

However, there is a tendency for us to focus on the teacher rather than the learner. As you may be aware, central to any successful teacher is the impact they have on the learning achieved by their pupils. Thus, it is the progress of the pupils that rightly or wrongly defines the success of the teacher. Encouraging us as teachers to stop and think about what the actions/reactions of pupils mean, encourages us to think about how behaviours (of themselves) might subsequently change.

Models also encourage us to consider how we draw out reflections. In doing so, we should be thinking about some of the following.

- The rationale behind why we are doing something.

- A justification of why we have opted to undertake that activity.

- The alternatives we might have.

- The beliefs we hold towards an activity and how these might be reflected in the approaches we adopt.

- How we engage in the self-reflection process.

Sources of evidence

So how can the reflective process be evidenced or, more specifically, what sources of evidence can you use to support the reflective process? In your previous experience, you will have been encouraged to keep some form of portfolio to show evidence of your progress against the Teachers' Standards. However, as a beginner teacher with the associated stresses of starting in the classroom, the sources should be those that are easily accessible. As already suggested, the process of reflection can be time-consuming, therefore trying to generate lots of data will not be beneficial. On a day-to-day basis the following could be used.

- Observations – by ourselves and by others
  - What did others see in your lesson that you did not?
  - Did you note anything down as you taught the lesson?
- Personal evaluations of lessons
  - How did we feel about the lesson?
  - What went well?

- What would you do differently next time?

- Why would you make changes?

- Lesson plans

  - Did you make changes to the lesson as we taught it?

  - Did the differentiation you planned for the lesson work, or do you need to modify these moving forward?

- Pupils work

  - Did the pupils achieve what you wanted them to?

- The pupils themselves

  - Did you undertake an exit survey to see how the pupils felt about the lesson?

- Discussions

  - Did you talk through the lesson prior to and post its delivery?

In essence, when reflecting on our teaching, the evidence we have to hand will provide us with the data we need to understand whether the lesson has been successful (evidenced through the progress made by the pupils) and what changes we might make to improve next time. Thus, we can use similar methods to those we might use during our lessons to support pupils to reflect on themselves.

Focusing on reflective practice and its impact on the teacher

This section develops further some of the research previously alluded to which has focused on reflective practice and its impact on the teacher.

Developing the reflective process in teaching

Using an intensive observation programme to support reflection among a small sample of Singaporean physical education teachers, Lawrence et al. (2016) identified the positive impact of focused observations on teachers' reflective capacities. Specifically, they identified that over even a short period of time, teachers were able to increase the depth of their analysis, resulting in changes to their behaviours around planning, delivery and assess. A consequence of this were changes in pupil behaviour, resulting in the observation of greater progress in learning. The study included the use of a structured protocol to support the reflective process (as detailed later in the chapter), as well as the use of video-enhanced observation technology, whereby a video of the lesson is made and then used to focus post-lesson conversations.

What this research shows is that in engaging in a reflective process, not only are the tools you use important, but also how different roles evolve over time to allow the teacher to take greater ownership of the reflective process, rather than it being controlled by the observer. Therefore, the teacher becomes the learner.

Using video-stimulated recall (VSR)

Tondeur et al. (2013) looked at using video-stimulated recall to investigate teachers' use of information communication technology (ICT) strategies within their teaching. Their premise was based on the concept that using VSR allowed for *authentic understanding of teachers' practice* (p446). In videoing teachers' delivery of a lesson, they were able to use the information captured to encourage teachers, through a review of their lessons, to think about their thoughts and feelings at specific points within the lesson. Specifically, they challenged their participants to reflect on why they had chosen to adopt the practices they had at the times identified. In analysis of their findings, the use of VSR did allow participants opportunities to reflect in more depth, and as a consequence saw the process as allowing them to develop professionally rather than being an imposition.

In the classroom

So far, we have focused on the principles associated with reflective practice, examining definitions and moving to look at the research associated with it. This section focuses on how this might be implemented within the classroom setting. In particular, it will examine two key approaches that can be used to support reflection.

- Lesson conversations.

- Using video-stimulated recall in the classroom.

Lesson conversations

By far the most common approach to reflection is to undertake lesson observations whereby teachers are observed by other individuals who provide them with feedback based on their observations. Here the tendency is for the observer to provide an interpretation of the lesson based on his or her own perceptions of what makes a good lesson. What is not always evident is the voice of the teacher being observed, as in the worst cases the observer just describes what they think went well and what they think could be improved on. Thus, based on our earlier discussions, the reflection becomes descriptive and therefore you as the teacher have limited input on the process.

The central part of the reflective processes associated with lesson observation lies in the structuring of the conversations that are held around the planning, delivery and evaluation of the lesson. This is reflected in the identification of key questions on which to hang any thoughts and can be reflected in the establishment of the following structure.

1. A pre-observation conversation

Here a conversation is held about what the aim of the lesson is, what you are expecting pupils to achieve and what evidence you will seek to demonstrate that the pupils have indeed achieved your expectations. It should involve reflection on the choice of the activities you have planned and be based on a clear understanding of how you have used prior experiences to structure the learning episode.

2. The lesson

Here the focus in on observing pupils' behaviours. Are they working at the level you would expect, do you need to make any lesson adjustments? How do you make a note of any positive aspects or concerns?

3. A post-lesson conversation

Here the focus is on the lesson. Did the pupils achieve what you had expected of them? What evidence do you have for this? What went well in the lesson? What would you do differently if you taught the lesson again? How will you use this experience to plan you next lesson?

If structured appropriately, the same approach can be adopted when you engage in self-reflection. Thus, depending on who is involved in the reflective activity (is it just you, is it your mentor, is it a group?), the structure and content can predominantly remain the same; it is just the role of the individual that changes.

Using video-stimulated recall in the classroom

The use of video-stimulated recall as part of the reflective process allows teachers the opportunity to review their own performance as they teach, and therefore the focus is more subjective, rather than being based on what they feel has happened. This strengthens their opportunity to draw on specific evidence to support their reflections.

Once you have become used to the sound of your own voice and your mannerisms, the use of this technique can be very insightful. At last you see yourself in action rather than relying on someone else. However, it is important, as with the conversations discussed in the previous section, that the process is structured.

As you are likely to be capturing the behaviour of your pupils as well as yourself in this process, permissions will need to be sought from the school and the parents for this to take place. Most schools will have a policy in place with parents granting permission for use of images for training purposes, but how the physical recordings are used and stored does need to be clearly outlined in line with the safeguarding policies within the school.

You will need to consider what software you will use to support this. Commercially available programmes such as IRIS Connect (www.irisconnect.co.uk) and VEO (www.veo-group.com) allow you to tag, store and share videos, and use basic tablet cameras to capture the information. However, a simple recording facility will provide you with the basics, although I would encourage you to use some form of microphone facility as well. Positioning of the camera is important, as you will want to capture as much as you can, but without having a negative impact on the learning that is taking place. If used frequently, both you and your classes will become familiar with the equipment being *in situ* and therefore it is less likely to become a distraction.

Once captured, the analysis of the video can be undertaken either by a complete rewatch, or through focused observation around specific times during the lesson, or specific behaviours that have been seen. Using the structure of the post-lesson conversation allows you to reflect on the video.

While the common use of video capture is through recording the lesson and then reviewing after the event, some schools are now using live streaming technology. In this approach, predominantly seen in Chinese secondary schools or through the use of streaming technology,

> *a particular school arranges for experienced teachers working for the school to observe its teachers using remote live video technology with the ultimate aim of support teacher professional development. The experienced observers can view classroom practices without visiting actual classrooms.*
>
> (Liang, 2015, p238)

In such a way, teachers are less likely to change their practices to reflect someone being in their classroom, thereby reducing what Liang (2015) refers to as *observer effect* or *reactivity*.

 **CASE STUDY**

Using video-enhanced observation (VEO) to support self-reflection of one's teaching

Pete is a newly qualified teacher. As part of his continuing professional development, he is required to undertake a number of self-reflections based on the lessons he teaches. At the start of the lesson, he asked a colleague to record it so that he could use the recording to reflect on his delivery and interactions with the class. Following the lesson, he reviewed the recording and was able to see clearly key characteristics of his own practice – for example, use of voice, positioning at the board and hand gestures.

While Pete found this a challenging experience, it allowed him to appreciate how his interactions with the class varied during the lesson and in particular how restrictive the classroom layout was in terms of his ability to interact with some groups. Using these observations and his subsequent evaluation, modifications were made to aspects of his delivery during the next lesson. While the topic area was different, Pete was much more focused on his positioning and ensuring that he engaged with all the members of the group through questioning. This included making changes to the layout of the classroom.

 QUESTIONS FOR DISCUSSION AND REFLECTION

1. Why would using a video allow the teacher to 'see' the characteristics of their teaching?

2. Why would observing your own teaching be challenging?

3. What sort of behaviours might have been observed to allow the teacher to say that the layout of the classroom was restrictive?

4. How could the teacher use their next observation to reflect further on their use of questioning?

Conclusion

Engaging in the reflective process allows us to develop a deeper understanding of our teaching and the impact it has on pupils. A range of approaches can be adopted, but central to these is an open mind and willingness to engage.

Engagement in a reflective process can be beneficial not only to the individual involved in the focused reflection, but also to those who engage with them. From a mentor perspective, this might be reflected in changes in their own practice, and where communities of practice (see Lave and Wenger, 1991) become established, the opportunities for a wider field of teachers to work together to change their practice can become embedded within the school philosophy.

In many ways, by scaffolding our reflections and therefore continuing to actively engage with the learning processes we encourage our pupils to access, we are also reflecting on the principles associated with the construction of our own and others' knowledge, reflecting the social constructivist views of learning.

QUESTIONS FOR DISCUSSION AND REFLECTION

1. The transition from QTS to NQT can be challenging. Hobson (2016) identifies some of the issues associated with this and the negative consequence it might have on the individual as a whole. As a teacher embarking on your career, what strategies do you plan to engage with to ensure that you minimise any risk associated with engagement in the reflective process?

2. One of the most beneficial approaches to support reflections on your teaching is the use of visually stimulated recall, which allows you to observe yourself teaching.

   a. How would you feel about engaging in such a process?

   b. What strategies would you employ to ensure that this was a positive experience?

   c. How would you use the experience to inform your own practice?

   d. How would such a process support you in evidencing your progress towards meeting your NQT standards, and moving forward how could it be used to support your professional development?

3. Having reviewed the range of models of reflection, answer the following questions.

   a. Which approach do you feel would be the most effective in supporting your professional development?

   b. How do you plan to embed the reflective process in your day-to-day teaching to ensure that you plan and deliver high-quality lessons?

CHAPTER SUMMARY

Reflecting on your own teaching is an important skill if you are to develop as a teacher. The aim of this chapter was to engage you in the reflective process as a means of using the skills you developed during your initial training phase to embed in your role as a beginner teacher and to support your professional development.

(Continued)

(Continued)

In introducing you to a range of literature, models of reflection and associated approaches that can be used within the classroom environment, opportunities for you to think about how you engage in the reflective process and how the subsequent outcomes to develop and enhance as a teacher have been explored. In engaging with the discussion questions and further reading, you can now start to plan how you will continue to embed reflective practice in the roles you undertake to ensure that you show clear evidence of how you *reflect systematically on the effectiveness of lessons and approaches* and *take responsibility for improving teaching through appropriate professional development, responding to advice and feedback from colleagues*, as detailed in the Teachers' Standards.

■■■ FURTHER READING ■■■

Tripp, T and Rich, P (2012) Using video to analyse one's own teaching. *British Journal of Educational Technology*, 43(4): 678–704.

Drawing on over 60 published articles, this meta-analysis review of literature looking at the use of video to support analysis of your own teaching provides a range of strategies that can be used to support the process. It also provides a comprehensive review of the literature currently available in the field of video analysis and therefore supplies a launch pad for those who are looking to explore this area in more depth.

■■■ REFERENCES ■■■

Blandford, S (2013) Developing a global system of teacher education for a global economy: is there a role for a royal college? *Education Today*, 63(1). Available at: www.collegeofteachers.ac.uk/education today63_1/sonia-blandford (accessed 22.12.16).

Carter, A (2015) Carter review of initial teacher training. London: Department for Education.

Department for Education (2011) Teachers' Standards: guidance for school leaders, school staff and governing bodies. London: DfE.

Dewey, J (1933) *How We Think*. Chicago, IL: Henrey Regney.

Farrell, TSC (2014) 'Teacher you are stupid!' Cultivating a reflective disposition. *The Electorinic Journal for English as a Second Language*, 18(3): 1–11.

Gibbs, G (1988) *Learning by Doing: A Guide to Teaching and Learning Methods*. Oxford: Further Education Unit, Oxford Polytechnic.

Hobson, AJ (2016) Judgementoring and how to avert it: introducing ONSIDE mentoring for beginning teachers. *International Journal of Mentoring and Coaching in Education*, 5(2): 8–119.

Kayapinar, U and Erkus, A (2009) Measuring teacher reflection: development of TRS. *Eurasian Journal of Educational Research*, 37: 144–58.

Kolb, DA (1984) *Experiential Learning: Experience as the Source of Learning and Development*. Upper Saddle River, NJ: Prentice-Hall.

Lave, J and Wenger, E (1991) *Situated Learning: Legitimate Peripheral Participation*. New York: Cambridge University Press.

Lawrence, J, Low, K and Phan, J (2016) The impact of a high intensity observation programme in Singapore. Paper presented at 6th Annual International Conference on Education and e-Learning, 26–27 September, Singapore.

Liang, J (2015) Live video classroom observation: an effective approach to reducing reactivity in collecting observational information for teacher professional development. *Journal of Education for Teaching: International Research and Pedagogy*, 41(3): 235–53.

Loughran, JJ (2002) Effective reflective practice: in search of meaning in learning about teaching. *Journal of Teacher Education*, 53(1): 33–43.

McFadden, J, Ellis, J, Anwar, T and Roehrig, G (2014) Beginning science teachers' use of a digital video annotation tool to promote reflective practices. *Journal of Science Education Technology*, 23: 458–70.

Rhine, S and Bryant, J (2007) Enhancing pre-service teachers' reflective practice with digital video-based dialogue. *Reflective Practice: International and Multidisciplinary Perspectives*, 8(3): 345–58.

Schön, DA (1933) *The Reflective Practitioner: How Professionals Think in Action*. New York: Basic Books.

Shanks, R (2014) A study of learners' situational vulnerability: new teachers in Scotland. *Education in the North*, 21: 2–20.

Standal, OV and Moe, VF (2013) Reflective practice in physical education and physical education teacher education: a review of literature since 1995, *Quest*, 65: 220–40.

Tondeur, J, Kershaw, LH, Vanderlinde, R and van Braak, J (2013) Getting inside the black box of technology integration in education: teachers' stimulated recall of classroom observations. *Australasian Journal of Educational Technology*, 29(3): 434–49.

Tripp, T and Rich, P (2012) Using video to analyse one's own teaching. *British Journal of Educational Technology*, 43(4): 678–704.

6

USING EVIDENCE TO INFORM TEACHING

PAUL HOPKINS

 THIS CHAPTER

By reading this chapter you will develop your understanding of the following.

- The range of research on teaching and learning.
- The dynamics of the 'traditional' and 'progressive' positions.
- How to critically explore the research about teaching and learning.
- How you can be engaged in undertaking research in your own classroom and on your own practice.

LINKS TO THE TEACHERS' STANDARDS

This chapter will help you with the following Teachers' Standards.

2. Promote good progress and outcomes by pupils

- Demonstrate knowledge and understanding of how pupils learn and how this impacts on teaching.

3. Demonstrate good subject and curriculum knowledge

- Demonstrate a critical understanding of developments in the subject and curriculum areas, and promote the value of scholarship.

3. Demonstrate good subject and curriculum knowledge

- Have a secure knowledge of the relevant subject(s) and curriculum areas, foster and maintain pupils' interest in the subject, and address misunderstandings.

8. Fulfil wider professional responsibilities

- Take responsibility for improving teaching through appropriate professional development, responding to advice and feedback from colleagues.

Depending on the research/study carried out the use of evidence could develop teachers' progress in Standards 4, 5, 6 and 7 as well (see Teachers' Standards in full on pp8-10).

Introduction

This chapter will explore how the beginning teacher should start to explore the range of ideas and literature that is available and how to consider undertaking research in their own classroom. It will start by looking at what is often labelled 'traditional' and 'progressive' learning, and explore how these terms are being used in the debate. It will then go on to look at some key papers in thinking about evidence and *what works* (EEF, 2013) or, as Wiliam said, *What works when* (Wiliam, 2006). The chapter will then explore how teachers themselves can use or undertake research in order to inform their own practice.

The first years of teaching are a time to develop one's pedagogical understanding and to explore ideas and practices in the real world of the classroom after having had the opportunity to explore these during training. The first few months of teaching tend to focus on establishing routines and embedding your own practice as well as developing relationships within the classroom. Now it is time perhaps to think about evidence-informed practice.

Impact

At the heart of the discussion over evidence-based practice is the question of impact – or what we think schooling is for. In recent years this has opened up a debate which has become polarised, especially in the social media sphere, around terminology such as 'progressive' and 'traditional'. Claxton and Lucas (2015) argue that these labels are the ends of a spectrum which they caricature as the 'trads' (traditionalists) and 'roms' (romantics) and argue that there is a little of both in all of us, but that most classroom teachers are at some point along the spectrum with some of the characteristics of each. The debate on social media has been vociferous, as those who support a more traditional model have felt a favourable political wind since 2010 with Gove decrying Higher Education Institutes (HEIs), which some saw as the *hotbed of progressive ideology*, or as *the blob* and *enemies of promise* (Gove, 2013). Simply put, traditional teaching favours direct instruction from the teacher with a specific goal in mind. This is usually a test or assessment that will measure progress and be quantifiable. Progressive teaching sees schooling as part of a wider social and developmental progress, and will have ends in minds that are less quantifiable.

Chandler (2013, pp296–7) has a useful table indicating the differences between the philosophies.

	Traditional schools	**Progressive schools**
Instruction	Direct instruction by the teacher; homogeneous grouping.	Self-directed learning; discovery learning; working co-operatively with others; heterogeneous groupings.
Reading	Reliance on a phonics approach.	Reliance on a whole-language approach.
Mathematics	Reliance on direct instruction; drill, computation skills.	Reliance on discovery and student-initiated learning.
Assessment	Reliance on periodic testing with norm-referenced, objective tests. Grades are assigned by comparing performance with age/grade peers.	Reliance on portfolios which feature individual and collaborative projects. Grades are downplayed in favour of teacher narratives on progress.
Outcomes	Emphasis on academic skills as demonstrated in the traditional core areas.	Emphasis on the whole-child approach; psychological, social and cultural aspects of child development.
Curriculum	Narrow, focused on academic areas.	Encompasses a range of issues; a balance between academic and social concerns.
Standards	Set so that all children seek the same level of minimal competency.	Adjusted, recognising the differences among individual learners.
Teacher sole	Academic instructor, authority figure.	Facilitator, counsellor, mentor.

Evidence

The phrases 'evidence-based practice' and 'evidence informed teaching' are used to define the parameters so we need to consider what we think of as evidence. Evidence could be defined as *the use of formal research, practitioner enquiry and the interpretation of routinely collected data use to inform action* (Brown and Rogers, 2014, p246). The notion of using evidence is not without some debate

(Hargreaves, 1996; Tooley and Darby, 1998; Biesta, 2007) and it is unlikely that there is ever a direct line between the practice that is outlined in research and the practice that is put into place in the situation of the classroom. There are too many variables that cannot be controlled, so there will be, by necessity, an amalgam of the research and the context (Virtanen and Tynjälä, 2008; Rexvid et al., 2012). This necessary compromise is reflected by the Department for Education (DfE) which uses the term 'evidence-based practice' (EBP) which it suggests is a combination of the knowledge from research and the more tacit knowledge from the practitioner. A useful definition of evidence-based practice can be taken from the work of Barends et al., in which they say that *evidence based practice is about making decisions through the conscientious, explicit and judicious use of the best available evidence from multiple sources* (2014, p2).

The argument about what is evidence is important if we are to have evidence-based practice.

 **CASE STUDY**

The visual environment

A study on visual environment concluded that *Children were more distracted by the visual environment, spent more time off task, and demonstrated smaller learning gains when the walls were highly decorated than when the decorations were removed* (Fisher et al., 2014, p1362). From this we might conclude that all displays should be removed from classrooms forthwith; indeed, this was the call from some newspaper headlines. This was contested by those arguing that the methodology of the study was flawed. Kohn (2014) on his blog argues that this was drawing causal links where only correlative ones could be drawn, arguing that children will adopt other behaviours.

This was supported by Willingham who argued that even if the study were correct, other social or affective reasons might exist for display in a room, including the need for building a community (Willingham, 2014). Willingham in his blog goes on to talk about the complexity and interactivity of classroom factors. It is tempting to want to find simple causal 'what works' solutions for classrooms – the truth is these rarely exist.

 QUESTIONS FOR DISCUSSION AND REFLECTION

1. What do you know about the difference between correlation and causality? How are these related?

2. Is there research that supports your own ideas about learning and teaching in the classroom?

3. What are the factors that effect learning in your classroom?

Coe (1999, p1) says that evidence should be *more than trendy jargon* and that *the only worthwhile kind of evidence about whether something works is to try it out*. However, as we have seen above, we need to be careful to distinguish between the correlative effects and the causal reasons. Coe (1999) argues that evidence is problematic as it is not values free, as there are rarely quick and simple solutions, that evidence is often incomplete and that is it complex. As Wiliam (2006) said in a lecture at the Cambridge Assessment for Learning keynote: *In education, 'what works?' is not the right question because everything works somewhere and nothing works everywhere, so what's interesting, what's important in education is: 'Under what conditions does this work?'* Allen (2013) supports this, arguing that *The social science model of research is not 'what works?' but rather 'what works for whom and under what conditions?'* The social context of a child shapes their learning more than it does for medicine – RCTs (Randomized Control Trials) may tell us about the schools involved in the experiment, but translating this to other schools is fraught with difficulty.

A focus on the research

This section will look at three meta-reports on evidence-based teaching with a short synopsis of each. These are available on-line and worth reading for both the content and the extensive reference lists.

The science of learning

This short text from the Deans for Impact (2015) looks at six key questions about learning and gives a summary of the cognitive science that has underpinned the research. It describes its own purpose as *to summarise the existing research from cognitive science related to how students learn and connect this to its practical implications for teaching and learning* (p2). The six key questions that the text explores are as follows.

1. How do students understand new ideas?

2. How do students learn and retain new information?

3. How do students solve problems?

4. How does learning transfer to new situations in or outside the classroom?

5. What motivates students to learn?

6. What are the common misconceptions about how students think and learn?

The work is based on the work of Daniel Willingham and Paul Bruno, and is strongly rooted in a positivistic methodological approach within the discipline of cognitive science. It is focused on measurable items, but the combination of research evidence from a range of studies and practical ideas on how to implement these makes this an important contribution to learning.

What makes great pedagogy? Nine claims from research

In this report by Husbands and Pearce (2012), there is a strong consensus that high performance in education systems is dependent on the quality of teaching. This reflects on an earlier work by Barber and Mourshed (2007, p13) in which they say that *the quality of an education system cannot exceed the quality of its teachers*. Husbands and Pearce's report gives supporting evidence for nine claims, as follows.

1. Effective pedagogies give serious consideration to pupil voice.

2. Effective pedagogies depend on behaviour (what teachers do), knowledge and understanding (what teachers know) and beliefs (why teachers act as they do).

3. Effective pedagogies involve clear thinking about long-term learning outcomes as well as short-term goals.

4. Effective pedagogies build on pupils' prior learning and experience.

5. Effective pedagogies involve scaffolding pupil learning.

6. Effective pedagogies involve a range of techniques, including whole-class and structured group work, guided learning and individual activity.

7. Effective pedagogies focus on developing higher order thinking and metacognition, and make good use of dialogue and questioning in order to do so.

8. Effective pedagogies embed assessment for learning.

9. Effective pedagogies are inclusive and take the diverse needs of a range of learners, as well as matters of student equity, into account.

The report concludes as follows.

The evidence which has been reviewed suggests that outstanding pedagogy is far from straightforward. Classrooms are complex, multi-faceted and demanding places in which to work and successful pedagogies are correspondingly sophisticated. Highly successful pedagogies develop when teachers make outstanding use of their understanding of the research and knowledge-base for teaching in order to support high-quality planning and practice. The very best teaching arises when this research base is supplemented by a personal passion for what is to be taught and for the aspirations of learners.

The Evidence Endowment Foundation: Teaching and Learning Toolkit

The Sutton Trust–EEF Teaching and Learning Toolkit (https://educationendowmentfoundation.org.uk) was originally produced as the Pupil Premium Toolkit by Durham University (Wiggins et al., 2011). It aims to be an accessible summary of educational research that provides guidance for teachers on action they can instigate to improve the attainment of disadvantaged pupils. The toolkit examines a wide range of practices and provides a summary of their average impact on attainment, the strength of the evidence supporting them and their cost. This is reported as an impact score. The top ten contributors to learning success (2016) were as follows.

1. Feedback

2. Metacognition and self-regulation

3. Homework (secondary)

4. Mastery learning

5. Peer tutoring

6. Reading comprehension strategies

7. Collaborative learning

8. Oral language interventions

9. One-to-one tuition

10. Early years intervention

 # Classroom focus

Research in your own classroom

This section explores two ways of undertaking research in your own classroom. This could be by implementing some of the practices you have read about above or explored in the linked reading, in undertaking research in your own institution or by becoming involved in some of the wider research that is taking place via the research schools (see the case studies below).

Practitioner research

As a teacher, you are most likely to want to research your own practice with the intention of improving your practice and the outcomes of your children (Jones, 2015). Thus, it is very likely that if you undertake research it will be as a practitioner researcher. The key aspect of the practitioner researcher is that the focus is on the improvement of practice rather than the establishment of theory or generalisable results (Verma and Mallick, 1999). Hammersley (2002) suggests a distinction between scientific and practical research.

So, practitioner research is very much rooted in Wiliam's (2006) *what works here* rather than trying to find out *what works*. Practitioner research does not demand any particular paradigmatic approach but often *borrows from a range of paradigms using qualitative and/or quantitative methods as appropriate* (Burton and Bartlett, 2005, p25). So, while quantifiable performance indicators may be important, they are not essential to the practitioner researcher.

The Educational Endowment Foundation (EEF), currently the largest funder of educational research, favours a more positivistic approach with a favoured method of randomised control trials, but practitioner research can be carried out in other ways.

As practitioner research is focused on improvement, it often used an action research or multi-cycle approach. Action research is one specific form of practitioner research, although some researchers use the term interchangeably (Bartlett and Burton, 2006; Kemmis, 2006). The key concepts (EdFutures) in undertaking practitioner researcher areas are as follows.

Teacher initiated	The driving force for the research is the improvement in practice.
Small-scale	It should fit within the practice of the teacher, be manageable and not be a significant burden on their resources.
Collaborative	Working with teachers in their school on shared problems and for the good of all.

Democratic All involved see this as valuable.

Empowering Giving teachers a voice in the improvement of their own practice and the power and responsibility so to do.

Open to scrutiny The results should be made public to other practitioners within and without the institution.

Example of a practitioner research study

Jane is concerned about the impact on the new requirements for assessing practical work in GCSE science. She has noticed that her students find these difficult and uninspiring, so she wishes to explore ways to carry these out that will engage the students more and thus increase their achievement at GCSE. She designs a small-scale interpretative piece of research working with colleagues in her department to observe the students undertaking practical work to look for particular 'pinch points' where there is a lack of engagement or where misunderstandings occur. As well as the observations, she intends to interview students so she can triangulate her data. She will use the data she collects to redesign the school's approach to the practical assessments and also hopes to be able to share her work with the examination board if this is suitable.

 QUESTIONS FOR DISCUSSION AND REFLECTION

1. Is this the kind of study you could carry out in your school?

2. What support/training would you need in order to do so?

3. What are the strengths/weaknesses of this approach?

4. What might be the impact of such a study?

Lesson study

Lesson study is rooted in a model of coaching and mentoring. It is a highly specified form of action research focusing on the development of teacher practice knowledge (Dudley, 2011) and has been in use in Japan since the 1870s (Dudley, 2011). It has grown in popularity in the West after some large-scale studies in the US showed the impact on the development of teacher pedagogy and subject knowledge (Stigler and Heibert, 1999; Lewis et al., 2012).

Lesson study is a collaborative cyclical process following a reflective practice model. The key components of a lesson study are as follows.

Plan A pair, or small group, of teachers will plan a 'research lesson' together addressing a specific enquiry question (which could be drawn from evidential enquiry).

Identify Three 'case pupils' will be chosen, each of whom should typify a group of learners in the class and their reaction to the lesson should be predicted by the research team.

Observe	Teach the 'research lesson' while colleagues observe, paying particular attention to the case study pupils; the case study pupils are then interviewed to gain their understanding and perspective.
Discuss and analyse	Consider the impact of the teaching on the case study pupils and wider.
Reflect	On the accuracy of the predictions and on changes that might need to be made.

Example of a lesson study

A primary school has identified the need, via data analysis of pupil performance, to improve writing outcomes for children. Using critical reading of the EEF toolkit, research has been planned to develop sentence structure and punctuation. The English co-ordinator was given time to observe the planned lessons to embed the use of guided writing strategies with all four of the teachers in Year 2 and Year 4. All the teachers took turns in delivering the planned lesson to their classes and observing the other teachers over the course of the week with the English co-ordinator observing them all.

The lessons were planned so that pupils could be interviewed at the beginning of lunch and then the teachers could all meet for a working and reflective session for the rest of lunch to consider the impact of the new lesson structure on teaching and learning. From observing, discussing and reflecting on their shared practice, the teachers had clear direction on how to improve their practice. This was shared with the whole staff in a staff meeting led by these teachers.

 QUESTIONS FOR DISCUSSION AND REFLECTION

1. Is this the kind of study you could carry out in your school?
2. What support/training would you need in order to do so?
3. What might be the impact of such a study?
4. What are the strengths/weaknesses of this approach?

Examples from research-led schools

Two of the new research-led schools talk about their experience.

Teachers who are new to the profession have it hard. They have to make hundreds of meaningful decisions every day, based on relatively speedy training, high-pressured practice and a handful of practical tools to hold fast in the storm. Once in the thick of practice, where is the time to reflect, research and think hard?

Buffeted by such daily challenges, teachers can soon see their critical faculties drained by tiredness. It is crucial that every support is in place to ensure that teachers have the time and tools to critically reflect on their practice and to make sustainable improvements to their work in the classroom.

As a busy secondary school and a national Education Endowment Foundation (EEF)/Institute for Effective Education (EEF) Research School, predominantly serving Yorkshire and the Humber, we are tasked to help school leaders and teachers with this task. We hold to the principles of what the Behavioural Insights Team calls the 'EAST Framework' – that is to say, we need to ensure that teachers can access research evidence in a way that is Easy, Attractive, Social and Timely.

First, teachers need easy access to research evidence and tools that develop the research into useable knowledge. At Huntington, we promote the EEF Teaching and Learning Toolkit, which distils research evidence into an accessible summary. We also work hard at sharing useful research summaries, like Rosenshine's (2012) 'Principles of Instruction' or converting the research of Dunlosky et al. (2013) into useful tools for effective student revision. We aim to make the research attractive by ensuring that the language of such summaries is accessible and that teachers can connect the theory with their practice (which is no mean feat in many cases).

The social aspect of new teachers researching about teaching and learning is crucial. Here, it is the duty of the school to provide a regular rhythm of high-quality professional development time (at Huntington, we have a fortnightly cycle). Teacher enquiry is supported by links to relevant research and we aim to attach such enquiry and critical reflection to improve student outcomes.

Regular newsletters, blog posts and shared resources based on robust evidence, all contribute to support our teachers to critically explore their practice. Schools and teachers need this bridge to access research evidence and to act on it, with our research school work being directed towards that aim.

(Alex Quigley, English teacher and Director of Huntington
Research School, York)

 QUESTIONS FOR REFLECTION

1. What research evidence is available in your school? (e.g. journals, books)

2. How easy do you find it to access research? (Explore the MESH guides at www.meshguides.org)

3. How often is current research discussed at your school?

4. How often is research discussed at PD events either in or out of school?

The Kyra Research School explores the ways that teachers can be engaged in undertaking research in their own classroom and on their own practice, or looking at how teachers can critically explore the research about teaching and learning.

Research evidence (Hattie, 2012) suggests that effective feedback has a significant impact on pupil progress. With this evidence in mind, 21 schools across Lincolnshire were involved in a research-engaged project focusing on effective feedback through digital technology. A range of different interventions was piloted by groups of schools working in collaborative partnerships of up to six schools.

Over the year, strong collaborative work between a small number of partnerships developed a range of interventions, which suggested an impact on raising attainment. Data took time to gather, though, as schools spent considerable time engaging with research evidence and interpreting this in terms of their context.

Initial data analysis showed a significant variation in impact between schools and this enabled the teachers involved to re-evaluate the approaches used – not only for the development of effective practice but also for how professional development played a key role.

The work was refined and focused on specific 'interventions', which showed the most promise. In year two, the research focused on using digital feedback via iPad and developing 'E-portfolios'. A Professional Learning Community model in the second year was used to encourage a more uniform approach to implementation across 16 schools. In addition, ten of the schools, involving Key Stage 2 pupils, undertook a randomised control trial (RCT), examining the impact of digital feedback compared to written feedback, using a small amount of funding by the National College for Teaching and leadership as part of the Closing the Gap: Test and Learn project. Some 230 pupils participated in the RCT.

The gains matched current research evidence around the impact of feedback on closing the gap in attainment and the intervention produced the greatest gains for disadvantaged and SEND pupils, and may be an effective intervention for closing the gap. Pupil perceptions of digital feedback indicated that pupils felt they made better progress in their written work following digital feedback.

In the third year of the project, teachers refined their work and shared their research. An application was made to the Education Endowment Foundation for funding for a larger scale trial, which was ultimately successful, taking three years of work from many teachers through to a larger scale evaluation (https://educationendowmentfoundation.org.uk/our-work/projects/digital-feedback-in-primary-maths/)

James Siddle (Krya Research School)

 QUESTIONS FOR DISCUSSION AND REFLECTION

1. Is this the kind of study you could carry out?
2. What are the strengths and weaknesses of this study?
3. Is there a 'professional learning community' in your school?

Conclusion

This chapter will develop your awareness of the range of research and evidence that is 'out there' as an important part of your own development in these first years of teaching. Using this evidence allows you to develop your own teaching and learning rooted in a wider evidence base than your own personal experience, which might be *highly susceptible to systematic errors* (Barends et al., 2014, p12), and where cognitive and information-processing limits make us prone to biases that can have negative impacts on the decisions we take (Simon, 1997; Kahneman, 2011).

EBP does not demand that teachers get involved in the conduct of research, rather that they *make decisions using the best available current evidence in order to improve pupil outcomes* (Jones, 2015, pxx). They should evaluate the impact of the research on their own children with an emphasis on the improvement of their own practice and on pupils' outcomes. It may be that as teachers, you then want to get involved more formally in the process of research. This may be via enrolment in a research degree at a local faculty of education in a Higher Education Institution (HEI) or via involvement in the Research Schools network (https://researchschool.org.uk).

When accessing research evidence about 'what works' or 'what might work' in your classroom, how do you approach this critically in order to be able to see how you could apply the idea, concepts or results of this research to your own classroom? A list of questions adapted from Bassey (1990, in Hitchcock and Hughes, 1995) can help you be a critical reader of research.

1. What contributions to knowledge are claimed?

2. What conceptual frameworks/theories are quoted/used?

3. What methodology underpins the research?

4. Was the collection of data suitable, appropriate, sufficient and ethical?

5. Does the author have a vested (commercial) interest?

6. Was the analysis of data suitable, appropriate, sufficient and ethical?

7. Does the evidence substantiate claims to new knowledge?

8. Does the presentation allow these questions to be answered?

 QUESTIONS FOR DISCUSSION AND REFLECTION

1. How do I go about getting involved in research?

Explore the issues outlined in the chapter and start to think about your own practice.

a. Where do you fall in the traditional v. progressive debate outlined in Chandler (2000)?

b. Which of the studies outlined in the evidence section do you find more compelling or interesting?

c. Are there areas you want to explore to find out, to paraphrase Wiliam (2006), *if they work here?*

A starting place is to use social media (blogs and Twitter) to explore the debate that is taking place. If you would like to know more, contact the author of this chapter on @hullpgce

There are two possible routes for you to explore in order to progress these. One might be to contact a local HEI to consider undertaking a Master's degree with research linked to one of the studies above. The other is perhaps to see if you have a research school (https://researchschool. org.uk) such as Kyra or Huntingdon in your area.

CHAPTER SUMMARY

Having read this chapter and reflected on its contents and your own practices, you should now have an understanding of research as follows.

1. Be aware of the range of research on teaching and learning.

2. Have an understanding of the dynamics of the 'traditional' and 'progressive' positions in learning.

3. Be confident in how you can critically explore the research about teaching and learning.

4. Have some ideas about how you can be engaged in undertaking research in your own classroom and on your own practice.

FURTHER READING

Adey, P and Dillon, J (2012) *Debunking Myths in Education*. Berkshire: Open University Press.

This book explores the evidence behind a number of claims that 'we all know' in education, and sets out the process of exploring and looking at the evidence. It explores why these myths may have come about and how evidence is used.

Burton, D and Bartlett, S (2005) *Practitioner Research for Teachers*. London: Paul Chapman.

Most teachers, if they engage in research, become practitioner researchers. This book is full of good advice and good ideas for the beginning researcher in school settings.

Hattie, J (2012) *Visible Learning for Teachers: Maximising Impact on Learning*. Abingdon: Routledge.

This is a huge set of meta-analyses looking at those things that have most impact on classroom practice. While many of these might be beyond the scope of the individual teacher to change, this book will raise awareness of the key and wider issues in education.

Zwozdiak-Myers, P (2012) *The Teacher's Reflective Practice Handbook: Becoming an Extended Professional through Capturing Evidence-informed Practice*. Abingdon: Routledge.

This is a very useful book for helping you to reflect on and explore your own practice in your classroom using the lens of pedagogical thinking and research evidence. It aids in the complexities on combining explicit and tacit knowledge in research and practice.

REFERENCES

Allen, R (2013) Evidence-based practice: why number-crunching tells only part of the story. Available at: https://ioelondonblog.wordpress.com/2013/03/14/evidence-based-practice-why-number-crunching-tells-only-part-of-the-story/ (accessed December 2016).

Barber, M and Mourshed, M (2007) *How the World's Best Education Systems Come Out on Top*. London and New York: McKinsey.

Barends, E, Rousseau, DM and Briner, RB (2014) *Evidence-Based Management, The Basic Principles: In Search of Evidence.* Leiden: Center for Evidence-Based Management.

Bartlett, S and Burton, D (2006) Practitioner research or descriptions of classroom practice? A discussion of teachers investigating their classrooms. *Educational Action Research*, 14(3).

Biesta, G (2007) Why 'what works' won't work: evidence-based practice and the democratic deficit in educational research. *Educational Theory*, 57(1): 1–22.

Brown, C and Rogers, S (2014) Measuring the effectiveness of knowledge creation as a means of facilitating evidence-informed practice in early years settings in one London borough. *London Review of Education*, 12(3).

Burton, D and Bartlett, S (2005) *Practitioner Research for Teachers.* London: Paul Chapman.

Chandler, LA (2013) Traditional and progressive schools: identifying two models of educational practice. *Journal of Catholic Education*, 3(3): 296–7.

Claxton, G and Lucas, B (2015) *Educating Ruby: What Our Children Really Need to Learn.* Carmarthen: Crown House.

Coe, R (1999) Manifesto for evidence-based education. Available at: www.cem.org/attachments/ebe/manifesto-for-ebe.pdf. Durham: CEM.

Deans for Impact (2015) The science of learning. Austin, TX: Deans for Impact.

Dudley, P. (2011) How Lesson Study orchestrates key features of teacher knowledge and teacher learning to create profound changes in professional practice. Presented at the World Association of Lesson Studies Annual Conference, Tokyo.

Dunlosky, J, Rawson, K, Marsh, E, Nathan, M and Willingham, D (2013) Improving students' learning with effective learning techniques: promising directions from cognitive and educational psychology. *Psychological Science in the Public Interest*, 14(1): 4–58. DOI: 10.1177/1529100612453266

EdFutures (n.d.) Available at: http://edfutures.net/Practitioner_Research (accessed December 2016).

Education Endowment Foundation (EEF) (2013) Available at: http://educationendowment foundation.org.uk (accessed December 2016).

Fisher, A, Godwin, K and Seltman, H (2014) Visual environment, attention allocation, and learning in young children: when too much of a good thing may be bad. *Psychology of Science*, 25(7):1362–70. DOI: 10.1177/0956797614533801

Gove, M (2013) I refuse to surrender to the Marxist teachers hell-bent on destroying our schools. Mail on-line. Available at: www.dailymail.co.uk/ debate/article-2298146/I-refuse-surrender-Marxist-teachers-hell-bent-destroying-schools-Education-Secretary-berates-new-enemies-promise-opposing-plans.html (accessed December 2016).

Hammersley, M (2002) *Educational Research, Policymaking and Practice.* London: Paul Chapman.

Hargreaves, DH (1996) Teaching as a research-based profession: possibilities and prospects. The Teaching Training Agency Annual Lecture.

Hattie, J (2012) *Visible Learning for Teachers: Maximizing Impact on Learning.* London: Routledge.

Hitchcock, G and Hughes, D (1995) (2nd edn) *Research and the Teacher: A Qualitative Introduction to School-based Research*. London: Routledge.

Husbands, C and Pearce, J (2012) What makes great pedagogy? Nine claims from research, National College of School Leadership, Autumn.

Jones, G (2015) The BERA blog: research matters. Available at: www.bera.ac.uk/blog/evidence-based-practice-some-common-misconceptions (accessed December 2016).

Kahneman, D (2011) *Thinking, Fast and Slow*. London: Penguin.

Kemmis, S. (2006) Participatory action research and the public sphere. *Educational Action Research*, 14(4).

Kohn, A (2014) Alfie Kohn: the blog. Available at: www.alfiekohn.org (accessed December 2016).

Lewis, C, Perry, R, Friedkin, S and Roth, J (2012) Improving teaching does improve teachers: evidence from lesson study. *Journal of Teacher Education*, 63(5): 368–75.

Rexvid, D, Blom, B, Evertsson, L, and Forssen, A (2012) Risk reduction technologies in general practice and social work. *Professions and Professionalism*, 2(2): 1–18.

Rosenshine, B (2012) Principles of instruction: research based strategies that all teachers should know, *American Educator*, Spring.

Simon, HA (1997) *Models of Bounded Rationality*, Vol. 3. Cambridge, MA: MIT Press.

Stigler, JW and Hiebert, J (1999) *The Teaching Gap: Best Ideas from the World's Teachers for Improving Education in the Classroom*. New York: Simon & Schuster.

Tooley, J and Darby, D(1998) Educational research: a critique. London: Office for Standards in Education.

Verma, G and Mallick, K (1999) *Researching Education: Perspectives and Techniques*. London: Falmer Press.

Virtanen, A and Tynjälä, P (2008) Students' experiences of workplace learning in Finnish VET. *European Journal of Vocational Training*, 44: 199–213.

Wiggins, M, Austerbury, A and Ward, H (2011) Implementing evidence-based programmes in children's services: key issues for success. London: HMSO.

Wiliam, D (2006) Using assessment to improve learning: why, what and how. Keynote and the Cambridge Assessment for Networking Seminar on Assessment for Learning.

Willingham, D (2014) Bare walls and poor learning? The trouble with headlines. Available at: www.realcleareducation.com/articles/2014/06/05/bare_walls_and_poor_learning_the_trouble_with_the_latest_headlines_1004.html (accessed December 2016).

7

TECHNOLOGY AND THE NEW TEACHER

PAUL HOPKINS

 THIS CHAPTER

By reading this chapter you will develop your understanding of the following.

- The range of research on using technology in teaching.
- The integration of technology and pedagogy.
- How to reflect upon and develop your competencies in using technology for teaching and learning.

LINKS TO THE TEACHERS' STANDARDS

This chapter will help you with the following Teachers' Standards.

2. Promote good progress and outcomes by pupils

- Demonstrate knowledge and understanding of how pupils learn and how this impacts on teaching.

3. Demonstrate good subject and curriculum knowledge

- Have a secure knowledge of the relevant subject(s) and curriculum areas, foster and maintain pupils' interest in the subject, and address misunderstandings.

3. Demonstrate good subject and curriculum knowledge

- Demonstrate a critical understanding of developments in the subject and curriculum areas, and promote the value of scholarship.

8. Fulfil wider professional responsibilities

- Take responsibility for improving teaching through appropriate professional development, responding to advice and feedback from colleagues.

Introduction

Technology is pervasive today in a wide variety of shapes and sizes. If you are under 25, you will almost certainly be a user of 'new' technology. You are what Prensky (2001) called a 'digital native' or Veen (2006) a 'Homo Zappiens'. It is very likely that technology is a core part of your daily, non-teaching life. Your smartphone, your tablet and access to the Internet are probably things you take for granted and miss when you do not have them. Indeed, some psychiatrists consider is even possible now to be addicted to technology (Aboujaoude and Koran, 2006; Muñoz-Maralles, 2016), although others are sceptical about this suggesting that *by labelling technology as an addition before we understand the processes at work we run the risk of removing our own responsibility for how we use technology* (Byron, 2014).

In your training and as you start your career in school you will also expect to use a range of technologies. It is rare to find a classroom now that does not have an interactive whiteboard or smart TV, when only a few years ago there would have been a chalkboard. However, there are concerns that this technology is not being used effectively, or at all (Educational Technology, 2015), as teachers *lack the confidence and proper training to use it.*

The first years of teaching are a time to develop your pedagogical understanding, as you are able to explore ideas and practices in the real world of your 'own' classroom. This chapter will explore some conceptual and practical ideas around the use of technology in the classroom.

When to, and when not to, use technology

At the core of good technology use is the understanding of when to, and when not to, use technology. There is much debate over the impact of technology on learning and how this is measured.

The OECD (2015) reports that moderate computer use has a positive effect, but heavy use can be negative; other analyses show a positive impact on language acquisition (Zhao, 2005; O'Hara et al., 2011) and a large-scale meta-analysis shows one-to-one laptop usage improving student scores (Zheng et al., 2016).

Thus, it is essential that we have these models on which to draw and consider how we best integrate technology into learning. As the Education Secretary in 2015 said, *there has never been a more exciting time to think about the way in which emerging technologies can transform the world of education* (Morgan, 2015). At the heart of technology use are two questions.

- How is the technology supporting or enhancing the pedagogy in my classroom?

- How does the technology challenge the pedagogy in my classroom?

For the purposes of this, we are going to briefly explore three pedagogic models for technology usage, which you can then use to make judgements for yourself on when you should use technology.

The SAMR model

This model was developed by Puentedura (2008) and while is has not been empirically tested, it provides a framework for exploring how we plan technology use in our classrooms. This model is rooted in a constructivist methodology and roots technology use into pedagogic change.

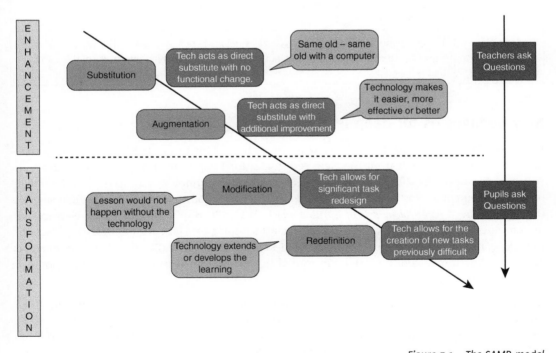

Figure 7.1   The SAMR model

Source: Hopkins (2016) based on Puentedura (2008).

The four stages of the models are as follows.

Substitution	Technology acts as a direct tool substitute with no functional change.
Augmentation	Technology acts as a direct tool substitute, with functional improvement.
Modification	Technology allows for significant task redesign.
Redefinition	Technology allows for the creation of new tasks previously inconceivable.

This process is not technology-specific but pedagogy-specific, so we can apply this to most methods of teaching and learning – for example, teacher delivery of information.

Substitution	The whiteboard and the interactive board often become just an option to all the presentation of material with a little more functionality or efficiency.
Augmentation	The use of a presentation tools such as ©Powerpoint or ©Keynote allows for the presentation of materials with the addition of multi-media material, which augment and develop the presentation of the materials. These supplant the use of multi-technologies amalgamating them into a single technology.
Modification	The use of a presentation tool such as ©Prezi (www.prezi.com) allows for the presentation of materials to be organised more pedagogically where the presentation more reflects the ways in which the students are learning and organising those materials in their minds.
Redefinition	The use of more interactive Web-based technologies such as ©Nearpod (www.nearpod.com) allows for student data to be collected and supported, redefining the nature of the learning that is taking place.

New pedagogies for deep learning

Fullan and Langworthy (2013) offer a view where technology is integrated fully into the curriculum. Drawing on research from the New Pedagogies for Deep Learning Partnership, Barber (in Fullan and Langworthy, 2013, Foreword) reflects that where technology has been used, the impact on learning outcomes has been disappointing. In order to support greater impact, Fullan suggests that schools need *powerful models of learning and teaching* (2013, pi). The three core elements are underpinned by the potential offered through new technologies. These technologies allow schools to make connections to the world beyond: what Kearney and Maher (2013) called *authentic tasks*. The key is the move from a curriculum rooted in information consumption to one rooted in knowledge creation.

In this new model, technology is not added on in order to support existing teaching and learning approaches, but is *pervasive and is used to discover and master content knowledge and to enable the deep learning goals of creating and using new knowledge in the world* (Fullan and Langworthy, 2013, p3). Technology is at the heart of a learning model that allows the creation and use of new knowledge in the real world and this is enabled by the ubiquitous technology.

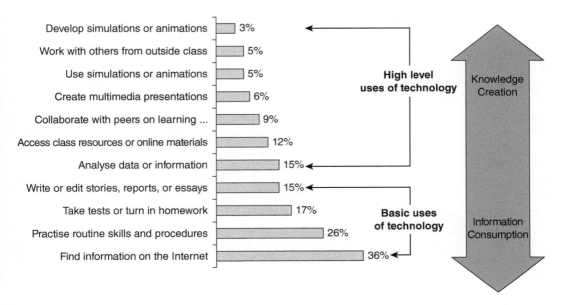

Figure 7.2   High-level and basic levels of technology use

Source: Fullan and Langworthy (2013, p31)

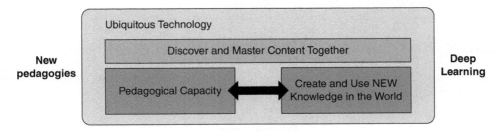

Figure 7.3   The new technology

Source: Fullan and Langworthy (2013, p3)

The prevalence of online and always-accessible technologies changes the traditional roles of teachers and their relationship to pupils and also the access to information. Access to information becomes much more open and available, and thus new skills are needed to access this knowledge. The new technologies move problem-solving from the closed domain of the school to the wider and more authentic domain of the outside school world. This is the real potential of technology: not just access to knowledge, but also the use of this knowledge and its use in communities and systems. Again, this is facilitated by technology, especially social media and online communities.

Tablet pedagogy

This last model focuses on the use of tablet technologies. These have become more and more prevalent in classrooms in the last few years. It is hard to believe the first iPad was launched in April 2010.

There has been incredible growth in the use of tablet devices in last few years, especially in primary and secondary education, and thus there is the need to have a pedagogic approach that focuses on the use of these devices. In 2015, tablet sales approached those of PCs (Gartner, 2015) and over 70 per cent of UK schools are estimated to be using tablets (BBC, 2014). Over the past two decades, technology has moved from the 'desktop' to the more mobile, personal and networked, and the access to, and use of, these devices have become more and more common among a wide range of groups (Newhouse et al., 2006). There is, however, a lack of studies in this area looking at theoretical or pedagogical underpinnings and particularly a lack of support and training (Peng et al., 2009; Cochrane, 2012). There is also limited research on the process of supporting and preparing preservice and new teachers to use these technologies (Kearney and Maher, 2013; Baran, 2014; Ekanayake and Wishart, 2014). As these devices become established in schools, they both support and develop existing practice (Burden et al., 2012; Baran, 2014), but are also starting to challenge some existing models of thinking and pedagogy (Fullan and Langworthy, 2013; Kearney et al., 2012) and also teachers' attitudes towards learning and teaching (Ertmer, 1999; Burden and Hopkins, 2015). Offering opportunities for learning to become more authentic, personal and collaborative (Kearney et al., 2012), there is potential for teachers to start to redesign the ways in which learning takes place (Puentedura, 2010; McCormick and Scrimshaw, 2001). Traxler defines mobile learning as *an educational process, in which handheld devices or palmtops are the only or dominant used technology tools* (2007, p2). Kearney et al. (2012) argue that it has the potential to revolutionise the learning process by allowing individuals to determine their own independent paradigms and frameworks of learning. These devices are also sophisticated producers of digital artefacts, and children and teachers are capable of being co-producers of learning materials.

A framework for the use of mobile technologies

This has been developed by Kearney et al. (2012) for the iPAC framework – a pedagogical framework for the use of mobile technologies.

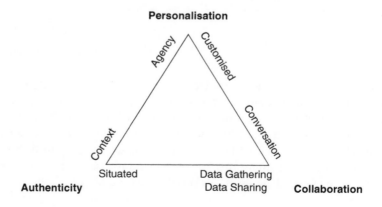

Figure 7.4   The iPAC framework

Source: Hopkins (2016) based on Kearney and Maher (2013)

There are three core concepts.

- **Personalisation**: How the technology supports learning tailored to the needs of the individual and contains the following subconstructs.

  - *Agency*: What choices the individual has in the learning process.

  - *Customisation*: How is the learning tailored to suit the individual?

- **Authenticity**: How learning reflects real-world relevance and personal meaning, and contains the following subconstructs.

  - *Context*: Where does the learning take place?

  - *Situated*: How was the learning relevant to the learner's experience?

- **Collaboration**: How learning supports interaction with more capable peers or adults and contains the following subconstructs.

  - *Conversation*: How are students encouraged to share in dialogue?

  - *Data sharing*: What new data are generated and how are they shared?

Classroom focus

Technology in the classroom

In this section a range of ways that technology can develop and enhance the learning in our classroom will be considered. These will offer you some ways of thinking pedagogically about the teaching and learning in your classroom, and also offer you some tools that you can start to explore and use in your classroom. The nature of new technologies is that they develop very quickly, so the tools you will have access to in your classroom may be different from those talked about here. The important thing is not the tool but the pedagogical application.

We will use three areas of competency that have been developed, drawing on the Digital Competence Framework developed by the European Commission's science and knowledge framework (DIGCOMP 2.0, 2016). This can be accessed at: https://ec.europa.eu/jrc/en/digcomp/digital-competence-framework

The three areas have been chosen as they are: 1) areas in which it is likely the reader will have some existing competence; 2) areas that will most impact on the teaching and learning in the classroom, and 3) aids for the development of early career teachers. These are:

- information handling;

- communication;

- content creation.

Information handling

The Internet has opened up an incredible range of information and resources for teachers and students. However, navigating this can be complex and difficult, and a number of skills are needed for both teachers and pupils. A simple search on a search engine can yield an impossible number of results. Searches in December 2016 for some simple terms yielded the following.

The Tudors	3.3 million
Change of state	3.8 million
Fronted adverbial	11,900
Long division	433,000

This means that teachers, and especially children, rarely go beyond the first pages of Internet search results, and often use imprecise and ambiguous language when doing do (Jansen et al., 1998). They may then formulate very short questions, which tend to be informational rather than navigational, looking for specific answers rather than patterns (Gossen et al., 2011).

A key aspect of being better at searching online is the use of more sophisticated personal search strategies (OECD, 2016), including Boolean search operators. Two good resources to assist with this can be found at:

- www.ct.gov/kids/search/search_INKinstr.asp

- www.youtube.com/watch?v=ZbVY8F7KGfw

Alongside the difficulties in just finding information is the complexity of being able to discern the quality of information. The usability of a Web search is very important for children, since their cognitive abilities are not fully formed (Gossen et al., 2012) and also their reading ages will often be considerably lower than the reading ages of the pages they are accessing. This will be especially true of very young children (Gossen et al., 2012).

Once we have found resources online from the wide range of sources available, we need to organise these materials so we are able to use them effectively to create artefacts of learning or make them accessible to the children we are teaching. The organisation of these resources can be thought of as analogous to the role of the museum curator whose role is to select from the large range of resources. There are two options for the digital educator: one is to use the growing number of digitally curated resources (Porcello and Hsi, 2013) and the other is to use one of the digital curation tools to construct your own archives of resources, both for your own and your children's uses.

The already created repositories you might find, and use, will depend on your phase and subject interests. To aid in finding these, make critical use of search (see above) as well as links from subject associations or from your social media contacts and networks (Porcello and Hsi, 2013). Some of these will be free and some will be paid, and one of the judgements to make is the cost of access to the resource archive (e.g. TES online: www.tes.com/teaching-resources) and the skills of the archivists against the cost of your own time. However, you can also use a range of curation tools to develop your own archive, or one in conjunction with colleagues in your institution or with a virtual group. Some of the best curation tools are as follows.

- Pinterest: https://uk.pinterest.com

- Scoop.it: www.scoop.it

- Livebinders: www.livebinders.com

- Bag the Web: www.bagtheweb.com/featured/Education

- Evernote: https://evernote.com

- Slideshare: www.slideshare.net

The digitally competent teacher (OECD, 2013) is one who is able to:

Use a wide range of search strategies when searching for information and browsing on the Internet. Who can filter and monitor the information they receive. Who can use a range of search strategies using a range of databases and who is critical about information and cross-checks sources to assess validity and credibility. Who can apply different methods and tools to organise files, content and information. Who can deploy a range of strategies for retrieving the content that they have organised and stored and who can share access to these resources among appropriate groups.

 **CASE STUDY**

Collating resources

A subject leader for science in a primary school is looking for a range of different sources to support the teaching of science enquiry and subject knowledge. She has searched a number of different sources and databases across a range of different media. She has checked the information that they have found and removed those that cannot be verified in at least two places.

These sources have then been checked for age suitability and collated under the nine subject areas of the primary curriculum, and Pinterest has been used to organise these and make them available to the teachers in the school and wider. These can be found at: https://uk.pinterest.com/primaryscience/

 QUESTIONS FOR DISCUSSION AND REFLECTION

1. Where do you find your resources for teaching?

2. How do you check their voracity?

3. What tools could you use for the collation of materials?

4. How would this most benefit your teaching and learning?

Communication

Digital tools allow teachers and children to communicate via a range of different media, communicating their resources and ideas and forming collaborative communities of practice (Lave and Wenger, 1991). Learning takes place across time and space. Communication covers a range of areas, but for the developing teacher the creation of personal learning networks (PLNs) can offer support and professional development in the first years of teaching. These can be divided into two areas: tools for collaboration and access to networks via social media.

Collaborative tools allow the formation of networks that can be in virtual space and in asynchronous time, and thus are more flexible, and in the development of virtual support communities in order to share ideas and resources and form support communities. This can include the reading and writing of blogs.

There is also the capability to share resources via online communities (see above) and for us to join virtual support communities. This is sometimes called grassroots professional development (Forte et al., 2012) and teachers have reported positive effects, both personally and professionally (Hur and Brush, 2009; Badge et al., 2012). Those in favour (Lu, 2011) suggest a range of positive benefits such as enhanced communication, collaboration and engagement. Krutka et al. (2016) suggest there are three primary benefits of these communities: communication, class activities and professional development.

Netiquette

When working and collaborating online, it is important to respect the views of others and display common courtesy. This is known as 'Netiquette', a portmanteau word from 'Internet' and 'etiquette'. While various online groups have their own behaviours, there are some common rules for online behaviour, which include the following.

- Refrain from personal abuse – tackle the arguments not the person.

- Write as clearly as possible – this can be tricky on Twitter where you are limited to 140 characters, so tailor the message to the medium and try to avoid ambiguity.

- Remember that posts on social media could end up anywhere, so post as though you are posting to a public site.

- Be aware of copyright and IPR.

The digitally competent teacher (OECD, 2013) is one who is able to use a range of communication tools for professional purposes, who can share content and actively participate with others via online communities and networks, who uses these channels to collaborate with others in the production and sharing of resources, knowledge and content, who has a developed sense of Netiquette.

CASE STUDY

Keeping a blog

As part of his reflective practice in his first year of teaching, a teacher decides to keep a blog of his growing relationship with his class. The blog gains a number of followers and via this, the teacher starts to form a network of colleagues, all of whom are in their first few years of teaching. This leads to the teacher joining the Twitter community (www.twitter.com) and starting to follow other new teachers who often Tweet about issues in their own classes, and offer support and useful links to materials, resources and ideas for teaching. This growing community decides to organise a TeachMeet in their local area and also to collaborate online in the development of teaching materials using Google Docs (http://docs.google.com). While the teacher is supported by his mentor, this virtual support community gives both professional and personal support to the new teacher.

QUESTIONS FOR DISCUSSION AND REFLECTION

1. What learning communities are you a member of?

2. How could being a member of an online community support your professional development?

3. What 'wisdom' do you have that you would like to share with your peers (and how is this supported by wider evidence - see Chapter 6)?

Content creation

Digital tools are superb for content creation and offer opportunities for teachers and students to capture and then create a range of materials. The first stage of creation is data capture, and the digital tools available to the teacher in the classroom allow for a range of digital capture. The digitally competent teacher is one who is aware of, and able to capture, data in a range of formats including:

- text;
- still images;
- video;
- audio.

As well as these 'generic' forms, there are sensors that plug into smartphones or tablets that allow for the capture of a range of other data. These are most useful for teachers of STEM areas. Once data have been captured, it is easy to manipulate these by cropping, editing, integrating and re-elaborating in order to produce new material for use in classrooms; it is then relatively easy to find video tutorials on how to perform these functions on video storage sites such as YouTube (www.youtube.com) or Vimeo (www.vimeo.com). One excellent tool for reformulating video is EdPuzzle (https://edpuzzle.com), which allows you to interspace videos with questions, reflection points or quizzes.

Reformulation

As you develop your digital skills, you will move on from the creation of multi-media presentations to consider how the content you create will impact on the teaching and learning in your classroom. This might be to enable the model of the 'flipped classroom' (Milman, 2012) where the rich multi-media content can be used by students outside the classroom as the vehicle for knowledge transmission, giving more time inside the classroom for interactions between the teacher and the children.

The digitally competent teacher can select suitable material (text, images, video, exemplar materials, quizzes etc.) and the 'wrapper' (the software tool) that these are presented using. These may be the increasingly sophisticated standard presentation tools such as PowerPoint or Keynote, or Web-based presentation tools such as:

- Prezi (www.prezi.com);
- Glogster Edu (http://edu.glogster.com);
- Animoto (https://animoto.com);
- Kizoa (www.kizoa.com);
- Slideful (http://slideful.com).

They may also be tools that allow the teacher not only to present data, but also to capture data responses. These response data may be from questions, activities or quizzes:

- Nearpod (https://nearpod.com).
- Zeetings (http://about.zeetings.com).

Teachers can now also create interactive digital textbooks at low cost with software such as:

- Book Creator (www.bookcreator.com);
- Creative Book Builder (http://getcreativebookbuilder.blogspot.co.uk);
- iBooksAuthor (http://www.apple.com/uk/ibooks-author/).

These allow the integration of multi-media along with interactive 'widigts' from companies such as BookWidigts (www.bookwidgets.com) and Bookry (www.bookry.com).

These content-rich resources for the teacher are not just to produce a replacement textbook, but also to capture the children's learning whether this is an activity in PE, a piece of drama, an investigation in science or the children speaking in a foreign language. The data can then be used by the children as retention and reinforcement as practice for examinations, or just to share with others as examples of their own practice.

Copyright and intellectual property

As you create more sophisticated materials, you should be aware that materials found online and wider materials have copyright. Digitally competent teachers are aware of the limitation of the materials they are using and reformulating, and also how to protect or share their own copyrighted materials. Many educational materials are released under:

- Creative Commons licenses (https://creativecommons.org);
- Copyleft rules (https://en.wikipedia.org/wiki/Copyleft);
- Public domain licenses (https://en.wikipedia.org/wiki/Public_domain).

The digitally competent teacher (OECD, 2013) is one who is able to:

> Capture and produce digital content in different formats and use a variety of digital tools. Who can integrate multi-media in order to present ideas to children and can mash up existing content to form new content, which allows pedagogic challenge. Who can use cloud based tools to integrate media and use this to both present data to and collect data from children.

 **CASE STUDY**

Video instruction in PE

A PE teacher has set up a carousel of activities but finds she spends a significant amount time at the beginning of each lesson demonstrating and explaining how the equipment should be used, and that when the children arrive at their third or fourth piece of equipment, they have forgotten the instructions they have been given. The teacher thus finds she spends a lot of time in the lesson repeating simple instructions rather than assisting them.

Instruction cards do not convey the necessary information, so the teacher creates short instruction videos using videos of 'expert' children using the equipment with her own narration over the top of the video. These short videos are placed on a closed YouTube channel and the teacher then creates a simple presentation slide with links to the video.

Tablet computers are then fixed with Velcro® to the wall of the gymnasium. At the beginning of the lesson the teacher directs the students to the equipment and tells them to listen to the videos. If they are unsure, they can replay the video while the teacher focuses on assisting other children.

QUESTIONS FOR DISCUSSION AND REFLECTION

1. What elements of your own practice could be 'automated' in this way?

2. What skills/training do you need in order to be able to do this?

3. How might doing this benefit the teaching and learning in your classroom?

Conclusion

Technology should not be used to entertain or pacify, but to present new topics in engaging and rich ways in order to help children access and retain information, and to allow them to work independently and collaboratively, both with and without their teachers present. It can give them instant feedback by using low-stakes quizzes and practices, and enable them to access learning that is more personalised, authentic and situated.

Douglas Adams said that *we are stuck with technology when what we really want is stuff that works* (Adams, 2002, p115). There are two key questions to ask as you consider how you can use technology in your teaching and how children can use it in their learning:

• How is the technology supporting or enhancing the pedagogy in my classroom?

• How does the technology challenge the pedagogy in my classroom?

If you cannot answer either of these questions in a positive manner, then you should not be using that particular technology, whatever it is, be it a pencil, a book, an interactive whiteboard, a tablet or a VR headset; if you can answer positively, then the technology is working for you and your children, and you have found 'stuff that works'.

QUESTIONS FOR DISCUSSION AND REFLECTION

1. How are you currently using technology?

Given the categories outlined above, consider how you are using technology in your classroom and how this fits into the schema outlined. You might start by considering what you think of as technology and what you do not.

    1.1 Make a list of the technologies you are using without thinking about them.

    1.2 Make a list of those you use but could do with more personal development.

2. What things do you want to try out?

We hope that the ideas explored above will have given you the desire to try out some of them in your own classroom. Starting with your own learning, you should explore how these tools can enhance or develop the teaching and learning in your classroom.

2.1 Can you identify one technology usage you want to try out?

2.2 Can you identify which part of your curriculum this might enhance?

2.3 How will you measure the impact of this innovation?

3. What are your core competencies and what professional development (PD) support do you need?

As you have seen in the section above, the European Union's framework for Developing and Understanding Digital Competence in Europe (DIGCOMP, 2013) developed a number of core areas for digital competence for the teacher of the C21st. You can download a full version of this document from: https://ec.europa.eu/jrc/en/digcomp/digital-competence-framework

3.1 Which of these competencies do you feel you score well on?

3.2 Which of these do you feel you score badly on?

3.3 What evidence are you using to support this?

3.4 Now draw up a personal digital development plan to discuss with your mentor.

4. What Personal Learning Networks can I develop?

One of the most exciting elements of the new technologies is the opportunity to develop your learning networks. Siemens (2005) has written about the concept of connectivism as a *learning theory for the digital age* and postulates that learning will take place more and more as a group rather than as an individual activity. Martindale and Dowdy (2010, p178) talk about Personal Learning Environments, which they describe as a *manifestation of a learner's informal learning processes via the Web*. These PLNs, or Personal Learning Networks, are a growing important part of support and development structures for teachers. Consider how you could develop these. Twitter (www.twitter.com) is a valuable mechanism for this process. A good place to start this exploration is: www.teachertoolkit.me/2014/11/30/101-great-teachers-to-follow-on-twitter-by-teachertoolkit/

4.1 What PLNs are you already a member of?

4.2 What PLNS are you aware of?

4.3 What kinds of collaboration/cooperation could be enhanced?

 CHAPTER SUMMARY

Having read this chapter and reflected on its contents and your own practices, you should now have the following.

1. Be aware of some pedagogical approaches to using technology.

2. Have a greater understanding of your own capabilities.

3. Be more confident in ways you can use technology to enhance your teaching and the learning of your students.

FURTHER READING

Beetham, H and Sharpe, R (2013) *Rethinking Pedagogy for a Digital Age* (2nd edn). London: Routledge.

This text explores in a deep way the idea of pedagogical design when considering the challenges that digital technologies bring to teaching and learning. It does so via deep theory and practice examples of the ways in which learning will need to change into the twenty-first century.

McFarlene, A (2015) *Authentic Learning for the Digital Generation*. London: Routledge.

This book explores young people's use of personal devices, online creative communities and digital gaming. It questions the idea of the digital native and explores the help young people need to learn in a digital world.

Poore, M (2013) *Using Social Media in the Classroom*. London: Sage.

This is a useful book if you are just starting off with considering using social media. It links the digital technologies with pedagogical ideas and offers a comprehensive set of ideas for teaching with these technologies.

Younie, S, Leask, M and Burden, K (eds) (2015) *Teaching and Learning with ICT in the Primary School* (2nd edn). London: Routledge.

This text gives a wealth of theory and practical ideas across the curricular subjects for teachers in the primary sector, but it would also be useful for those in the early years of secondary.

REFERENCES

Aboujaoude, E and Koran, LM (2006) Potential markers for problematic Internet use: a telephone survey of 2,513 adults. *CNS Spectrums*, 12.

Adams, D (2002) *The Salmon of Doubt: Hitchhiking the Galaxy One Last Time*. London: Macmillan.

Badge, J, Johnson, S, Moseley, A and Cann, A (2012) Observing emerging student networks on a microblogging service. *Journal of Online Learning and Teaching*, 7(1): 90–8.

Baran, E (2014) A review of research on mobile learning in teacher education. *Educational Technology and Society*, 17(4): 17–32.

BBC (2014) Tablet computers in 70% of schools. Available at: www.bbc.co.uk/news/education-30216408 (accessed December 2016).

Burden, K and Hopkins, P (2015) How do mobile technologies challenge preservice teachers' pedagogical thinking? Conference paper. Mobile Initial Teacher Education. Galway, Ireland.

Burden, K, Hopkins, P, Male, T et al. (2012) iPad Scotland evaluation. Hull: University of Hull.

Byron, T (2014) Interview on BBC *Newsnight*. Available at: www.youtube.com/watch?v=iW5nqfurlPs (accessed December 2016).

Cochrane, TD (2012) Critical success factors for transforming pedagogy with mobile Web 2.0. *British Journal of Educational Technology*, 45(1): 65–82.

DIGCOMP (2013) A framework for developing and understanding digital competence in Europe. EU Joint Research Centre, European Union.

DIGCOMP 2.0 (2016) The digital competence framework for citizens. EU Joint Research Centre, European Union.

Educational Technology (2015) Is classroom technology actually being used by teachers? Available at: http://edtechnology.co.uk/Article/is-classroom-technology-actually-being-used-by-teachers/ (accessed December 2016).

Ekanayake, T and Wishart, JM (2014) Developing teachers' pedagogical practice in teaching science lessons with mobile phones. *Technology, Pedagogy and Education*, 23(2): 131–50.

Ertmer, PEA (1999) Examining teachers' beliefs about the role of technology in the elementary classroom: *Journal of Research on Computing in Education*, 32(1): 54–72.

Forte, A, Humphreys, M and Park, T (2012) Grassroots professional development: how teachers use Twitter. Proceedings of the 6th International AAAI Conference on Weblogs and Social Media, Dublin, Ireland (pp. 106–13).

Fullan, M and Langworthy, M (2013) *A Rich Seam: How New Pedagogies Find Deep Learning*. London: Pearson.

Gartner (2015) Gartner says worldwide devise shipments to grow 1.5%, to reach 2.5 billion units in 2015. www.gartner.com/newsroom/id/3088221 (accessed 27.3.17).

Gossen, T, Hempel, J and Nürnberger, A (2012) Find it if you can: usability case study of search engines for young users. *Personal and Ubiquitous Computing*, DOI:10.1007/s00779-012-0523-4

Gossen, T, Low, T and Nürnberger, A (2011) What are the real differences of children's and adults web searches? Conference paper at the 34th International ANC SIGIR Conference on Research and Development in Information Retrieval. DOI: 10.1145/2009916.2010076

Hopkins, P (2016) A support website for PGCE teachers. Available at: www.hullpgce.org.uk (accessed December 2016).

Hur, JW and Brush, TA (2009) Teacher participation in online communities: Why do teachers want to participate in self-generated online communities of K–12 teachers? *Journal of Research on Technology in Education*, 41, 279–303.

Jansen, M, Spink, A, Bateman, J and Saracevic, T (1998) Real life information retrieval: a study of user queries on the web. *ACM SIGIR Forum*, 32(1): 5–17.

Kearney, M and Maher, D (2013) Mobile learning in math teacher education: using iPads to support pre-service teachers' professional development. *Australian Educational Computing*, 27(3): 76–84.

Kearney, M, Schuck, S, Burden, K and Aubusson, P (2012) Viewing mobile learning from a pedagogical perspective. *Research in Learning Technology*, ALT Journal, 20.

Krutka, D, Carpenter, J and Trust, T (2016) Elements of engagement: a model of teacher interactions via professional learning networks. *Journal of Digital Learning in Teacher Education*, 32(4): 150–8.

Lave, J and Wenger, E (1991) *Situated Learning: Legitimate Peripheral Participation*. Cambridge: Cambridge University Press.

Lu, A (2011) Twitter seen evolving into professional development tool. *Education Week*, 30(36): 20, 13 July.

Martindale, T and Dowdy, M (2010). Personal learning environments. In Veletsianos, G (ed.) *Emerging Technologies in Distance Education*. Athabasca University Press, pp. 177–93.

McCormick, R and Scrimshaw, P (2001) *Education, Communication and Information*, Vol.1, No.1.

Milman, N (2013) The flipped classroom strategy: what is it and how can it best be used? *Distance Learning* 9.3 (2012): 85–7.

Morgan, N (2015) Nicky Morgan speaks at the 2015 BETT show. Available at: www.gov.uk/government/speeches/nicky-morgan-speaks-at-the-2015-bett-show (accessed December 2016).

Muñoz-Miralles, R et al. (2016) The problematic use of Information and Communication Technology (ICT) in adolescents by the cross-sectional JOITIC study. *BMC Pediatrics Journal*, 16(1): 140.

Newhouse, CP, Williams, PJ and Pearson, J (2006) Supporting mobile education for pre-service teachers. *Australasian Journal of Educational Technology*, 22(3): 289–311.

OECD (2013) DIGCOMP: A framework for developing and understanding digital competence in Europe. Paris: OECD Publishing.

OECD (2015) Students, computers and learning: making the connection. Paris: OECD Publishing. DOI: http://dx.doi.org/10.1787/9789264239555-en

O'Hara, S, Pritchard, R and Pella, S (2011) The teaching using technology studio (TUTS): learning to use new technologies through responsive teacher professional development. In Koehler, M and Mishra, P (eds) *Proceedings of Society for Information Technology & Teacher Education International Conference 2011* (pp3702–10). Chesapeake, VA: Association for the Advancement of Computing in Education (AACE).

Peng, H, Su, Y-J, Chou, C and Tsai, C-C (2009) Ubiquitous knowledge construction: mobile learning re-defined and a conceptual framework. *Innovations in Education and Teaching International*, 46(2): 171–83.

Porcello, D and Hsi, S (2013) Crowdsourcing and curating online education resources. *Science Education*, 341: 240–1.

Prensky, M (2001) Digital natives, digital immigrants: part 1. *On the Horizon*, 9(5): 1–6.

Puentedua, RR (2008) Transformation, technology, and education. Available at: http://hippasus.com/resources/tte/ (accessed December 2016).

Siemens, G (2005) Connectivism: a learning theory for the digital age. Available at: www.elearnspace.org/Articles/connectivism.htm (accessed December 2016).

Traxler, J (2007) Defining, discussing, and evaluating mobile learning: the moving finger writes and having writ ... *International Review of Research in Open and Distance Learning*, 8(2): 112.

Veen, W (2006) Homo Zappiens: growing up in a digital age. New York: Network Continuum Education, ePub.

Zhao, Y (2005) Technology and second language learning promises and problems. Michigan State University, unpublished conference paper.

Zheng, B, Warschauer, M, Lin, CH and Chang, C (2016) Learning in one-to-one laptop environments: a meta-analysis and research synthesis. *Review of Educational Research*.

8

SPEECH, LANGUAGE AND COMMUNICATION NEEDS

CLAIRE HEAD

THIS CHAPTER

By reading this chapter you will develop your understanding of the following.

- The impact that speech, language and communication difficulties can have on a child's learning and life skills.
- Some examples of effective school-based provision for children with speech, language and communication needs.
- That children need the right environment in order to develop effective communication skills and to develop their language for thinking, responding and for expressing feelings.
- A range of starting points, further reading and online support that can help teachers access training and guidance throughout their careers.

LINKS TO THE TEACHERS' STANDARDS

This chapter will help you with the following Teachers' Standards.

3. **Demonstrate good subject and curriculum knowledge**

5. **Adapt teaching to respond to the strengths and needs of all students**

Introduction

An effective start for life-long communication and learning

Children build their sense of self and find their voices through interaction (non-verbal and verbal communication) with the key people who inhabit their world. Research on this process highlights the importance of this formative interaction with trusted adults at key stages of development, particularly in the first few years of life (Selleck, 1965; Siraj-Blatchford et al., 2002; Siraj et al., 2015). As children grow and develop their language skills, the following factors provide the optimum nurturing environment for these skills to flourish: the opportunity to play; to engage in meaningful conversations; to help solve problems, and to share narratives that promote thinking, reasoning and language development (David et al., 2003; Hartshorne, 2006). Being treated with love, warmth, respect and interest is unsurprisingly the best foundation for social, emotional, cognitive and language development (Rose, 2006; Evangelou et al., 2009).

Children who do not experience this positive start in life may enter school with impoverished language skills and will be at risk of potentially experiencing a negative impact on their relationships, learning, behaviour and life-long employment opportunities (Sylva et al., 2012). Research by I CAN, the children's communication charity (2008–16), and The Communication Trust (2011) indicates some of the significant risk factors for children with Speech, Language and Communication Needs (SLCN) who do not receive effective support.

- *Only 25% of pupils with SLCN achieve the expected level in English at the end of Key Stage 2.*

- *Two thirds of 7–14 year olds with serious behaviour problems had language impairment.*

- *60% of young people in young offender's institutions have communication difficulties.*

(Communication Trust, 2011, p9)

Identifying children with SLCN

Teachers play a vital role in supporting pupils' speech, language and communication skills. Language is the thread that runs though every school day, and it should unite pupils and teachers in shared understanding and learning. Talk is often the medium of instruction and a tool for enquiry; it is also how pupils connect with each other and make friends. It is therefore critical

that teachers appreciate the many added challenges that children with SLCN face when inter-
acting, socialising and learning. Children who have SLCN often experience one or more of the
following difficulties.

- *Problems forming sounds and words.*

- *Problems formulating sentences and expressing ideas.*

- *Problems understanding speech and language.*

- *Problems using language socially.*

- *Delays and disorders in the development of speech and language skills.*

(Gadhok, 2007)

Some of these difficulties are as a result of language delay, which is sometimes referred to as 'impoverished language'. Children with impoverished or delayed language tend to have poorly developed
communication skills characterised by limited vocabulary, immature sentence structure, poor articulation, and some difficulties understanding instructions and maintaining attention. This type of
SLCN can be transient and therefore the good news is that with the right kind of intervention and
support, these children are often able to catch up with their peers. In some areas of social and economic disadvantage in the UK more than 50 per cent of children start school with this type of SLCN
(I CAN, 2006: Cost to the Nation of Children's Poor Communication, 1).

Approximately 10 per cent of all children have a persistent (rather than transient) SLCN and this
relates to children who have SLCN in conjunction with another SEN condition (such as hearing
impairment, cerebral palsy or autism), and 7 per cent of children with persistent and SLCN difficulties who have a specific language impairment (SLI), which is their main area of difficulty. Some of
these difficulties can be supported and improved over a short period of time with targeted support
(often from a speech and language therapist), but for other children these difficulties can be severe
and persistent, and can affect talking, understanding and learning. Research indicates that in 5-year-
olds, SLI affects about 7 per cent of children with SLCN (this is around two children in every class)
and that it is more common in boys than girls (I CAN, 2006).

These children will need specialist support throughout their schooling and I CAN's *Cost to the Nation
Report* (2006) warns educators that 50–90 per cent of these children will experience difficulties with
literacy, particularly reading and spelling.

I CAN refer to all aspects of SLCN as a *hidden* or *invisible disability* (2009) as the impact children
experience in struggling with some or a range of these needs often means that they also experience
difficulty with controlling their emotions, frustration spills over into behavioural issues, and has an
impact on social relationships and making friends. It can adversely affect or delay learning to read
and write, leading to later literacy problems as older children try to access the wider curriculum. All
of these difficulties hinder the healthy development of children's self-esteem and confidence. As
children with SLCN often find it difficult to talk about their feelings and to articulate their needs,
this can lead to children withdrawing and feeling angry, upset or alone. Inevitably, this affects children's literacy skills, resilience, learning power, well-being and future life chances (Hartshorne, 2006;
Claxton, 2008; DCSF, 2008; Freeman and Hartshorne, 2009).

 **RESEARCH/EVIDENCE FOCUS**

The Bercow Report

In 2008 the publication of The Bercow Report (Bercow, 2008, p16) drew national attention to the *grossly inadequate recognition across society of the importance of communication development, let alone the active steps needed to facilitate it.* The Bercow review team spent ten months gathering and reviewing evidence in order to provide the government with practical recommendations to improve SLCN provision for children and their families. One of the key messages reported was how variable current provision is across England and how important it is to raise the national status and profile of SLCN throughout the sector, but especially in the early years where that vital language acquisition process and early intervention are so crucial. Key recommendations centred around five main themes.

- *Communication is crucial.*
- *Early identification and intervention are essential.*
- *A continuum of services designed around the family is needed.*
- *Joint working is critical.*
- *The current system is characterised by high variability and a lack of equity.*

(DCSF, 2008)

Following publication of Bercow's recommendations, a range of government-funded and supported strategies was implemented to promote understanding of SLCN among the educational workforce and parents and carers (e.g. Every Child a Talker, 2008; National Literacy Trust, 2010; the Early Language Development Programme, 2011). The Nutbrown Review (2012) highlighted the importance of maintaining a qualified workforce leading early years education. Similarly, Field's (2010) review of early years practice confirmed that communication and language development at age three is one of the main National Life Chances Indicators for children. The impact of related policy and practice is due to be reviewed in 2018 after a ten-year implementation process. This period has been influenced by some major political, educational and societal transformations, including changes to the way government policy affects school budgets (e.g. some teaching alliances and academy chains engage their own speech and language therapist rather than relying on diminished local authority services), the implementation of a revised Early Years Foundation Stage Framework (2011), which now features communication and language as prime aspects to be embedded before later literacy skills are formally taught, and a new National Curriculum (DfE, 2013) with an increased emphasis on spoken language as part of pupils' linguistic, cognitive and social development implemented. There have also been changes to the health service and available support for families in need (such as the healthy child programme and two-year-old health check). The implementation of a new statutory SEND Code of Practice (DfE, 2014b) with the emphasis on inclusivity and meeting individual needs has led to personalised planning and joint services provision for 0–25-year-olds. Finally, the growing role of technology as a tool for leisure, learning and work has undoubtedly had an unprecedented impact on the way everyone communicates and shares experiences. Some of these changes will be discussed further in this chapter.

Raising teachers' awareness of SLCN through professional development

One of the initiatives introduced to address the main concerns highlighted in the Bercow Report (2008) was the introduction of the Early Language Development Programme (ELDP) from September 2011 to March 2015. This training programme was designed to upskill the early years workforce and raise awareness of the vital and active role that early years practitioners and family members play in early language development. ELDP was promoted and led by the children's charity I CAN and enabled lead practitioners to share professional development training with over 16,000 early years practitioners, recognising their instrumental role in supporting early communication with the 0–5 age range. This built on previous initiatives such as Every Child a Talker (ECat), Talk of the Town (Communication Trust) and Early Talk 0-3. An evaluation of the programme (EDLP, 2015) reported many positive outcomes including the following.

- *95 per cent of practitioners who completed the training felt that it had helped them to support children's early language development.*

- *93 per cent of practitioners felt that they were more confident in identifying children with language delay.*

- *87 per cent of parents surveyed commented on how engagement in the ELDP had increased their knowledge about how children learn to talk and how parents could support children at home.*

(EDLP, 2015, p3)

The following quote from a parent who participated in the programme activities summarises the positive impact that home–school links can have in this area.

> *I wouldn't have known that reading to your child helps them to talk, and that it is hearing words constantly which helps. Instead of saying 'what's this, what's this?' now I say words related to what he is saying, to extend his language.*

(Parent, cited in EDLP, 2015, p4)

Early years practitioners and primary school teachers are at the forefront of identifying and supporting pupils' speech, language and communication needs at strategic points in their development and sharing this with parents. It is important that teachers have the ability to identify children's emerging needs and are aware of how to support, intervene or seek help to meet these needs. Early intervention is essential if children are to be supported in making progress and ideally catching up with their peers and consequently avoiding the ongoing risk factors documented in the Bercow Report.

> *If a child does not benefit from early intervention, there are multiple risks – of lower educational attainment, of behavioural problems, of emotional and psychological difficulties, of poorer employment prospects, challenges to mental health and, in some cases, of a descent into criminality.*

(Bercow Report, DSCF, 2008)

The new Special Educational needs and Disability (SEND) statutory Code of Practice (DfE) came into force in September 2014b (the 2001 Code was revised to match the changes introduced by the Children and Families Act, 2014). All schools must adhere to this Code when taking action to meet children's individual needs and to help individuals make progress, and must ensure that children are supported across the following aspects of provision.

1. *Communication and interaction.*

2. *Cognition and learning.*

3. *Social, mental and emotional health.*

4. *Sensory and/or physical.*

(DfE, 2014b)

As discussed throughout this chapter, it is significant that children with SLCNs often experience related difficulties across a range of learning and teaching experiences, and that the majority of children with SEN such as dyslexia, hearing impairment, autistic spectrum disorders, specific and general learning difficulties also have SLCN (Lee, 2013). When the government published statistics on types of difficulties prevalent in schools in England (DfE, September 2014) it was noted that the most common need identified for support is children with SLCN, and children with behavioural, emotional and social needs. Primary school teachers identified 11 per cent more pupils with SLCN as their pupils' main needs and secondary teachers reported a 5 per cent increase compared to figures in 2012 (DfE, 2014a).

All the evidence suggests that teachers need further professional development to help children with SLCN to reach their potential and this must begin with early identification and assessment before personalised planning can be put in place. One of the main changes to be implemented in the new Code of Practice (DfE, 2014b, p13) is a greater emphasis on inclusive practice which supports professionals in identification, assessment and intervention to provide Education and Health Care (ECH) plans to help pupils make progress throughout their school lives and into young adulthood.

This focus on raising teachers' awareness and improving their knowledge and skills in supporting children with SLCN, through ongoing professional development training, is echoed in the draft framework of core content for initial teacher training (ITT) in England. This was created in response to recommendations made in the Carter Review (DfE, 2016b) which reported on the quality of ITT and indicated that the standard of training in key areas, such as supporting children with SEND, was variable. The new professional standard, proposed for implementation in 2017–18, aims to

ensure that trainees understand the principles of the SEND Code of Practice, are confident working with the four broad areas of need it identifies, and are able to adapt teaching strategies to ensure that pupils with SEND (including, but not limited to, autism, dyslexia, attention deficit hyperactivity disorder (ADHD), sensory impairment or speech, and language and communication needs (SLCN)) can access and progress within the curriculum.

(DfE, 2016b, p17)

Ofsted (2012) noted that Newly Qualified Teachers often struggled to adapt their lessons and language to meet the needs of children with SLCN and did not have a secure understanding of language development in order to effectively inform their professional practice. Similarly, in a Communication Trust Survey in 2007, qualified teachers also expressed doubts about their ability to effectively identify and support children with SLCN.

 **RESEARCH/EVIDENCE FOCUS**

ICAN

Research carried out by I CAN highlighted the urgent need to respond to the *communication skills short-age* and teachers' ability to support pupils based on the growing number of pupils identified with SLCN on school entry.

- *7 per cent of five-year-olds entering school in England – nearly 40,000 children in 2007 – have significant difficulties with speech and/or language.*
- *1 per cent of five-year-olds entering school in England – more than 5,500 children in 2007 – have the most severe and complex SLCN.*
- *50 per cent of children and young people in some socio-economically disadvantaged populations have speech and language skills that are significantly lower than their peers.*

(Kamini Gadhok, Chief Executive of the Royal College of
Speech and Language Therapists, 2007)

What is the impact of SLCN?

Children who have difficulties in articulating speech sounds, understanding how to construct sentences, using language expressively, processing what people say or using language to communicate in different situations often have difficulties with many aspects of learning across the curriculum and the school day. The link between good spoken language skills and later academic achievement has been well documented, and the Evangelou Report (2009) and the Tickell Review (2011) used this evidence to highlight the crucial role that parents and early years teachers play in supporting oral and language development as vocabulary at age five is a strong predictor of academic success at school leaving age. Findings reported in EPPSE 3–14 led the research team to conclude that early childhood experiences at home and pre-school *created the 'platform' on which the marks of primary and secondary school are then etched* (Sylva et al., 2012). In a direct response to address these findings, the SSTEW scale (sustained shared thinking and emotional well-being) was launched in March 2015. Its aim was to support high-quality interaction and to promote sustained shared thinking in early years settings by providing practitioners with guidance on:

- *building trust, confidence and independence;*
- *social and emotional well-being;*

- *supporting and extending language and communication;*

- *supporting learning and critical thinking;*

- *assessing learning and language.*

(Siraj et al., 2015)

The emphasis placed in Foundation Stage and Key Stage One classrooms on systematic synthetic phonics instruction has perhaps masked the importance of developing children's vocabulary and comprehension skills through interaction with adults and immersion in a rich language and literacy environment in parallel with phonological awareness.

> *Children's phonological skills are important in learning to read but so is vocabulary. Phonological skills at age 5 are better predictors of reading at the age 7 than at the age 11. Vocabulary at age 5 is a better predictor of the more complex tasks of reading at age 11.*

(Evangelou et al., 2009, p15)

The 2016 Early Years Foundation Stage Profile (EYFSP) results show that 86 per cent of children with no identified special educational needs achieved the expected standard in phonics, but only 46 per cent of children with SLCN achieved the expected standard, which confirms the link between SLCN and later literacy difficulties and speech and language processing.

Classroom focus

Social constructivist theory (Vygotsky, 1978) suggests that language development is primarily a social process and the best conditions for learning are through opportunities for adults, children and their peers to make meaning together, to co-construct understanding, to model vocabulary use, to scaffold syntax development by recasting sentences and finding ways to express ideas and solve problems in real conversational contexts. In order for this to be replicated in the classroom, teachers must consciously create a classroom culture that values talk and encourages children to be patient with each other, and to sensitively seek clarification when communication breaks down. Teachers must show children that they are willing to work hard to become active listeners themselves and ensure that all children, including those with SLCN, can make their voices heard and can work collaboratively with others in a mutually respectful environment.

One of the 12 aims that the Cambridge Primary Review team (2010) hoped would guide policy makers when revising the Primary National Curriculum is this notion of the central role, that

> *learning is an interactive process and that understanding builds through joint activity between teacher and pupil and among pupils in collaboration, and thereby to develop pupils' increasing sense of responsibility for what and how they learn*

(2010, p199)

Useful classroom strategies to support children with SLCN

Useful stragegies include the following.

- Encourage children to watch the speaker (and ask individuals to sit near the teacher if necessary).

- Break information down into manageable chunks and provide visual support when possible to support each stage – e.g. visual timetables, story maps, photographs.

- Give a simple overview of each part of the lesson or task before expanding in more detail during the lesson.

- Use multisensory teaching techniques, practical activities and role play to provide memory hooks for children.

- Find opportunities in your lessons for children to check understanding by explaining what they have heard and through teaching their peers.

- Use a variety of methods to teach new vocabulary and to check understanding of this – e.g. word banks, word wheels, encourage children to 'talk around the word' if they can't find the one or need a broader definition, writing frames with minimal word prompts.

- Allow children to use drawings, apparatus, IWB, models or recording devices as a starting point to capture their ideas before talking about them with others.

- Continually identify, praise and reward good listening and attention skills throughout the school day; use visual prompt cards to support individuals or display a class poster as in the following examples.

   Am I a good listener?

   Do I like to listen to my friends when they talk to me?

   Do I try to understand what people are saying?

   Do I look at the speaker?

   Do I ask questions to encourage speakers to explain their ideas?

   (Education Department of Western Australia, 1994, p59)

If a teacher feels that a child has a speech or language impairment such as a severe delay, with persistent difficulties with voice, speech, language or fluency, then support from the school SENCO should be sought initially; consultation with parents should take place, and then a referral to the local speech and language therapy service. Joint working between therapists, school-teachers and parents is essential as the child's needs are assessed, and an intervention and individual support programme is implemented.

One child in ten in your class is likely to have some form of SLCN. The majority of these children in primary classrooms will have transient needs as a result of language delay, and with support they can make significant progress and catch up with their peers in some cases. Effective intervention programmes for 4–7-year-olds include I CAN's 'Talk Boost' which aims to support language-delayed children by focusing on key skills, led by a teaching assistant working in close partnership with the class teacher following attendance at a professional development training course. The children are taught in groups of four, three times per week, in sessions lasting 30–40 minutes over a ten-week period. Evaluation of this programme indicates that children typically make between 14 and 18 months' progress (I CAN, 2011). In addition to providing a specific intervention for individuals who need this type of support, it is also beneficial to involve the whole school in 'talking' initiatives that promote communication and language skills.

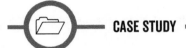 **CASE STUDY**

Placing talk at the heart of the curriculum

No Pens Day Wednesday – whole school initiative

Following the success nationally of 'No Pens Day Wednesday', showing that by 2015 over 4,800 schools had registered to become involved in the Communication Trust's initiative, a school in North Yorkshire decided to take part in this initiative. A staff meeting launched the project, focusing on the importance of supporting speaking and listening skills. The literacy coordinator explained that they needed to teach at least one day when 'pens' are not required, and speaking and listening skills would lead learning. Detailed plans for the whole school were agreed and the day started with a whole school assembly when it was explained to the pupils. Messages were sent on social media to ensure that parents were fully informed and involved. Examples of activities throughout the day included a debate on the issue of litter and fly-tipping in the local area in Year 6, which culminated in creating a news report which was filmed and sent to the local TV programme. A visit from a storyteller in Year 5 led to storytelling in pairs and stories were later recorded using iPads to capture the gestures, body language and stories to be later shared with other classes. Examining portraits by famous artists in Year 3, children worked in groups and were given key questions to explore each portrait style, followed by presentations to the class. In years 1 and 2, children carried out forest school activities in the school grounds, including lighting fires and listening to stories set in forests. In Reception, children explored the local area, taking a listening walk, recording sounds around them. A final assembly at the end of the day celebrated the achievements of each class, with a slide-show of the many different ways they had been learning through speaking and listening.

In the 2014 evaluation of No Pens Wednesday, carried out by the Communication Trust, participants reported that:

> 95 per cent said they'd do things differently around school as a result of their involvement and one in five respondents reported they identified pupils who were struggling with spoken language that they'd not known about before.
>
> (www.thecommunicationtrust.org.uk/media/311441/npdw_e<<valuation_short_final.pdf)

A full resource activity pack to support this initiative is available at: www.thecommunicationtrust.org.uk/projects/no-pens-day-wednesday/

You can also find resources and lesson plans to support No Pens Wednesday available from TES online at: www.tes.com/teaching-resource/no-pens-day-primary-lesson-plans-6215889

QUESTIONS FOR DISCUSSION AND REFLECTION

1. What do you think are the benefits of 'No Pens Wednesday'?

2. What would be the challenges of implementing this in your classroom?

3. Review the lesson plans and resources and consider how you could make use of these in your class.

Make your classroom 'communication friendly'

Start by reviewing The Communication Trust checklist, which you can download from: www.thecommunicationtrust.org.uk/publications/checklists. Also download the *Primary Talk* poster that will help you identify typical stages of language development for children aged 4–11. It also gives you a useful description of how children may act or respond in the classroom to help you identify potential difficulties, as in the following example.

Age range	Examples from the Primary Milestone Poster: 'What's typical talk at primary?'
4-7	Knows to look at who's talking and think about what they're saying.
5-7	Starts to ignore unimportant information.
7-9	Listens to key information and makes relevant, related comments – e.g. 'So all mammals are warm-blooded, have fur or hair and their babies all drink milk.'
9-11	Sustains active listening to both what is said and the way it is said.

Source: www.thecommunicationtrust.org.uk/media/1590/primary_milestone_poster_-_final.pdf

Supporting children with SLCN in everyday classroom activities

Download a free copy of *The Communication Cookbook* from: www.ican.org.uk/cookbook

Think about how you can introduce short activities into your lessons with groups and individuals who need targeted support with the five core strands of language development identified by I CAN and based on Ann Locke's Living Language programme (1995).

- *Attention and listening skills.*

- *Vocabulary.*

- *Building sentences.*

- *Telling stories.*

- *Conversations.*

Source: www.thecommunicationtrust.org.uk/media/12285/
let_s_talk_about_it_-_final.pdf

For example, go on a listening walk – take your group or class on a 'listening walk' around the school grounds. Pause at strategic points to listen, describe the sounds heard and try to identify them. Encourage the children to draw a map of their walk, drawing pictures or noting down the different sounds they experience.

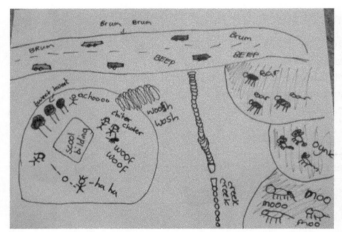 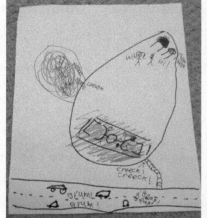

Figure 8.1   Some examples of children's maps

You or the children can record sounds at the 'pausing time' on a dictaphone or an iPad (to record and take photographs) and these can be played back during a revisiting and discussion session in the classroom. The maps and pictures can be used to create a learning story in the form of a book, which the children can take on the literacy walk to see if they spot and hear the same things on a different day.

In a similar style, older children can be encouraged to take work in pairs and use an iPad to document their favourite places in the classroom or school (or to show a visitor or new pupil around the school) and then make a short slide-show with a narrated voice-over to accompany the pictures and express how they feel about them.

Once children have experimented with listening to and identifying sounds through listening walks and playing with musical instruments, the following activities tend to provide more challenges and meaning for older children.

- Creating the background sounds to match a picture or a story.

- Listening to the background soundtrack and then drawing or describing the story that the children think is taking place based on the sound clues.

Play games that help children to listen and remember

Everyone knows how to play the traditional game 'Grandma's shopping basket', but this time ask children to say ' **S**am (child's name) went shopping and he bought some **s**ausages'. The next child starts with Sam's sentence and then adds on her name and shopping item 'and **M**andy bought some **m**ilk'.

Older children need a further challenge and are always keen to spot the teacher making a mistake (even if it is a deliberate one). Ask the children to listen to a sentence carefully and then tell them that you will change one (or two words) when you repeat it – can the children spot the difference? For example: I like walking in the rain with my little dog/I love walking in the rain with my little dog/I like running in the rain with my little dog/I like walking in the sunshine with my small dog, etc. Children can try this in small groups by thinking of a sentence first, saying it out loud, rehearsing the change in their head (or writing it down) and then changing a word on their second turn.

Use the guidance available from The Communication Trust to learn more about identifying children's SLCN and skills. This is available at:

The Communication Trust. Explaining speech, language and communication – www.thecommunication trust.org.uk

The Communication Trust. The Speech, Language and Communication Framework – www.the communicationtrust.org.uk

Conclusion

We know that children learn to talk by being talked to and that *talkative parents have talkative children* (Talk To Your Baby research project, 2010). We have also learned that *by the age of five a middle class child has heard 32 million words more than a child from a deprived background* (ibid.). Interaction in the formative years is crucial to later language and literacy development. If this process is delayed or impaired, it also has a significant influence on children's well-being and social skills. Children who have SLCN are disadvantaged in an education system and society that prize good communication skills as the gateway to forming relationships, academic success and employment opportunities. Educators must work closely with pupils and their families to ensure that these needs are identified at an early stage and priority is given to addressing them to provide a strong starting point for later life chances.

 CHAPTER SUMMARY

You should now know:

- about key theories and contemporary research, which help us to understand how children's cognition and language skills develop, and use this knowledge to underpin pedagogy and classroom practice;

(Continued)

(Continued)

- that early childhood is a critical phase of language development and that children need interaction with supportive adults and their peers in the right environment in order to develop effective communication skills;
- that teachers play a crucial role in enabling children to use their developing language and communication skills for thinking, enquiring, responding and learning, and for expressing feelings and ideas.

FURTHER READING

Saxton, M (2010) *Child Language: Acquisition and Development*. London: Sage.

This offers a very thorough account of language acquisition and focuses on the nature v. nurture debate.

Let's Talk About IT: what new teachers need to know about children's communication skills. Available at: www.thecommunicationtrust.org.uk/media/12285/let_s_talk_about_it_-_final.pdf

www.talkingpoint.org.uk/resources/don't-get-me-wrong – checklist to support teachers in identifying children's SLCNs.

www.thecommunicationtrust.org.uk/publications – Communication Trust website which combines online resources with news articles and case studies to support teachers and families.

www.londonsigbilingualism.co.uk – support for teachers identifying children with English as an additional language who may have SLCN.

REFERENCES

Bercow, J (2008) The Bercow Report: a review of services for children and young people (0–19) with speech, language and communication needs. London: Department for Education.

Claxton, G (2008) *What's the Point of School? Rediscovering the Heart of Education*. Oxford: One-world Publications.

Communication Trust (December, 2011) Let's talk about it: what new teachers need to know about communication skills. London: The Communication Trust.

David, T, Goouch, K, Powell, S and Abbott, L (2003) Birth to three matters: a review of the literature. London: Department for Education and Skills.

DCSF (2008) Every child a talker. Nottingham: DCSF.

DfE (2013) *National Curriculum in England*. London: DfE.

DfE (2014a) SFR 15/2013: School workforce in England, November 2012, issue 30, April 2013.

DfE (2014b) *SEND code of practice: 0 to 25 years* – Publications – GOV.UK. Available at: www.gov.uk/government/publications/send-code-of-practice-0-to-25

DfE (2016a) Carter review of initial teacher training (ITT). London: DfE.

DfE (2016b) A framework of core content for initial teacher training (ITT), July. Available at: www.gov.uk/government/uploads/system/uploads/attachment_data/file/536890/Framework_Report_11_July_2016_Final.pdf (accessed 11 January 2017).

EDLP (2015) Summary evaluation carried out by the University of Sheffield. Available at: www.ican.org.uk/~/media/Ican2/Whats%20the%20Issue/Evidence/ELDP-Evaluation-%20Report-OPM-6Feb2015%20Final.ashx (accessed 11 January 2017).

Education Department of Western Australia (1994) *First Steps Oral Language Resource Book.* Melbourne: Longman Publishing.

Edwards, C, Gandini, L and Forman, G (eds) (1998) *The Hundred Languages of Children: The Reggio Emilia Approach to Early Childhood Education* (2nd edn). Norwood, NJ: Ablex Publishing.

Evangelou, M, Sylva, K, Kyriacou, M, Wild, M and Glenny, G (2009) *Early Years Learning and Development Literature Review.* DCSF Research Report, University of Oxford.

Field, F (2010) The foundation years: preventing poor children becoming adults. The report on the Independent Review on Poverty and Life Chances. Available at: http://webarchive.nationalarchives.gov.uk/20110120090128/http://povertyreview.independent.gov.uk/media/20254/poverty-report.pdf (accessed 11 January 2017).

Freeman, K and Hartshorne, M (2009) *Speech, Language and Communcation Needs in the Early Years: I CAN Talk Series,* Issue 7, I CAN.

Gadhok, K (2007) Speech, language and communication needs – a definition. National Literacy Trust website. Available at: www.literacytrust.org.uk/talk_to_your_baby/news/2528_Speech_langauge_ and -communiation_needs (accessed11 January 2017).

Hartshorne, M (2006) *I CAN Talk* series: The cost to the nation of children's poor communication. Issue 2. London: I CAN. Available at: www.ican.org.uk/~/media/Ican2/Whats%20the%20Issue/Evidence/2%20The%20Cost%20to%20the%20Nation%20of%20Children%20s%20Poor%20Communication%20pdf.ashx (accessed 11 January 2017).

I CAN (2009) SLCN – What is the issue? Available at: www.ican.org.uk/What_is_the_issue.aspx (accessed 11 January 2017).

I CAN (2011) Impact Report 2011–12. Available at: www.ican.org.uk (accessed 27 March 2017).

I CAN (2016) Speech, Language and Communication Needs and Literacy Difficulties. I CAN Research Paper, Issue 1. Available at: www.ican.org.uk/~/media/Ican2/Whats%20the%20Issue/Evidence/1%20Communication%20Disability%20and%20Literacy%20Difficulties%20pdf.ashx (accessed 11 January 2017).

Lee, W (2013) A generation adrift: the case for speech, language and communication to take a central role in schools' policy and practice. The Communication Trust, available at: www.thecommunicationtrust.org.uk/media/31961/tct_genadrift.pdf (accessed 11 January 2017).

National Literacy Trust (2010) Highlights from a literature review prepared for the Face to Face research project, funded by the Department for Education's Children, Young People and Families Grant Programme. Available at: www.literacytrust.org.uk/assets/0000/6770/F2F_literature_highlights. pdf (accessed 11 January 2017).

Nutbrown, C (2012) Foundations for quality: an independent review of early education and child-care qualifications. London: DfE.

Ofsted (2012) From training to teaching early language and literacy: the effectiveness of training to teach language and literacy in primary schools. Available at: www.gov.uk/.../From_training_to_teaching_early_language_and_literacy.pdf (accessed 11 January 2017).

Rose, J (2006) Independent review of the teaching of early reading, final report, March. London: DfES (ref: 0201-2006DOC-EN).

Selleck, R (1965) (cited in DfES, 2003) *Birth to Three Matters*. Nottingham: DfES Publications. Available at: http://webarchive.nationalarchives.gov.uk/20130401151715/http://www.education.gov.uk/ publications/eOrderingDownload/BIRTHCD-PDF1.pdf (accessed 11 January 2017).

Siraj, I, Kingston, D and Melhuish, E (2015) *Assessing Quality in Early Childhood Education and Care*. Stoke-on-Trent: Trentham Books.

Siraj-Blatchford, I, Sylva, K, Muttock, S, Gilden, R and Bell, D (2002) *Researching Effective Pedagogy in the Early Years*. London: Department for Education and Skills, Research Report 356.

Sylva, K, Melhuish, E, Sammons, P, Siraj-Blatchford, I and Taggart, B (2012) Effective Pre-school Primary and Secondary Education 3–14 project (EPPSE 3–14). Final report from the Key Stage 3 phase: influences on students' development from age 11–14. London: DfE/Institute of Education.

Tickell, C (2011) The early years: foundation for life, health and learning. An independent report on the Early Years Foundation Stage to Her Majesty's Government. London: DfE. Available at: www. education.g ov.uk/tickellreview/ (accessed 11 January 2017).

Vygotsky, LV (1978) *Mind and Society: The Development of Higher Mental Process*. Cambridge, MA: Harvard University Press.

YouGov/The Communication Trust Survey, June 2007.

9

BUILDING ACADEMIC LANGUAGE IN LEARNERS OF ENGLISH AS AN ADDITIONAL LANGUAGE: FROM THEORY TO PRACTICAL CLASSROOM APPLICATIONS

KAMIL TRZEBIATOWSKI

THIS CHAPTER

By reading this chapter you will develop your understanding of the following.

- How to build academic language for English as an Additional Language (EAL) learners by utilising language-appropriate and level-appropriate strategies.
- Which second-language acquisition theories underpin these strategies and the reasons for these strategies, so that you can adapt your approaches to individual children and not use EAL strategies 'on' all EAL children.

Introduction

In January 2016, there were 1,233,416 'English as an Additional Language' pupils in maintained primary and secondary schools in the UK, a very significant rise from 499,000 in 1997 (NALDIC, 2013; DfE, 2016). The numbers continue to grow. Nowadays, the likelihood of working at a school with no learners with EAL is extremely slim; all teachers need to have a firm grasp of EAL pedagogy.

This chapter looks at some of the most important theories and insights into second language acquisition (SLA) and research into effective EAL provision at schools which form the basis for the distinctive EAL pedagogy. The highly influential Jim Cummins's Basic Interpersonal Communication Skills (BICS) vs Cognitive Academic Language Proficiency (CALP) theory of language development (Cummins, 1979) will be discussed, as will his Thinking Skills Quadrants Framework; it suggests different types of tasks for learners at different stages of English language acquisition. The US-based research by Thomas and Collier (1997) into what constitutes effective EAL support will be discussed, as well as corresponding British-based research from Birmingham into similar issues (BASS, 2006).

Several EAL pedagogy-based strategies to be used in classrooms for the benefit of EAL learners will be considered: substitution tables, graphic organisers, Directed Activities related to texts (DARTs) and ways to teach language explicitly.

EAL students

There are now over a million EAL students in British maintained primary and secondary schools. They are certainly not a uniform group: some are new arrivals to the country, some were born here. Some are literate in their home language, some are not. They may have different levels of school experience and come from varying cultural, social and economic backgrounds. They may have had no prior schooling or a disrupted one. Some might not know the Roman script at all, some are completely multiliterate.

NALDIC (1999), in their publication *The Distinctiveness of EAL*, sum up the task ahead of EAL learners very well. First, they need to learn *the English (language)* and do this *through English (the school curriculum*). In addition, they need to socialise with other children in the yet unlearnt language, acquire often radically new social skills and accommodate new values, culture and expectations, and potentially balance them with the ones expected at home. EAL learners' lives are, therefore, diametrically different from those of EFL (English as a *foreign* language) learners, who by and large learn in their own cultural environments and do not need the new language for general schooling. Thus, the EAL pedagogy is *distinct* from EFL pedagogy.

Since they need to learn *through* English, it is of vital importance that language is explicit in your teaching. Gibbons (1999) suggests that to a competent language user language is like a clear window – transparent; you know it is there, but it is hard to see. To an EAL learner, the window is frosted: their understanding of your content is affected by their language skills. Focusing on content alone makes language the invisible curriculum in school and disadvantages EAL learners.

Figure 9.1   The Prism Model (from Thomas and Collier, 1997, p42)

Thomas and Collier's (1997) *Language Acquisition for School Prism Model* theory deals with how English language learners (ELLs) best acquire language at school. They point to the interdependence of the aspects of schooling that you see in the image to the right. While language development is important (first and second), care needs to be taken that students do not remain in withdrawal sessions indefinitely: the curriculum does not wait and, consequently, students will not have the time to catch up on their academic curricular (subject-/content-based) development. The prism addresses cognitive development as well: Thomas and Collier stress it begins at birth, is subconscious in nature and related to the first-language development. Finally, social and cultural processes – in the school, community and broader society – may influence SLA – for instance, the experience of racism can have an adverse effect on the attitude towards a target language. Thomas and Collier remind us that English is only one part of the learning process. Thus, withdrawing learners completely from the mainstream for EAL interventions interferes with three out of the four aspects of the prism.

Additionally, Thomas and Collier state that in order to close the achievement gap, ELL learners need to make 1½ years of progress, relative to native speakers of English, for 6 years. In England, extensive research conducted in Birmingham (BASS, 2006) suggests that the gap can be closed for a student literate in their first language (L1), arriving in year 7, by year 11 (5 years = accelerated progress), and argues that students need to be mainstreamed and receive language support for this to occur.

No introduction to EAL pedagogy can be complete without mentioning the work of Jim Cummins. Cummins is probably the best-known name in the EAL/ESL teaching field. He has made a distinction between the two types of language skills that learners can possess (Cummins, 1979). One is *BICS – Basic Interpersonal Communication Skills*. This is the type of language that we use for social and basic conversational communication purposes, such as when pupils get their lunch in a school's canteen. It is highly dependent on context and such visual context is usually provided – for example, in a school playground, you can see what 'a swing' looks like. BICS, according to Cummins, develops usually within two years of exposure (Cummins, 2008). *CALP – Cognitive Academic Language Proficiency* – the more abstract, complex, syntactically and grammatically sophisticated language (as required for GCSEs), takes 5–7 years to develop (Cummins, 2008).

Context and contextualised learning features are perhaps the most important aspect of EAL pedagogy, as is evident in the paragraph above. NALDIC, the largest EAL association in Britain, concurs and suggests in *The Distinctiveness of EAL* that the provision of rich contextual background is crucial if the input that EAL learners receive is to be comprehensible (NALDIC, 1999). Mohan suggests using graphic organisers (Mohan, 1986) as a highly contextualised and comprehension-enabling tool. Presenting students with the content of their lessons in the form of diagrams, cycles, mind maps, spidergrams and other similar visual representations of knowledge (i.e. graphic organisers) can be very effective in lowering the linguistic demands on them, allowing learners to use their cognitive thinking skills and facilitating understanding. I explore this topic further elsewhere in this chapter.

As has been seen, Thomas and Collier (1997) place emphasis on harnessing the English language learners' command of their home language for their academic, cognitive and linguistic development. Nowadays, bilingualism is recognised as an asset, including by the British government (DfE, 2012). Cummins' model of language interdependence ('dual iceberg') (Cummins, 1981, p37) also

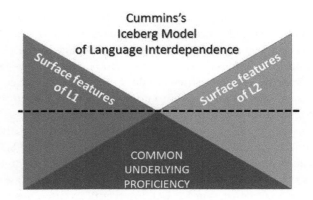

Figure 9.2   Language Interdependence Theory (adapted from Cummins, 1981, p37)

speaks to the importance of the mother tongue for SLA. He claims that proficiency involving more cognitively demanding tasks is shared between languages, and that concepts first learned in L1 can be applied in the second language (L2); or, stated more simply, the development of L2 – in our case, the English language – will be helped not only by taking advantage of but also by the continuing development of L1.

 **RESEARCH/EVIDENCE FOCUS**

Cummins' Thinking Skills Quadrant Framework – from BICS to CALP

Based on his BICS and CALP language development stages distinction, Cummins provides suggestions on what type of EAL-friendly strategies this may entail. This is shown in the images below, which Milton Keynes Council has adapted from Cummins' work for their comprehensive guide (Milton Keynes Council, 2004).

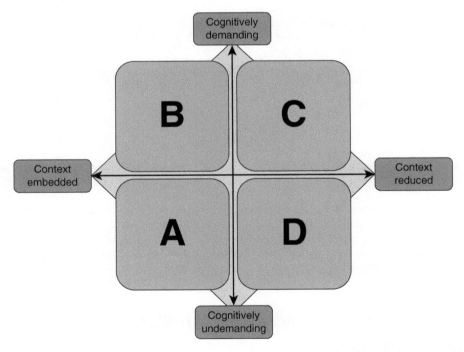

Figure 9.3   BICS and CALP quadrants (adapted from Milton Keynes Council, 2004, p7)

The D quadrant tasks are to be avoided at all cost: repeating or copying phrases without any understanding is unproductive for the learners. Quadrant A represents the type of tasks that beginner learners would engage in, and one can observe that these tasks are less demanding but far more

(Continued)

(Continued)

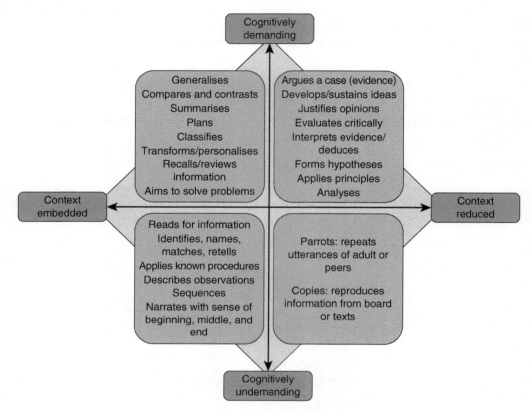

Figure 9.4   BICS and CALP quadrants (adapted from Milton Keynes Council, 2004, p8)

contextualised – for example, sequencing a selection of images, matching pictures to vocabulary items or applying procedures observed in a science lab. The journey would take the learners from such quadrant A tasks to quadrant C tasks, which rely on being able to read, interpret and evaluate large bodies of text and information, involving far more abstract language than the more visual-, kinaesthetic- and realia-based tasks in A and B.

Bernard Mohan's Knowledge Framework and Graphic Organisers

Please look at the table below. Mohan (1986, in Slater and Gleason, 2011) contends that whichever subject you teach, your lessons will involve teaching the Knowledge Structures shown. Descriptions require an ability to classify and categorise; sequencing and ordering events or items requires understanding the principles behind the order; making choices requires forming an opinion of the worth or value of the items you are choosing from.

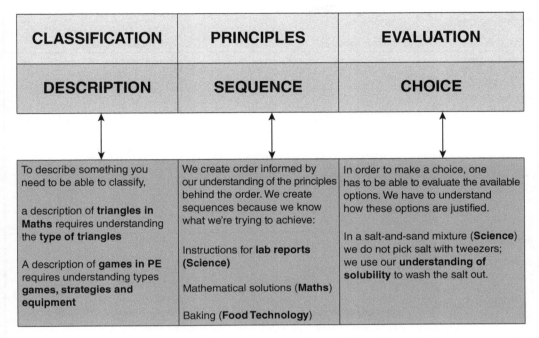

CLASSIFICATION	PRINCIPLES	EVALUATION
DESCRIPTION	SEQUENCE	CHOICE
To describe something you need to be able to classify, a description of **triangles in Maths** requires understanding the **type of triangles** A description of **games in PE** requires understanding types **games, strategies and equipment**	We create order informed by our understanding of the principles behind the order. We create sequences because we know what we're trying to achieve: Instructions for **lab reports** (**Science**) Mathematical solutions (**Maths**) Baking (**Food Technology**)	In order to make a choice, one has to be able to evaluate the available options. We have to understand how these options are justified. In a salt-and-sand mixture (**Science**) we do not pick salt with tweezers; we use our **understanding of solubility** to wash the salt out.

Figure 9.5   Knowledge structures (adapted from Slater and Gleason, 2011, pp8–10)

Mohan then suggests that each such knowledge structure is related to the kind of thinking skills that we require of students. In turn, these are linked to key visuals (graphic organisers). These do lower the verbal demands on our English language learners, but, more to the point, specific associated language can – and should – be taught so that students can talk about and/or write about their thinking – translating their cognitive thinking processes into linguistic outcomes. The table below, adapted from Mohan's own website, provides examples of this approach.

Classroom focus

Language teaching needs to be explicit in your classroom practice. You should aim to use the *metalinguistic* rather than the *referential function of language*, explained by Creese (2005): the metalinguistic function is the ability of the language to comment on itself – for example, 'Are you going to use an *adjective* or *adverb* here?' or 'Would it be better if this sentence was in the *passive voice*?'), while the referential is language used to talk about something else (i.e. refer to matters other than the language itself). This also means that, to serve your EAL learners well, you may need to refresh your knowledge of English grammar terminology. It is difficult to advise students on language if you do not have the words to talk about it.

To serve your EAL learners well, understanding your students' backgrounds and the past is crucial. You need to be aware of the linguistic and cultural backgrounds of your EAL learners. Are

Knowledge structure + thinking skills	Key visuals (graphic organisers)	Associated language
Classification Classifying, grouping, defining, talking part/ whole		"Being" verbs (e.g. *be, have*) Additive conjunctions (e.g., *and*) Part/whole lexis (e.g. nouns: *types, classes, kinds, categories, ways;* verbs: *classify, sort, group, organize, categorize, divide, comprise*) Passives (e.g. *are classified, are grouped*)
Principles Explaining, predicting, drawing conclusions, applying causes, effects, ends, rules, formulating, testing, establishing hypotheses		Action verbs Consequential conjunction and adverbials (e.g. *since, due to, in order to, consequently, because, thus, if-clauses*) Cause-effect lexis (e.g. nouns: *cause, effect, result;* verbs: *cause, produce, bring about*) Passives + agency (e.g. *is caused by, are produced by*)
Evaluation Evaluating, ranking, judging, criticising		"Thinking" verbs (e.g. *believe, think, value, consider, rank, judge*) Comparative conjunctions (e.g. *likewise, however, while*) Evaluative lexis (e.g. nouns: *best, worst;* adjectives: *good, bad, right, wrong, boring, acceptable;* verbs: *rank, approve, value, like*)
Description Identifying, labelling, describing, comparing, contrasting		"Being" verbs (e.g. *be, have*) Additive conjunctions (e.g. *and*) Attributive lexis (e.g. *adjectives of colour and size*) Language of comparison and contrast (e.g. *the same as, similar to, like, different from*)

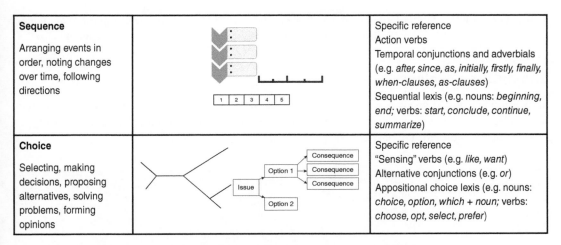

Sequence		Specific reference
Arranging events in order, noting changes over time, following directions		Action verbs Temporal conjunctions and adverbials (e.g. *after, since, as, initially, firstly, finally, when-clauses, as-clauses*) Sequential lexis (e.g. nouns: *beginning, end*; verbs: *start, conclude, continue, summarize*)
Choice		Specific reference
Selecting, making decisions, proposing alternatives, solving problems, forming opinions		"Sensing" verbs (e.g. *like, want*) Alternative conjunctions (e.g. *or*) Appositional choice lexis (e.g. nouns: *choice, option, which + noun*; verbs: *choose, opt, select, prefer*)

Figure 9.6   Knowledge structures and thinking skills (adapted from Knowledge Framework. Available at: http://tslater.public.iastate.edu/kf/structures.html and http://tslater.public.iastate.edu/kf/powerpoint.html, 2012)

they indeed literate in their home language? What are their own and their parents' expectations of school? Are they refugees? Do they have experience of schooling? If so, was it diametrically different from the one provided in the UK? If they are from, say, Somalia, it might be; if they are from Poland, perhaps less so. Answering these cultural and social questions will be important to you to differentiate your resources for these learners. There is no point devising an 'activating prior knowledge' starter around an episode of *The Simpsons,* if your student has never heard of the programme and it is of no significance to them.

This links to Krashen's *Affective Filter Hypothesis*, part of which proposes that *Low anxiety appears to be conducive to second language acquisition, whether measured as personal or classroom anxiety* (2009, p31). In essence, if your beginner EAL learners are stressed, the chances are that your well-designed activities are not likely to reach the part of their brain responsible for language acquisition. The solution to that is to truly include EAL learners in your classroom: provide them with a buddy who speaks the same language as they do or a friendly language-interested English speaker, and also provide them with tasks they can perform in your classroom – for example, distributing books – and will make them feel useful. Beginner learners will usually pass through a period known as 'the silent period', where they will choose not to speak until they feel confident to do so. This is normal, and can last up to six months, depending on the child (Roseberry-Kibbin, 1995, in Roberts, 2014).

Crucially, you will need to understand the level of English language acquisition of your students. Hopefully, your school will have a member of staff responsible for providing you with this information. Ideally, you will receive a profile on these students with their listening, speaking, reading and writing skills described and relevant teaching strategies provided. If this is not the case, you might need to take matters into your own hands: the *EAL Mesh Guide* (Flynn, n.d.) lists several EAL assessments you could use.

Three types of EAL-friendly language-made-explicit and contextualised strategies – *substitution tables*, *graphic organisers* and *directed activities related to text* (also known as DARTs) – are considered below.

Substitution tables

Substitution tables, as you can see in the examples below, aim to break long strings of language (sentences) into smaller, grammatical, manageable chunks. We can discern, broadly, between two types of substitution tables for EAL learners.

I	like love	read**ing**	books.
You	enjoy don't like dislike hate	listen**ing** to	the radio.
He	likes loves	read**ing**	books.
She	enjoys doesn't like	listen**ing** to	the radio.
It	dislikes hates		
We	like love	read**ing**	books.
You	enjoy don't like	listen**ing** to	the radio.
They	dislike hate		

Figure 9.7   An example from K Trzebiatowski's classroom

The first one is an example of a *basic grammar substitution table*, intended for beginner EAL learners (Cummins' quadrant A). Here, the first column lists the pronouns/subjects of the sentences. The next column has only verbs. The last two columns represent objects of the sentences, but as you can see, they have been divided into gerunds (the -ing verbs that follow verbs such as *like, love* and *enjoy*; i.e. we say *I like reading* rather than *I like read*) and nouns/noun phrases. The students create their sentences by selecting one item from each column. Largely, due to their limited command of the English language, they become locked into fixed pre-set sentences, which repeat the same grammatical structure, again and again. The -s suffix is added to the third-person singular pronoun verbs – these students should have their attention drawn to this fact. The opinion words (*like, love, enjoy, hate*) can be changed, of course, to reflect the students' opinions.

I do believe it is evident that we have just made our language teaching *explicit*. The next most important factor is to contextualise the language teaching. For beginner learners, less verbal elements need to be provided, particularly if they struggle with the vocabulary provided. There is no better tool for this purpose than the Google Images search engine. For instance, you can add emotions emojis for *like/love/enjoy/don't like/dislike/hate* to your table and/or images for *books* and *radio*.

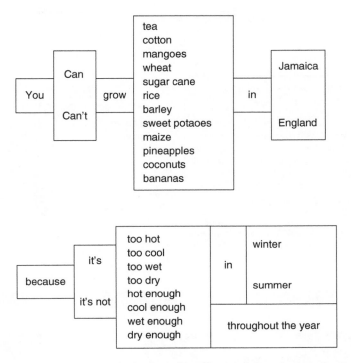

Figure 9.8   Substitution tables (from Collaborative Learning Project). Available at:
www.collaborativelearning.org/whatcanyougrow.pdf, 2010

Let us now consider learners on the B level of English language acquisition. As your learners' aware-ness of the English language grows, the proportions of the focus on language and content in your teaching and differentiation need to change. While the A quadrant learners need the *language inte-grated with content* approach, B quadrant learners might need the *language/content* approach (i.e. more content and less language).

This is what this next type of substitution table aims to do. In the example in Figure 9.8, structured around a geography lesson, the focus is on the type of plants that can be grown in either Jamaica or England in different seasons, and learners need to show their understanding of this topic – the table allows them to do so while focusing on grammatical elements such as *can/can't grow, too hot/hot enough* and *in winter/summer*. The repetition of these linguistic structures is built into this exercise, but learners are not as locked into the use of language as they were before. As they are now more adept at the English language, we can focus more on the content.

Graphic organisers

Graphic organisers ought to be used as frequently as possible in your work with English language learners. As graphic organisers need to be accompanied by language, while the organisers in them-selves are a huge help, teachers need to offer support with describing the relations between their different items by suggesting what language can be used when talking or writing about them.

The first example is for a science lesson on photosynthesis.

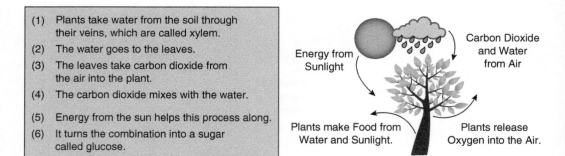

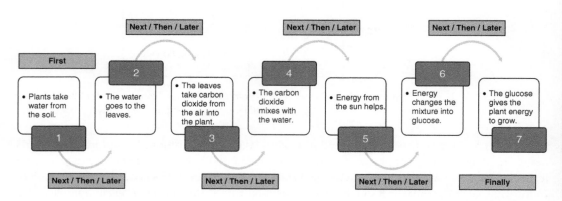

Figure 9.9   An example from K Trzebiatowski's classroom.

Source: All About Photosynthesis: Basic Photosynthesis Process Explained (Easy Science for Kids, 2016)

In this example, the sentences are given to students alongside an image/diagram of the process. The sentences given have been simplified for students for easier access. What we really want the students to do, however, is to use the sequencing connectives (*first, next, then, later*) to move from one sentence to the next.

You may have more than one EAL in your class; therefore, how do you differentiate this task for a learner in Cummins' B quadrant? While in the first graphic organiser, all the learners were asked to do was to use connectives without altering the sentences at all. This is no longer possible in the Figure 9.10 example: to take advantage of *when/as/this is when, present simple tense* has to be used. This can be pre-taught or revisited prior to this task, and students can be reminded that it is present simple that is used to write about factual (repeatable) processes.

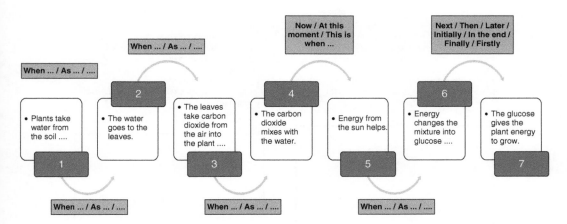

Figure 9.10   An example from K Trzebiatowski's classroom

In the graphic organiser in Figure 9.11, after reading the book *Azzi in Between* (Garland, 2015), my group of beginner learners use sequencing words and connectives to write about the story. The arrows indicate moving from the beginning of the story to the end, as does the axis at the bottom. The colours of the clouds indicate which words are to be used for the beginning, middle and end of the story. The present simple tense was pre-taught, and students were using the sentences from their book to write their one-paragraph summaries.

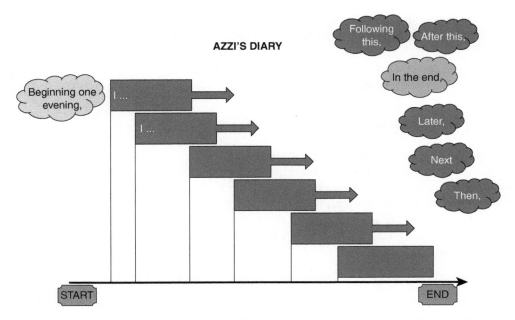

Figure 9.11   An example from K Trzebiatowski's classroom

> There are three kinds of dogs that I like best. I like Pugs because they are companion dogs and have cute faces. Boston Terriers are on my list because they are intelligent and not too big. I also like Golden Labrador Retrievers because they are faithful, loving, and fun to play with.

> There are three types of triangles: equilateral, isosceles and scalene. Equilateral triangles are made up of three equal sides and three equal angles. Isosceles triangles are made up of two equal sides and two equal angles. Scalene triangles are made up of unequal sides and unequal angles. Scalene triangles look the most unsymmetrical.

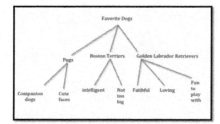

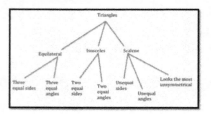

Figure 9.12   Knowledge structures and thinking skills (after Knowledge Framework).

Source: *http://tslater.public.iastate.edu/kf/powerpoint.html, 2012*

Cognitive thinking skills, activated and supported by graphic organisers, allow English language learners to access the complex curriculum content of your classroom. Above is one example, provided by Mohan at his own website.

On the left, we have a grammatically simple piece of text, categorising favourite dogs and the reasons for liking them. One could find such a piece of writing in an EFL textbook unit for beginner learners. On the right, the exact same graphic organiser is used to categorise types of triangles in Maths. What are the only differences? 'Kinds' in the first sentence in the text about dogs is now 'types' and 'have' has become 'are made up of' (an example of a passive voice phrase) in the triangles passage. Learners can now write about what they know about triangles and use a more formal register of language while doing so.

Directed Activities Related to Texts (DARTs)

DARTs are a group of activities that focus students' attention on elements of a text as opposed to learners answering a standard set of comprehension questions after reading it. This can be a gap-fill (cloze), sequencing paragraphs, grouping parts of a text according to categories, labelling a diagram, giving each paragraph a title and highlighting particular language elements (for instance, all adjectives or prepositions) in the text. While you will have taught some of these activities before, the crucial aspect of DARTs is that you focus on the *language* of the text rather than the content.

First, we focus on different types of cloze activities – please examine Table 9.1.

A similar approach can be taken to gap-fill exercises. Rather than focus on removing subject content-based words, remove language-specific words – for instance, prepositions as in Figure 9.13. Prepositions do not translate across languages easily (e.g. the phrase *I am at home now* usually translates as *I am in home now* in the Polish language) and this can represent a stumbling block for your

Table 9.1   Types of cloze (after Gibbons, 2009)

Type of cloze	Explanation/examples

Specific cloze	Rather than randomly removing content words, we remove specific words to do with *language*. Two subtypes of such cloze work can be distinguished:
	
	• Many different possibilities, e.g.
	
	  A school is a _____ where students and teachers gather to _____ and _____.
	
	• Limited amount of words possible, e.g.
	
	  ___ school is ___ building _____ students and teachers gather ___ learn and teach.
	
	Discuss with your class why some words, linguistically and grammatically, have to always be there and others are changeable.

Vanishing cloze	At the end of your lesson, during a plenary, write one sentence on the board summing up that session. For instance: **William Shakespeare, who lived in the 16th and 17th century, was a playwright who wrote *Macbeth* and *Hamlet*.** Ask students to read this sentence and proceed to erase one word. Ask students to read it again and discuss the language and grammar of the words that disappear (e.g. *the* precedes *16th and 17th century*). Carry on the procedure until no words are remaining.

A PREPOSITION GAP FILL

She was dressed__rich materials - satins, and lace, and silks-all__white. Her shoes were white. And she had a long white veil dependent_____her hair, and she had bridal flowers__her hair,__her hair was white. Some bright jewels sparkled__her neck and__her hands, and some other jewels lay sparkling__ the table. Dresses, less splendid than the dress she wore, and half-packed trunks were scattered_____. She had not quite finished dressing,__she had__one shoe__ the other was__the table_____her hand - her veil was half arranged, her watch and chain were not put__, and some lace__her bosom lay_____those trinkets and_____her handkerchief, and gloves, and some flowers, and a prayer-book-, all confusedly heaped_____the looking-glass.

Choose from the words in the box			
In	near	an	of
with	about	but	from
for			

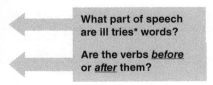

What part of speech are ill tries* words?

Are the verbs *before* or *after* them?

Figure 9.13   An example from K Trzebiatowski's classroom

EAL learners in your lessons rather than your content. For more advanced EAL learners and, indeed, native English-speaking children, you can simply remove the box at the bottom of the exercise. Reorienting yourself towards considering *language within your content* makes it possible to differentiate many other activities. For instance, consider the following sentences.

Table 9.2   Language-focused gap-fill activities

Task: fill in the missing words	Language focus (metalinguistic function)
The atom is made up _____ protons, neutrons and electrons.	Prepositions
Plants take water _____ the soil.	Prepositions
_____ occurs when egg and sperm meet. (change the word CONCEIVE to a NOUN)	Word building / word formation
This process results in _____ (change the word ERODE to a NOUN)	Word building / word formation
___ school is located in ____ particularly deprived part of ____ country.	Articles (a/an)

 **CASE STUDY**

Pupil: Anna, a new arrival from Poland. Full schooling in Polish education system (five years of primary school). In my class, she only used telegraphic language to communicate needs (pen, toilet, book), but did not string sentences together. She appeared to understand basic instructions where context was provided.

Below you can see an example resource from my classroom. The lesson's objective was to write sentences about certain historical figures (despotic tyrants) using paragraphs of text, in the past tense, using the connective *who*. I produced the following (Figure 9.14) for her. In the lesson, I drew attention to the subject–verb–object structure, and 'was' used in the past. Anna was also provided with images, access to a tablet and a paper bilingual dictionary.

SUBJECT	VERB	OBJECT	CONNECTIVE	VERB	PREPOSITION	NOUN
NAME	WAS	WHO WAS HE?		WHAT DID HE DO?	IN	WHERE WAS HE?
Saddam Hussein	was	a dictator	who	ruled	in	Iraq.
1	2	3	4	5	6	7

Figure 9.14   A substitution table by K Trzebiatowski, based on an activity by the British Council, 2016

QUESTIONS FOR DISCUSSION AND REFLECTION

Consider the following.

- How the language is made explicit.
- How the substitution table is contextualised to the content of the lesson.
- How the use of L1 was allowed and encouraged in this activity.
- How Anna is able to do the same type of activity as everyone else in the class.

CASE STUDY

Pupil: Georgina has so far spent two years in the UK and now has a fully developed BICS. She is an advanced EAL learner. Her tenses still show inaccuracies. She writes at length, but her vocabulary is simple and imprecise.

Below, there is an example of a DARTs activity (the original text was much longer). The students are asked to replace the underlined words with more formal/academic alternatives from the box.

Mogadishu Mothers <u>GET HELP</u> (_____) in Fight To Keep Kids FED (_____)

Fatia and Halima are fighting to protect their children from <u>eating badly</u> (_____).

Despite their age, the two young women are mothers of <u>a lot of</u> (_____) experience. Halima is 24 years old and has seven children while Fatia, a year older, is a mother of six. Both are firm believers in the value of the specialized food packets they <u>are getting</u> (_____) every month from the World Food Programme to keep their children healthy.

"I don't want my babies to become weak and <u>eat badly</u>," (_____) says Fatia. "It's important to keep the little ones strong," adds Halima, cradling her youngest, eight-month-old Hashim, on her knee.

get a hand	be malnourished	are receiving	Being undernourished
	nourished	significant	

Figure 9.15   A DARTs activity by K Trzebiatowski; original text: AQA, 2012, p[3]

QUESTIONS FOR DISCUSSION AND REFLECTION

- How an individual aspect of language is focused on here (formal language).
- The higher level of cognitive demand asked of students in this task.
- There is no visual support – why is that?

Conclusion

EAL pedagogy is quite different from English as a Foreign Language (EFL) teaching approaches. The school context for EAL learners means that they need to learn English and the curriculum content through English – the EAL pedagogy, calling for contextualised content-based language teaching, reflects this reality. The linguistic, the academic, the cognitive and the social aspects of EAL learners' development need to be taken into consideration if they are to realise their full potential. As both Cummins (1981) and Thomas and Collier (1997) argue, students' first language is crucial to the development of their second one, and you are strongly advised to take advantage of this while teaching these learners.

English language teaching needs to be present and explicit in your lessons. The strategies suggested in this chapter – substitution tables, graphic organisers and DARTs – all position *language* at the forefront, but teach it in a contextualised way, at no point becoming distant from the school curriculum. What it requires of you, however, is dedicated space in your planning time where you pay close attention to the linguistic demands of your lessons. If you do so, you will serve the EAL learners well.

 QUESTIONS FOR DISCUSSION AND REFLECTION

1. How are you going to ensure that language is not the invisible curriculum of your school and make it explicit in your lessons?

Pick a random lesson, either from a textbook you might be using, a reading you might choose, or a resource you would expose your entire class to next week. Spend five minutes distancing yourself from *what* it says; rather, look at *how* it says it. In other words, what makes it the frosted glass for your EAL learners? What language demands does it place? What *tense* is used throughout? Is the *active* or *passive voice* being used? Is the passage written in a particularly *formal register*?

You might wish to pick one aspect of language to focus on in the lesson you are planning. Which strategy would you use to accomplish this goal? Are substitution tables more suitable than graphic organisers here or, perhaps, a combination of the two is going to achieve your goal? Are you making certain that you are not teaching the grammar of the English language in isolation, but you are contextualising it to the content of your lesson?

2. How are you going to ensure that you do everything in your power to close the attainment gap between your EAL learners and native English-speaking pupils?

Think about how this question relates to both Thomas and Collier's prism. What steps can you take to ensure that your EAL learners are developing linguistically, cognitively and academically, as well as socially?

As we considered before, language learning needs to be contextualised, meaning that you are teaching language and content simultaneously. Consider how Davison's *Language to Content* continuum

(2001) is going to affect your differentiation for different types of English language learners. What types of activities will you provide them with?

Thomas and Collier as well as Cummins stress the importance of the home language for cognitive development. Consider how you might ensure that the first language truly does aid the acquisition of the English language – and in so doing cognitive and academic development – and does not become tokenistic in your classroom.

Finally, how can you address the social aspect of the prism and ensure that your students remain motivated to learn and keep the affective filter down for them? Consider your seating plan; where are your EAL students going to sit in relation to the other children? Who will be their buddy and why? In what ways are you going to value their language and identity? What message will you send to your entire class regarding other languages, bilingualism and the status of EAL learners in the wider school?

CHAPTER SUMMARY

You should now understand the following.

- Cummins' distinction between *Basic Interpersonal Communication Skills (BICS)* and *Cognitive Academic Language Proficiency (CALP)*

- Types of tasks appropriate for EAL learners at varying SLA levels.

- How your differentiation for EAL learners should be aligned to the cognitive demands and context of the tasks you present them with.

- The relevance of all the aspects of *Thomas and Collier's prism* to the way you teach and what you teach to EAL learners.

- Cummins' *Language Interdependence Theory* and the importance of your learners' first language for their second language acquisition.

- Some strategies that have been found effective for EAL learners – substitution tables, graphic organisers and DARTs.

FURTHER READING

Creese, A (2005) *Teacher Collaboration and Talk in Multilingual Classrooms*. Clevedon: Multilingual Matters.

This book represents an excellent body of research into how mainstream teachers and English language specialists collaborate (or not) in British schools, with implications for EAL practice.

Deller, S and Price, C (2007) *Teaching Other Subjects Through English*. Oxford: Oxford University Press.

An excellent resource book with numerous strategies for supporting EAL learners.

Gibbons, P (2009) *English Learners Academic Literacy and Thinking*. Portsmouth, NH: Heinemann.

An invaluable book with a myriad of strategies for the development of academic language in EAL learners; very accessible, teacher-friendly language.

Gibbons, P (1993) *Learning to Learn in a Second Language*. Portsmouth, NH: Heinemann.

Full of strategies and approaches to the teaching of EAL learners (mostly primary-oriented).

Gibbons, P (2002) *Scaffolding Language, Scaffolding Learning*. Portsmouth, NH: Heinemann.

Yet another book full of excellent, practical ideas for supporting EAL learners.

Graf, M (2011) *Including and Supporting Learners of English as an Additional Language*. London: A&C Black.

Written for student teachers; an introduction to the context, policies and pedagogy for EAL in the UK.

Mercer, N (1995) *The Guided Construction of Knowledge*. Clevedon: Multilingual Matters.

Promotes the idea of exploratory talk as a way to guide learning and constructing knowledge; highly applicable to EAL.

NALDIC (1999) Working Paper 5: The distinctiveness of EAL: a cross-curricular discipline.

An absolute must-have for any school and any teacher; a concise, accessible introduction to the basic tenets of EAL pedagogy and theories underpinning recommended practice.

Pim, C (2012) *100 Ideas for Supporting Learners with EAL*. London: Continuum.

A good strategies resource book for teachers of EAL learners.

▬▬ REFERENCES ▬▬

AQA (2012) English/English Language ENG1F. Available at: www.fbec.co.uk/fbec/dept/english/tests/Foundation/November%202012%20-%20F/AQA-ENG1F-INS-NOV12.PDF (accessed 17 December 2016).

BASS (2006) Distinguishing the difference: EAL or SEN? Available at: https://eal.britishcouncil.org/sites/default/files/document-files/Distinguishing%20the%20difference.pdf (accessed 3 December 2016).

British Council (2016) Not my business. Available at: https://eal.britishcouncil.org/sites/default/files/document-files/Dictators%20matching%20exercise.docx (accessed 17 December 2016).

Collaborative Learning Project (2010) What can you grow? Available at: www.collaborative learning.org/whatcanyougrow.pdf (accessed 3 December 2016).

Creese, A (2005) Is this content-based language teaching? In *Linguistics and Education*, 16(2): 188–204.

Cummins, J (1979) Cognitive/academic language proficiency, linguistic interdependence, the optimum age question .... *Working Papers on Bilingualism*, 19: 198–205.

Cummins, J (1981) The role of primary language development in promoting educational success for language minority students. In California State Department of Education (ed.) *Schooling and Language Minority Students: A Theoretical Framework*. California, LA: Evaluation, Dissemination and Assessment Center, California State University.

Cummins, J (2008) BICS and CALP: empirical and theoretical status of the distinction. Available at: http://daphne.palomar.edu/lchen/CumminsBICSCALPSpringer2007.pdf (accessed 17 December 2016).

Davison, C (2001) Current policies, programs and practices in school ESL. In Mohan, B, Leung, C and Davison, C (eds) *English as a Second Language in the Mainstream*. Harlow: Longman.

DfE (2011) Teachers' Standards. Available at: www.gov.uk/government/uploads/system/uploads/attachment_data/file/283566/Teachers_standard_information.pdf (accessed 3 December 2016).

DfE (2012) A brief summary of Government policy in relation to EAL learners. Available at: www.naldic.org.uk/Resources/NALDIC/Research%20and%20Information/Documents/Brief_summary_of_Government_policy_for_EAL_Learners.pdf (accessed 3 Deccember 2016).

DfE (2016) Schools, pupils and their characteristics: January 2016: National Tables. Available at: www.gov.uk/government/uploads/system/uploads/attachment_data/file/532038/SFR20_2016_National_Tables.xlsx (accessed 3 December 2016).

Easy Science for Kids (2016) All about photosynthesis: basic photosynthesis process explained. Available at: http://easyscienceforkids.com/all-about-photosynthesis (accessed 13 December 2016).

Flynn, N (n.d.) EAL MeshGuide. Available at: www.meshguides.org/guides/node/112?n=119 (accessed 3 December 2016).

Garland, S (2015) *Azzi in Between*. London: Frances Lincoln Children's Books.

Gibbons, P (1999) *Learning to Learn in a Second Language*. Portsmouth, NH: Heinemann.

Gibbons, P (2009) *English Learners Academic Literacy and Thinking*. Portsmouth, NH: Heinemann.

Knowledge Framework (2012) The knowledge framework. Available at: http://tslater.public.iastate.edu/kf/framework.html (accessed 3 December 2016).

Krashen, S (2009) Principles and practice in second language acquisition. Available at: www.sdkrashen.com/content/books/principles_and_practice.pdf (accessed 3 December 2016).

Milton Keynes Council (2004) Supporting pupils with English as an additional language. Available at: file:///N:/1.%20Supporting%20pupils%20with%20English%20as%20an%20additional%20language.pdf (accessed 13 December 2016).

Mohan, B (1986) *Language and Content*. Reading: Addison-Wesley.

NALDIC (1999) Working Paper 5: The distinctiveness of EAL: a cross-curricular discipline. Watford: NALDIC.

NALDIC (2013) Maintained primary and secondary schools: number and percentage of pupils by first language. Available at: www.naldic.org.uk/Resources/NALDIC/Research%20and%20Information/ Documents/Copy%20of%20EALpupils19972013.xls (accessed 3 December 2016).

Roberts, T (2014) Not so silent after all: examination and analysis of the silent stage in childhood second language acquisition. *Early Childhood Research Quarterly,* 29: 22–40.

Slater, T and Gleason, J (2011) Integrating language and content: the knowledge framework. Available at: www.academia.edu/2057644/Slater_T._and_Gleason_J._2012_._Integrating_language_and_content_ The_Knowledge_Framework._In_J._Morrison_Ed._Conference_proceedings_of_MidTESOL_Gateway_to_ global_citizenship_pp. _5_20_._Saint_Louis_MO_University_of_Saint_Louis?auto=download (accessed 13 December 2016).

Thomas, W and Collier, V (1997) School effectiveness for language minority students. Available at: http://files.eric.ed.gov/fulltext/ED436087.pdf (accessed 13 December 2016).

10

GRAMMAR, PUNCTUATION AND SPELLING (GPS)

FINDING YOUR WAY THROUGH THE FIRST YEAR OF TEACHING

JOHN BENNETT

THIS CHAPTER

By reading this chapter you will develop your understanding of the following.

- How you can continue to maintain momentum in developing your knowledge, skills and understanding of aspects of grammar, punctuation and spelling.
- What key information you need in order to meet national and school requirements for teaching and learning grammar, punctuation and spelling.
- Teaching activities and methods to support children's effective use of grammar, punctuation and spelling.

Introduction

Grammar, punctuation and spelling have gained increased attention in schools over recent years. They are given significant status in the national curriculum (DfE, 2013) and are formally tested, at least at Key Stage 2. They are also areas in which trainee teachers often have some difficulty, perhaps because of the way they were taught in these areas when at school themselves. NQTs must ensure that the steps they took to develop their knowledge and understanding, of both the subject content and the teaching approaches for these areas, are built on during the NQT year.

This chapter explores what an NQT particularly needs to think about regarding teaching grammar, punctuation and spelling (henceforth usually abbreviated to GPS) in order to become an outstanding accredited teacher. Those areas cover a breadth of knowledge and understanding, which require more consideration than possible within the confines of this chapter, so there are recommendations made for further reading to cover subject knowledge, teaching approaches, research and theory. The chapter approaches the areas from a primary NQT's perspective, given that the national curriculum for KS3 and KS4 assumes that the majority of content learning related to GPS occurs in primary schools, but aspects of the content presented here will also be useful for secondary NQTs.

Some suggestions are made for actions you may wish to take to help your first year of teaching GPS to go smoothly.

Grammar, punctuation and spelling are aspects of the national curriculum which can evoke strong feelings of concern in trainee teachers and NQTs, partly due to the amount of content. Unlike most curriculum areas, the national curriculum goes beyond the programmes of study to provide explicit detail and appendices, including a useful glossary of terms (DfE, 2013, p80). For most trainees, NQTs and many established teachers, what is presented is well beyond what they encountered in primary school and possibly beyond, or at least different from, what was covered at secondary level in their own education. This makes this area even more daunting, particularly for teachers who will be working with children in upper Key Stage 2. However, building on the work from their initial teacher training, NQTs can further develop the knowledge, understanding and skills to teach GPS in an engaging way, and thus help develop the quality of the writing and the understanding of the functions and forms of GPS, and how these contribute to effective writing.

In what follows, grammar and punctuation are deliberately linked in many sections, to take account of the fact that punctuation provides a method of structuring sentences and grammar provides the basis for that structure. Approaches to teaching grammar and punctuation are usually very similar, while teaching spelling uses a range of different strategies.

Classroom focus

Spelling

One of the benefits of having your own class (or classes) during the NQT year, when compared with the usually relatively short periods of time when you work with a class during school placements in initial teacher training, is that you are now able to observe and assess children over time, and this can be particularly useful when it comes to developing their spelling abilities. It is useful to keep some form of spelling error log to record common errors and which individuals and groups make them. This can be used to prompt planning for interventions, additional work and sometimes whole-class sessions to cover the mistakes the children make most often.

At the start of your NQT year, familiarise yourself with the spelling lists found within the national curriculum for the year group(s) you will be teaching. It would also be really beneficial to check with the previous teacher(s) of your class to find out how well the children dealt with learning the expected spellings and what strategies appeared effective. You will need to know if there were any words which the children continued to struggle with from previous lists, as obviously these still need to be learned, or they may indicate gaps in phonic knowledge which need to be addressed.

You need to find out about the school's use of particular strategies to develop spelling (e.g. Look, Say, Cover, Write, Check; Magic Spelling – http://magicalspelling.co.uk/; mnemonics) and get to know these, as with other aspects of matching the school approaches, through discussion and observation.

The school may also have a set system for dealing with times when children are unsure how to spell something. That system may be one that is expected to be used consistently across the classes in the school and is likely to be differentiated by age. Remember, if the school does not have a set routine for what children should do if they feel they can't spell a word, then early in your NQT year you should devise one and set the expectation that all children follow it. Sometimes at the beginning of a year and particularly with a new teacher, children will revert to the approach of putting their hands up or following the teacher around the room to get spellings. Do not fall into that unintentional trap. Early on, set the expectation and stick to it. It will make you more effective and the children more independent. There are various approaches to this, but for most schools following the national curriculum, children's first approach would be using their phonics knowledge to create phonetically plausible spellings. An example of an approach for children when they are not sure how to spell something might be as follows.

- Use your phonics.

- Think about spelling patterns.

- What word does it remind you of?

- Have a go (underline what you are guessing at).

- Use a dictionary.

- Ask somebody else.

When marking, correcting or reviewing the children's work, you should constantly look out for repeated errors, both from individual children and from groups. It is good to keep a note of spelling errors which occur frequently and then ensure that you do some direct teaching and provide activities to address those errors. If you just follow what the national curriculum dictates as the lists of words and spelling patterns children must know how to spell and don't address the results of your assessments, particularly with older children, it is possible that they will take spelling errors with them into secondary school.

One of the most common spelling error types relates to homophones. Such errors, once embedded, stay with children into adult life. In fact, these are often the most common errors encountered when reviewing the computer-assisted writing of trainee teachers, as spellcheckers don't identify issues with words like *there* and *their*, *where* and *were*, *practise* and *practice*, *to* and *too*. Grammar checkers may spot these, but in the classroom, writing is not always done electronically, and these errors may be taken into the NQT year and even passed on to children, which is clearly unhelpful. For children, the primary classroom is the place to eliminate such errors. Direct teaching about the differences between the different words and their different spelling is critical.

Be particularly careful when doing any form of shared writing with the children. Don't be afraid to admit your lack of knowledge to the children – assuming that will happen rarely. It is better to be honest about not being sure about a spelling and look it up, than go with what you think is either a guess or an incorrect spelling. Use these situations to demonstrate how you, as an adult, would use a dictionary (physical or digital) to check. Of course, if you are looking up many words, it does indicate that you need to develop your own knowledge more.

The effectiveness of spelling tests and learning spellings on a weekly basis is debatable, but with the advent of the spelling lists used in the national curriculum, there is a perceived pressure on schools to ensure that the children learn those spellings. You will need to find out how your school approaches the assessment of spelling and if spelling tests are used, what routine do they follow, how are the results recorded and, most importantly (but often the least successfully approached), what is expected to be done with those children who don't manage to learn the expected spellings?

Finally, regarding spelling, check your own (or better still get somebody else to). If you have any concerns about your own spelling, you are certainly not alone. In these times of almost ubiquitous use of spellcheckers, auto-correction and predictive text, we have come to rely so much on technology to help with spelling, that basic errors can creep in, particularly when that technology is not being used. It is unfortunately not uncommon when observing trainee teachers and NQTs to see spelling errors when they write on whiteboards or in comments on children's work. Errors made every now and then are perhaps to be expected, but this is more concerning when words are repeatedly incorrectly spelled and the children learn the incorrect spelling. This has been particularly noticeable with technical words within subject teaching. Always check and double-check words that you have not needed to use before or ones that you know you sometimes have problems with. One last tip – if you are writing to parents and have any insecurities at all with your own spelling, get somebody to check it. As well as the embarrassment you will feel when parents spot your spelling errors, your credibility as a teacher of English is undermined and parents could potentially bring this to the attention of the headteacher.

 **RESEARCH/EVIDENCE FOCUS**

Children's views on writing

The Literacy Trust 2015 survey into young people's writing raised some interesting points about primary children's perceptions of writing (Clark, 2016).

The survey found that almost a third of Key Stage 2 children thought there was *no point in learning spelling/grammar if you can use a spellchecker* (Clark, 2016, p13). Teachers therefore need to make the value of this as explicit as possible, while also acknowledging that spelling and grammar checkers have a purpose as well.

The third highest response from Key Stage 2 children when asked what makes a good writer was that the writer *uses punctuation correctly* (Clark, 2016, p14). This was higher than checking their work, reading or writing a lot and trying things out. Children therefore place a high value on punctuation, and it is interesting to consider whether this is due to it being a focus for marking which is easy to highlight.

When it comes to what the writing is about, there is perhaps an understandably high response - almost 80 per cent agreement at Key Stage 2 - to the idea that *writing is more fun when you can choose the topic* (Clark, 2016, p20). This clearly has implications for teachers trying to involve children in the design of writing activities.

Grammar and punctuation

The term 'grammar' is one that can sometimes be seen to relate to a set of rules which provide the way in which we construct sentences. Those rules can be learned through instructional methods, then applied in exercises, to develop and check understanding. Many NQTs will have been taught using this as the framework for learning grammar and may have negative perspectives on grammar as a result, as research by Watson (2015) has shown. Other NQTs may have had little formal grammar teaching while at school themselves, as there was a shift away from this in the past. It is important not to regard grammar purely as a set of particular rules and metalanguage to learn, and to see it as a set of tools that help to make writing as engaging as it can be for the reader. Many of the best authors bend the rules, but produce writing that still flows and enables them to communicate very effectively. Poets readily abandon standard grammar expectations in favour of creative uses of language to express meaning, and there are plenty of examples of authors whose writing includes examples where grammar rules have not been applied – the prize-winning novel *Solar Bones*, for example, which is written as a single long sentence (McCormack, 2016).

Teaching approaches

The current national curriculum in England and Wales expects grammar and punctuation, as a defined body of knowledge, to be explicitly taught and not simply be an understanding gained in an implicit way, through reading and correct usage (DfE, 2013).

The key question therefore becomes, given that we have to teach this, how do we do that? The answer, in many schools, is to do that through some form of contextualised instruction, so that the rules and terminology are learned explicitly, but immediately applied in real writing contexts, in order to show not just the rules, but the function of grammar and punctuation. A key aspect of this is that children recognise the impact of the grammar and punctuation on the reader. This ranges from simply ensuring that sentences make sense, to making what is written have meaning for the reader. Vocabulary choices are important, but children must also understand that varied and interesting sentences, using a range of punctuation, structures and cohesive devices, are what make writing effective when read. This may seem obvious, but simply teaching rules does not do this.

The key point that children need to understand when learning about any aspect of grammar and punctuation is why it is important. They need to know the difference that a particular feature makes to what people read. A simple example is the importance of the use of pronouns. Without those, text is repetitive and will be seen as boring by most people, as in the following example.

> *Sanjit went to see his friend Kayleigh. Sanjit took a favourite game with him. Sanjit was looking forward to playing with Kayleigh. When Sanjit got to Kayleigh's house, Kayleigh told Sanjit that she was not feeling well and Sanjit and Kayleigh did not get to play Sanjit's favourite game.*

If many of the proper nouns are replaced by pronouns such as he, she and they, the text flows more naturally for the reader. More complex examples can be found in the construction of complex or multi-clause sentences, which add layers of detail to the main clause and draw the reader deeper into the ideas that are being presented.

Beyond the basic purpose of any grammar element, children need to know how it enhances writing, and why it is important in helping meet the purpose of the text and the impact it has on the audience. They should have this explained and be expected to be able to describe why using particular aspects of grammar and punctuation makes a difference. When reviewing children's writing, to both assess and reinforce their understanding, they should also be asked to explain why they chose particular elements of grammar and punctuation.

It is important when teaching grammar and punctuation to ensure that these are taught in a meaningful context for the children, assuming that is the accepted approach at the school. At the start of the school year, you should look at the themes, topics and events which will be covered and identify possible contexts for the grammar and punctuation teaching, so the content and context can be linked as naturally as possible. Assuming you have some freedom to organise when particular things can be taught, mapping out the key grammar and punctuation content across the year is a useful thing to do.

 **RESEARCH/EVIDENCE FOCUS**

Research focus: Contextualised grammar teaching

Debra Myhill has researched and written on contextualised grammar teaching (Myhill et al., 2012). She argues that many children would benefit from an approach which situates learning about grammar within appropriate writing contexts, *not as a body of separate knowledge learned for its own sake* (Myhill et al., 2016, p3). While it could be argued that the intention of developing that knowledge is then to be able to apply it in writing, the evidence, from Myhill and the University of Exeter's Centre for Research in Writing, demonstrates that contextualised approaches lead to better writing outcomes. Myhill and her colleagues argue that there are key principles when teaching grammar in this contextualised way.

> *Always link a grammar feature to its effect on the writing.*
> *Use grammatical terms, but explain them through examples.*
> *Encourage high-quality discussion about language and effects.*
> *Use authentic examples from authentic texts.*
> *Use model patterns for children to imitate.*
> *Support children to design their writing by making deliberate language choices.*
> *Encourage language play, experimentation and risk-taking.*
>
> (Myhill et al., 2016, p3)

For an NQT, in a school where contextualised grammar teaching is an accepted approach, these principles should form the basis of an engaging grammar curriculum.

Many teachers use a class reading book as a context in which to explore grammar and punctuation. This strategy is particularly useful, as it means that the teacher can reasonably expect the children to have a good working knowledge of the content of the story, meaning that when grammar and punctuation activities are undertaken in this context, the children can focus on those aspects of their learning. However, activities should be designed to allow the children to explore language in the most interesting way possible, and playing with language, trying things out without feeling that any incorrect use of English will be criticised, is an essential part of a creative approach to exploring aspects of grammar and punctuation.

 **CASE STUDY**

Choosing a context

Ellie's class of Year 3 children were reading the Roald Dahl story *Fantastic Mr Fox* (Dahl, 1970). They were particularly enjoying Dahl's use of dialogue between the three farmers, Boggis, Bunce and Bean, whose interactions were full of argument and interesting language. At the start of the year, Ellie had identified

(Continued)

(Continued)

this story as a good one to use to introduce speech marks (inverted commas) and the three farmers provided an ideal vehicle for this.

Sourcing pictures of the three farmers from the animated film of the story, Ellie created an activity where the children could add speech bubbles to stills of the three farmers from the film. In small groups, the children created conversations between the farmers about their plans to get rid of the foxes, writing the dialogue in the speech bubbles and acting out the scenes, which helped them edit each character's speech until they were happy with it. Ellie then explained that the children were going to write out the conversations using speech marks, pointing out that it was the actual words that the characters said that would appear between the inverted commas and they already had that in the speech bubbles. Over a series of lessons, Ellie expanded on the basics, introducing what would happen in the written work if a character interrupted another, and how to break up the spoken sentence and where the speech marks would then appear.

Ellie used examples of incorrectly punctuated speech, again based on the conversations between the farmers, to help further illustrate the correct use of the inverted commas.

The context and form of activity were fun for the children and while the end product was basically a piece of correctly punctuated written work, the way it was developed led to very engaged children and excellent work.

 QUESTIONS FOR DISCUSSION AND REFLECTION

Why is it so important to contextualise grammar and punctuation learning?

What children's interests, current trends or TV shows could provide a context for approaching an aspect of grammar or punctuation (e.g. Pokémon GO is ideal for exploring prepositions)?

Revision

It is critically important to remember that once new grammar and punctuation skills, knowledge and understanding have been developed, they should be returned to as often as possible and in a number of different ways. This is a change in mindset for some NQTs, whose experience during training has been with classes for limited times, where there is often minimal time to return to previous learning.

You need to develop personal approaches to revisiting and revising content which has previously been introduced. This needs to be planned into the curriculum, and be part of a coherent and systematic approach to maintaining children's use of what they have learned. One of the best ways to do this is through games. There are many sources for excellent grammar and punctuation games (e.g. Corbett and Strong, 2015), but you should be creative and adapt games you know and find out about, as well as creating your own.

CASE STUDY

Story circle

Stefan was coming towards the end of his first term as an NQT with his Year 4 class. He felt he had achieved a lot of success in his grammar and punctuation teaching so far, with the children responding well to a range of new ideas, but when he returned to some of the themes he thought he had covered well, he was met by a classroom of blank and puzzled looks. It was at this point that he realised that apart from in the weeks when he had been specifically teaching the aspects of grammar and punctuation, he had never really returned to those topics and consequently neither had the children. He decided immediately to do two things. First, he sourced or created posters to go up around the classroom, providing constant reminders for the children about the language of grammar and what specific terms meant. He referred to those posters as often as necessary. Second, he introduced the 'story circle' game.

In the game, the children were given a topic for a story which would be very familiar to them and in groups they had to tell each other a story, one word at a time. The class responded very well to this, enjoying both the challenge and the freedom. Some children needed help and prompting, but overall it provided a successful basis onto which to add some grammar and punctuation revision.

Once the children understood the game, Stefan added actions and other movements which both encouraged children to listen and also to try to use particular aspects of grammar and punctuation. For example, whenever a comma was used the children had to put up their right hands, and whenever an adjective appeared, they stood up or sat down. In later iterations of the game, Stefan added challenges such as clapping which reversed the direction of the telling of the story, or giving more complex language features to try to include.

Not only did this activity reinforce some prior learning, but it also helped the children in developing their speaking and listening skills.

QUESTIONS FOR DISCUSSION AND REFLECTION

Why do you think the above game was so successful?

How could you help encourage reluctant children to take part?

What games have you seen played in classrooms? Can any of those be adapted to the GPS context?

Subject knowledge

Initial teacher training courses often ask trainees to audit their own subject knowledge in various areas, which includes the understanding of the metalanguage associated with teaching grammar and punctuation. Trainees have a lot of implicit knowledge about grammar and punctuation (if they didn't, then their academic work would be unlikely to meet the required standards for teacher training), which provides a good foundation upon which to build the explicit subject knowledge. The initial audits may be followed by creating action plans. You may still have areas to work on from those audits and plans, and it may be worth returning to these during your NQT year, particularly if working in Key Stage 2 or above, where the broad range of metalanguage needs to be understood in order to ensure that it is used appropriately with the children when commenting on and modelling language use in reading and writing. One approach to this could be to review the glossary from the national curriculum (DfE, 2013, p80), noting which of the following is the case for each of the terms, then creating a new action plan to address personal needs (for each term, consider which applies).

- I know this term.

- I can explain this term and why it is important.

- I could teach about this term with little preparation.

- I could teach about this term with some preparation.

- I need to find out much more about this term to develop my confidence.

Policies

One of the first things that you are likely to do when joining your first school is to collect copies of school policies. It is likely there will be an English (or possibly a literacy) policy, which will contain basic information about the approaches to English across the school. Obviously, it is very important that you read and digest these policies, noting key points to remember when planning, teaching and assessing. However, it is always worth checking the date of the policy and how current the practices described in it actually are. Things change rapidly and sometimes significantly in schools. The review and revision of the written policies do not always keep up with the rate of change, so it is often best to check with the English subject leader/coordinator to see if any new approaches are expected. A policy that is often closely linked to approaches to English is the school's marking policy and you will certainly need to know what the expected approach is to marking grammar, punctuation and spelling, and then stick to that, to avoid confusing the children.

Assessment of GPS

Marking of grammar, punctuation and spelling varies from school to school, and one of the first things you need to do is find out what the expected degree and format of marking should be for the year group(s) you will be working with. School marking policies will help with this and may give details of marking codes, symbols that are used on children's writing, the use of colours to indicate particular things (e.g. 'tickled pink' – a positive aspect of the work; 'green for growth' – an area to work on) and the extent and nature of teachers' comments on written work. You should not just rely on the content of a policy which is passed on, but also look at examples of marking from other teachers, to see exactly how the expectations are put into practice.

How assessment of GPS is recorded and how progress is analysed are further aspects of schools' approaches to these areas which you will need to know about, in relation to the systems used. No matter which year group you are working with in primary schools, it is very important to become familiar with the national GPS tests. At the time of writing, these were statutory for Key Stage 2, but non-statutory for Key Stage 1 (used instead to help inform teacher assessment).

Although the national curriculum, as noted earlier, promotes the contextualised use of grammar, the tests do not strictly use this as the basis for assessment. If they did, children would be expected to write more of the answers for themselves, demonstrating their understanding of how to use particular features, rather than what the tests tend to do, which is expect children to be able to identify and use features of grammar and punctuation. This focus on the metalanguage and the identification of features creates a situation where, while schools may wish to teach grammar as contextually as possible, they also need to ensure that children are able to use the terminology in more isolated ways. It has therefore become necessary not only to contextualise the teaching of grammar and punctuation, but also to explicitly teach the terminology and how to identify the use of different grammatical features and punctuation out of deeper contexts.

There is much variation in how schools approach the tests, with some devoting significant amounts of time to children practising the tests with past papers or other versions of the tests, then analysing and acting on the results, often as whole-class activities. Others approach this in more subtle ways, through perhaps a small number of 'mock' tests, but with revision activities built into the English curriculum. Whichever approach is used, it is important to spend some time looking at those tests and thinking about how your teaching can help to ensure that children are as successful as possible when they take them.

The school will probably have unused copies of the previous test papers and it is worth asking to see these. Although papers before 2016 will be of some use, ask to see one from 2016 onwards, as they are most clearly based on the expectations of the national curriculum introduced in 2014 (DfE, 2013). Previous tests are available online and it is useful to look at those, paying particular attention to the mark schemes to see the expectations.

One simple way to help children prepare for the tests, without making this explicit, is to incorporate the approach to presenting test questions into learning and teaching. This approach is strengthened through consideration of the types of errors being made and why they occur.

 **CASE STUDY**

Preparing for the GPS test

Sam, an NQT with a year 6 class, spent some time considering the year 6 GPS test to help him ensure that his class were fully prepared for it, but he did not wish that preparation to be endless test questions and papers. He decided to use one 'mock' test paper at the start of the academic year, which he created himself, based on the previous year's paper, to gain a picture of the needs of the class. He marked the test and analysed the results at a question level, noting the most common issues that arose. He then used the questions that had caused the most problems as review activities in the classroom, going through each question, over a period of a couple of weeks, in order to work out whether

(Continued)

(Continued)

the problems the children had with them lay in their subject knowledge or their interpretation of the questions. With that information, he was able to map out when he would address each particular issue as part of his teaching programme. As well as noting the gaps and misconceptions, Sam also realised that for some questions it was possible to guess an answer, simply by making sure the answers made sense, rather than using any knowledge of the focus of the question (e.g. multiple-choice answers). Sam stressed that these questions still needed thinking about, not just answering with what at first may feel like the best-fit answer.

For the question types where the format of the question had contributed to some of the errors, which became obvious through the review exercise, Sam wove similar formatting into written and whole-class activities over the year. This helped to ensure that, when faced with similar types of questions at the end of Year 6, the children had developed an understanding of how to approach those, resulting in good test results which truly showed their knowledge and understanding.

 QUESTIONS FOR DISCUSSION AND REFLECTION

1. Why is it important to prepare children for tests?

2. How can you ensure that this preparation is not simply looking at test papers and questions?

3. What aspects of the tests do you predict children will have the most difficulty with?

4. How could this approach be applied in other year groups?

While NQTs who work in Year 2 and Year 6 will have to become very familiar with whatever framework the government produces to support end of key stage teacher assessment (currently interim assessment frameworks which are available online – e.g. www.gov.uk/government/publications/2017-interim-frameworks-for-teacher-assessment-at-the-end-of-key-stage-1), it is important that NQTs in other year groups know what these contain, as they are clear statements of expectation to which work in other year groups must contribute. Alongside assessment frameworks, the Department for Education has published exemplification materials, which show examples of children's writing and how they demonstrate meeting the end of key stage expectations – e.g. www.gov.uk/government/publications/2016-teacher-assessment-exemplification-ks2-english-reading). These provide detail which will help an NQT continue to develop a picture of the end of Key Stage expectations.

Conclusion

The teaching of grammar, punctuation and spelling is a focal area of the latest version of the national curriculum and raises challenges for NQTs who may have gaps in their knowledge and understanding of those areas, and will need to get to grips quickly with their school's chosen approaches to these areas in order to develop their outstanding practice.

This chapter has provided a range of suggestions regarding gaining the required subject and school knowledge and has also explored a range of approaches which NQTs may encounter or build into their teaching and assessment repertoire.

QUESTIONS FOR DISCUSSION AND REFLECTION

1. **Grammar and punctuation**

   Considering the depth of knowledge that is required to teach grammar and punctuation as effectively as possible, how do you intend to ensure you will build on what you already know?

2. **Spelling**

   Given the common use of spellcheckers and predictive text, what arguments could be presented to justify learning spelling in the way it is presented within the national curriculum?

CHAPTER SUMMARY

You should now know a range of key things that you can or need to do as an NQT, in relation to teaching about grammar, punctuation and spelling, to help you develop outstanding practice. This includes the following things to find out about the school's approaches.

1. What information is already available about the class or classes you will be taking in relation to GPS?

2. What approach is used to ensuring the coverage of the spelling lists?

3. Are grammar and punctuation taught in discrete lessons, always in context or through a mixture of approaches?

4. What is the marking policy for spellings?

5. What codes are used as part of the marking policy (if any) and do these vary with year groups?

6. How are national tests prepared for?

7. Are spelling tests used, and if so how?

8. What records are kept in relation to these areas?

FURTHER READING

For developing your subject knowledge in relation to grammar, punctuation and spelling, the following are useful.

Medwell, J, Wray, D, Moore, G. and Griffiths, V (2014) *Primary English: Knowledge and Understanding* (7th edn). London: Sage/Learning Matters.

Wilson, A and Scanlon, J (2011) *Language Knowledge for Primary Teachers* (4th edn). London: David Fulton.

For exploring approaches to the teaching of grammar, punctuation and spelling, the following are useful.

Horton, S and Bingle, B (2014) *Lessons in Teaching Grammar in Primary Schools.* London: SAGE/ Learning Matters.

Waugh, D and Jolliffe, W (2016) *English 5–11: A Guide for Teachers* (3rd edn). London: Routledge.

Waugh, D, Warner, C and Waugh, R (2016) *Teaching Grammar, Punctuation and Spelling in Primary Schools* (2nd edn). London: Sage/Learning Matters.

Waugh, D, Allott, K, Waugh, R, English, E, and Bulmer, E (2014) *The Spelling, Punctuation and Grammar app*. Morecambe: Children Count Ltd (available through the App Store).

Useful websites

www.teachit.co.uk/spag Teachit

www.iboard.co.uk/skill-builders/grammar TES Spelling, Grammar and Punctuation

www.edufind.com/english/grammar/ Edufind – English Grammar Guide

www.ucl.ac.uk/internet-grammar/ The Internet Grammar of English

▬▬▬ REFERENCES ▬▬▬▬▬▬▬▬▬▬▬▬

Clark, C (2016) *Children's and Young People's Writing in 2015*. National Literacy Trust. Available at: www.literacytrust.org.uk/assets/0003/5710/Young_people_s_writing_2015_-_Final.pdf (accessed 18 November 2016).

Corbett, P and Strong, J (2015) *Jumpstart! Grammar: Games and activities for ages 6 –14* (2nd edn). London: Routledge.

Dahl, R (1970) *Fantastic Mr Fox*. London: George Allen & Unwin.

DfE (2013) English programmes of study: Key Stages 1 and 2 – National Curriculum in England. London: DfE.

McCormack, M (2016) *Solar Bones*. Basingstoke: Tramp Press.

Myhill, D, Jones, S, Lines, H and Watson, A (2012) Re-thinking grammar: the impact of embedded grammar teaching on students' writing and students' metalinguistic understanding. *Research Papers in Education*, 27(2): 139–66.

Myhill, D, Jones, S, Watson, A and Lines, H (2016) *Essential Primary Grammar*. Maidenhead: Open University Press.

Watson, A (2015) The problem of grammar teaching: a case study of the relationship between a teacher's beliefs and pedagogical practice. *Language and Education*, 29(4): 332–46.

11

SUPPORTING STRUGGLING READERS AND THE ROLE OF PHONICS

WENDY JOLLIFFE

THIS CHAPTER

By reading this chapter you will develop your understanding of the following.

- Different theoretical models to explain how children learn to read, including the Simple View of Reading.
- The role of phonics to support decoding, with a particular focus on the teaching of the complex alphabetical code.
- Effective interactive teaching methods for phonics.
- Methods of support for struggling readers.

LINKS TO THE TEACHERS' STANDARDS

This chapter will help you with the following Teachers' Standards.

3. Demonstrate good subject and curriculum knowledge

- Demonstrate a critical understanding of developments in the subject and curriculum areas, and promote the value of scholarship;
- Demonstrate an understanding of and take responsibility for promoting high standards of literacy, articulacy and the correct use of Standard English, whatever the teacher's specialist subject;
- If teaching early reading, demonstrate a clear understanding of systematic synthetic phonics.

Introduction

This chapter examines the key aspects involved in becoming an effective reader and focuses on how to support struggling readers. It starts by discussing the necessary subject knowledge for teachers and examines theoretical models which help explain how children learn to read. While much of this may have been covered in initial teacher education, the chapter aims to act as reinforcement for understanding the key components in reading and how they interact to help teachers in developing a balanced perspective on teaching reading. This is particularly important, as reading is subject to continual debate, both in the media and from academics. In the past this debate has even been called the 'reading wars' (Goodman, 1998). However, what is important for teachers is to have a clear 'roadmap' of the important elements and be able to plan appropriately to support children, and particularly those who may be struggling to become effective readers.

The chapter discusses the role of phonics in the teaching of reading and provides a summary of the essential subject knowledge for teachers in understanding our language and what is termed the 'alphabetic code'. It cites key research that has helped inform current thinking, but a considerable emphasis of the chapter will be on effective methods of teaching phonics to ensure this is engaging and interactive. This will set the essential foundations for the focus on supporting struggling readers. While this requires considerable expertise, it is hoped that the chapter will signpost the beginning teacher to appropriate responses to the many challenges teachers face. What is clear is that early diagnosis and intervention are key to ensuring that children are supported in becoming good readers. Evidence shows that too many children are finishing primary school with reading abilities that are below national expectations. While it has become difficult to compare results for the Standard Assessment Tasks (SATs) at age 11 due to major changes in 2016, the latest results showed a substantial drop in those achieving the expected standard for reading to 66 per cent. It is therefore important to ensure that children who are falling below expectations are accurately assessed and supported. Without further support, the danger is that many of these children will become disaffected pupils.

The role of phonics in the teaching of reading

Learning to read involves two main components. First, being able to decode the letters on the page and map these to the sounds of the language and then pronounce these to make words, building up a store of known words, called *word recognition*. The second key component is being able to comprehend what has been read, called *language comprehension*. These are integrated processes and both are equally important. Learning phonics supports the decoding element and helps unlock what is often termed the 'alphabetic code'. However, it is important to note that teaching phonics alone will not produce good readers. Children also need to develop the skills of language comprehension. As Brooks states (2013, p19):

> *Phonics teaching should normally be accompanied by graphic representation and reading for meaning so that irregular as well as regular patterns can be grasped.*

The terminology used in the teaching of phonics is often confusing for new teachers, but it is important for teachers to know the correct terms and many trainee teachers comment on how they have observed even very young children taking about phonemes and graphemes and other such terms. In order to check your understanding of terminology, look at the Glossary on pp195–6 and then ensure you can complete the quiz below.

 QUESTIONS FOR DISCUSSION AND REFLECTION

Checking terminology

1. What is a phoneme?

2. What is a grapheme?

3. How many letters are in a trigraph?

4. Give an example of a word containing a split digraph.

5. Give an example of a long vowel phoneme.

In order to help explain the complex processes involved in reading, a number of theoretical models have been developed and the most influential ones are discussed below.

 RESEARCH/EVIDENCE FOCUS

Theoretical models in learning to read

The Simple View of Reading

The Simple View of Reading is the most well known of the models that help explain the processes in learning to read. It was devised by Gough and Tunmer in 1986 and became much more widely known due to the Rose Review of the teaching of reading in 2006. This review for the government was the

(Continued)

(Continued)

springboard for a strong focus on phonics in schools in England and, since then, schools and teacher training institutions have been scrutinised on the teaching of phonics by Ofsted. The Simple View of Reading focuses on two aspects: word recognition – the ability to decode words out of context and to apply phonics rules as well as recognition of high-frequency irregular words. The second aspect is language comprehension, which refers to *linguistic comprehension*, and is defined by Gough and Tunmer (1986) as the process by which words, sentences and discourse are interpreted. The diagram below (Figure 11.1) is taken from the Rose Review (DfES, 2006, p40).

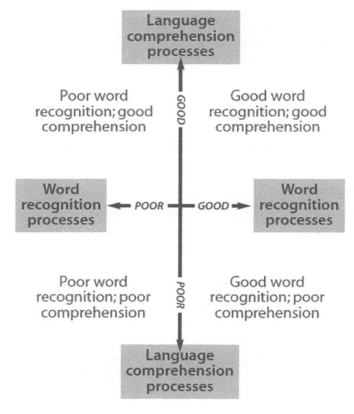

Figure 11.1   The simple view of reading

Source: DfES (2006) Independent review of the teaching of early reading. Final report. Ref: 0201-2006DOC-EN. Nottingham: DfES Publications, p40

The model is based on two axes and four quadrants, and children's strengths or weaknesses can be identified and categorised into the quadrants, enabling teaching to focus on specific aspects. The model is therefore useful as an overall diagnostic tool of the main area of difficulty a child may experience. However, critics have objected to the over-simplification of this model, but Hoover and Gough further developed this into the *Reading Acquisition Framework* (see Figure 11.2). This framework therefore explains the constituent elements within the two overarching areas of language comprehension and word recognition.

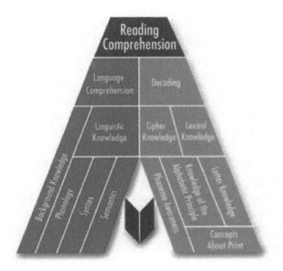

Figure 11.2   The reading acquisition framework

Source: Wren, S (2001) *The Cognitive Foundations of Learning to Read: A Framework.* Austin, TX: Southwest Educational Development Laboratory. Available at: www.sedl.org/reading/framework/framework.pdf

The strands of skilled reading

This model, developed by Scarborough (2009), helps visually to demonstrate the multifaceted strands involved in becoming a reader. Scarborough notes:

Skilled readers are able to derive meaning from printed text accurately and efficiently. Research has shown that in doing so, they fluidly coordinate many component skills, each of which has been sharpened through instruction and experience over many years.

(2009, p23)

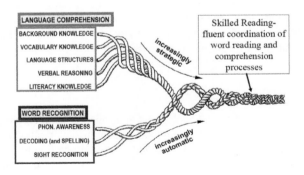

Figure 11.3   The strands of skilled reading

Source: Scarborough, HS (2009, p24) Connecting early language and literacy to later reading (dis)abilities: evidence, theory and practice. In Fletcher-Campbell, F, Soler, J and Reid, G (eds) *Approaching Difficulties in Literacy Development: Assessment, Pedagogy and Programmes.* Los Angeles, CA: Sage, pp23-38.

(Continued)

(Continued)

Figure 11.3 provides a diagrammatical representation of this model and shows how these strands are interwoven in the course of becoming a skilled reader. This diagram shows that as the strands become knotted together, comprehension becomes increasingly strategic and word recognition becomes increasingly automatic. Scarborough notes that most difficulties experienced by children in reading are associated with deficits in decoding and sight recognition of printed words. However, reading skills can also be seriously affected by deficits in the comprehension strands, particularly for children beyond age seven when reading material becomes more complex.

One important factor in understanding word recognition is to appreciate that while this largely relates to phonological knowledge, to become skilled readers, children also need to develop a stored sight vocabulary that provides fast access to meaning and pronunciation. Skilled readers create pathways between the visual and spoken words and their store of known words (semantic lexicon), and as readers become more proficient in recognising and understanding words, this develops into a store of correctly spelt words (an orthographic lexicon), which they can recognise automatically. Therefore, a stored sight vocabulary is an important factor in developing fluency.

While these theoretical models are complex, it is important to realise, as Stuart and Stainthorp (2016, p35) note, that *all contemporary models of reading are dual-route models*. That is, while they may disagree about the details, they agree on the two sets of processes: language comprehension and word recognition. This is helpful for teachers who need to translate theory into practice. The following case studies demonstrate that such models are helpful in practice in identifying the difficulties children may face.

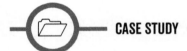 **CASE STUDY**

Christine was a newly qualified teacher who was faced with several children in her Year 2 class who demonstrated difficulties with reading. She was keen to identify the specific problems that each child was having and in order to find out more she listened to each of them read, followed by asking questions on the text and some related writing activities, such as completing the missing words in sentences from the text. Now consider what further support might be suitable to each child. You will find some suggested answers on p194.

Child A – Harry

Harry was reluctant to read. He had good phonic skills and relied on sounding out so that reading was very laborious and he often lost the sense or meaning of a sentence or the text in the process. He could answer questions orally once he understood the text, but needed prompting to talk about what was happening through the words and illustrations. Following this, with help he could complete the sentences about the text.

1. Considering the two main components of reading, which one is the key difficulty here?

2. What strategies might be used to help Harry?

3. What advice would you give to parents/carers to help Harry at home?

Child B - Ella

Ella was very shy. Her oral language was delayed and she had limited vocabulary. She was keen to read and showed that she had developed some word recognition skills. She remembered common irregular words and could use her phonic skills to read a growing number of words. Her comprehension of the text was limited, as often the subject was unfamiliar to her or she didn't know the meaning of words. She struggled to answer the questions orally and while she made a good attempt at the sentences, she picked words randomly rather than reading for meaning.

1. What strand according to the model in Figure 11.2 is Ella having difficulty with?

2. What strategies could be used to support her?

3. Is a particular intervention programme needed?

Child C - Archie

Archie was enthusiastic about most things at school. He was always keen to contribute orally and had a wide vocabulary. However, he disliked reading and really struggled with it. His phonic skills were limited and he seemed to have difficulty in discriminating sounds in words. He also struggled to recall common irregular words by sight. Once he had read with (rather than to) the teacher, he could talk about what he had read and answer the questions on the text orally. However, he struggled to write these answers due to his limited recall of words or how to make phonic attempts at writing them.

QUESTIONS FOR DISCUSSION AND REFLECTION

1. What aspect of the Simple View of Reading is Archie struggling with?

2. Is there a possible underlying issue here?

3. Is this a child who would benefit from assessment by an expert and an intervention project?

The complex alphabetic code

The alphabetic code refers to the concept that letters, or combinations of letters, are used to represent the sounds of our language. English has a complex alphabetic code as there are 26 letters and yet approximately 44 sounds. The correspondence between the letters (the graphemes) and the sounds (the phonemes) is inconsistent. You will find referring to the International Phonetic Alphabet helpful (see the National Curriculum, Appendix 1, p74). There are four principles that help explain the complex English alphabetic code.

1. Sounds/phonemes are represented by letters/graphemes.

2. A phoneme can be represented by one or more letters – for example, the phoneme //aɪ/ can be written as 'i' (in tiger), 'i-e' (in time), or 'igh' (in light). A one-letter grapheme is called a graph, a two-letter grapheme a digraph, and a three-letter grapheme a trigraph, and occasionally there are four-letter graphemes quadgraphs (as in 'eight' = /eigh/ /t/).

3. The same phoneme can be represented (spelt) more than one way, as in /eɪ/ spelt as 'ay' in pl**ay**, or 'a-e' as in 'm**a**k**e**', or 'ai' as in 'tr**ai**l', or 'a' as in 'b**a**by'.

4. The same grapheme (spelling) may represent more than one phoneme, as demonstrated by the letter 'c' which may make the sound /s/ in 'city', or /c/ in 'cat'.

Children start to learn phonics with the 'basic code', which refers to a single letter making one sound. Usually this begins with a few consonants and short vowel phonemes, (e.g. /s/ /a/ /t/ /p/ /i/ /n/) and then moves into blending these into consonant–vowel–consonant (CVC) words (e.g. 'sat', 'tin', 'pin', etc.). Children need to begin by learning one spelling for about 40 of the approximate 44 phonemes in the English language.

The complex code involves knowing that the phoneme can be represented by one or more letters, as in the phoneme /j/ which can be represented as 'j' as in **j**ug, or 'dge' as in ju**dge**, or 'g' as in **g**iant, or 'ge' as in bar**ge.** Details of phonemes and their common spellings can be found in a number of resources, including the National Curriculum, Appendix 1 (DfE, 2013) and *Letters and Sounds Notes of Guidance for Practitioners and Teachers* (DfES, 2007). You will also find a number of helpful charts on the Internet by searching for grapheme/phoneme correspondence charts.

English therefore has a high degree of inconsistency in grapheme/phoneme correspondences, particularly in vowel phonemes and their grapheme correspondences. Vowel phonemes can be short or long sounds and it is the long vowel phonemes, as in the words 'tree' and 'coat', where the /ee/ and /oa/ can cause confusion. Now look at the activity below to check your understanding of long vowel phonemes.

 QUESTIONS FOR DISCUSSION AND REFLECTION

Activity – long vowel phonemes

1. Which of these words contains a long vowel phoneme?

   rain, swan, stern, toil, house, me, jug

2. Name three alternative spellings for the long vowel phoneme /oa/ as in boat.

3. How many ways can you find to spell the phoneme /or/ as in 'horn'?

You will find answers on p194.

 **RESEARCH/EVIDENCE FOCUS**

Comparing alphabetic codes

It is important to understand that English has a complex alphabetic code, or what is termed an *opaque orthography* – that is, there is no direct one-to-one mapping of the sounds of the language on to the letters to represent them. Herein lies the key difficulty for children in learning to read in English and explains why in some countries where children start school much later they become fluent readers more quickly.

A number of European languages have a transparent alphabetic code, such as Finnish, Turkish, Spanish and Greek. A study by Seymour et al. (2003) compared learning to read in nine European languages and found that children learning English took twice as long as those from some other countries. Venezky (1973) studied 240 Finnish children in grades 1-3 and found how much easier it is to learn to read and write a transparent alphabet. Children begin reading in Finland at age seven and after twelve months of tuition, in a reading test of nonsense words denoting the complete Finnish orthography, the children scored 80 per cent, and the same test administered to college students showed 90 per cent correct. This showed that it takes only about a year to gain proficiency in reading Finnish.

In another language, Hebrew, which is a transparent writing system that uses symbols for consonants and diacritic marks for vowels, Geva and Siegel (2000) examined Canadian children who were learning to read and write both English and Hebrew together, with English as the first language. By the end of the first grade, the children scored 79 per cent correct on the Hebrew reading test, but only 44 per cent correct on the English version of the test, and they did not achieve 80 per cent competency until the fifth grade.

This helps explain the difficulty in learning to read and write in English and also goes some way to explain a history of reluctance to use phonics as a teaching method without a transparent mapping between the letters and sounds. However, this does not mean that phonics is not a valid teaching method: it demonstrates that a deeper understanding of the complex alphabetic code supports effective reading and particularly spelling.

Classroom focus

Interactive and engaging methods of teaching phonics

There are many ways to help provide interactive and engaging methods for teaching phonics. These principally include using multisensory approaches and ensuring regular opportunities to apply learning through reading and writing.

1. Examples of multisensory methods

   - Introducing actions to accompany each phoneme learned is particularly helpful for young children – for example, for the phoneme /f/ say 'five floppy fish flap' (which also uses alliteration) and flap your arms like a fish.

   - Use visual prompts to accompany learning a phoneme. Some phonic schemes provide these such as Read Write Inc. (Miskin, 2011) or Jolly Phonics (Jolly Learning, 1992). You can also download pictures from the Internet to create your own.

   - Using a range of different resources such as mini whiteboards for children to write words and hold up to show, or use of the interactive whiteboard with children participating in writing or selecting letters, etc.

2. Creating mnemonics, rhymes and raps

   Mnemonics, rhymes and songs, or raps, is a powerful way of supporting children's learning of phonemes. They are particularly useful to help to learn the long vowel phonemes and the varied ways of writing the same phoneme. As phonemes are learned, sayings can be linked together to form a 'rap'. Said in a lively way at the start of each phonics lesson, this acts as revision or overlearning of the phonemes taught and can be an engaging way of starting the lesson. Constant practice at saying a rap will support pupils in remembering the phonemes and their most common spelling choices/graphemes.

For example, when learning the phoneme /ai/ written 'ay', the rap is taught using the following steps.

1. Say the phoneme twice, e.g. /ay/ay/.

2. Say the mnemonic, e.g.'Play with hay' (and children can learn an action to show they are playing with the hay).

3. Say the letter names, e.g. 'A Y'.

(See Jolliffe, 2012 – *Quick Fix for Phonics* for further guidance.)

3. Building a chart

To provide a visual reminder, it is useful to create a chart of phonemes as you teach each one. The process is gradually built up and constantly referred to. Start by focusing on the most common graphemes for each phoneme, and then teach and add those that you feel are most

/ae/	/ee/
ay (hay)	ee (see)
ai (tail)	ea (beach)
a (baby)	e (he)
a-e (cake)	y (pony)

Figure 11.4   Section of a vowel phoneme chart

appropriate for the age of the children. You may wish to include pictures to represent each phoneme to make the chart more visually attractive, particularly for younger children. Using cards
similar to those shown in Figure 11.4 to regularly revisit phonemes taught is also very useful.
An extract of how a chart would look is shown in Figure 11.4 (for more information, see Jolliffe
et al., 2015, p61).

4. Applying learning in reading and writing is important, so all phonics lessons should include
   opportunities to hear the sound, say the sound, read the corresponding grapheme and write the
   graphemes – i.e. 'hear it, say it, read it, write it'. It is also helpful to provide opportunities to read
   level-appropriate decodable texts as practice in reading, alongside a rich diet of other texts. For
   older children, the difficulties of finding texts that are at their reading level and yet also of interest means that writing books with children is a very useful way of providing opportunities for
   practice. See the case study below for an example.

5. Using a range of games can be very useful way to practise phonics. A selection can be found in
   Letters and Sounds (DfES, 2007), such as Best Bet and the Full Circle game. There are also numerous games on the Internet – for example, see www.tes.com/articles/phonics-games-and-activities

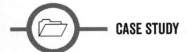 **CASE STUDY**

Making books

Liam was six and, like many boys of his age, had a fascination for dinosaurs. His bedroom resembled a
dinosaur forest with pictures, models and books all about dinosaurs. At school, Liam loved to be active
and found sitting at a desk for long boring. He was making progress with learning phonics, but found
reading his reading book a chore and was very reluctant to read at home or school. This led to him being
behind his peers in reading. His teacher discovered his fascination for dinosaurs and suggested to his
parents that they may like to create some dinosaur books with him and encourage him to write sentences alongside the adults to create books for him to read. Liam loved finding pictures on the Internet
and he knew the names of most of the dinosaurs. Together with his mum, they made a books by folding
a number of pages and Liam stuck in and drew pictures. Then they made up a scary story about the
dinosaurs with Liam as the main character. Every night he would ask to read this book and it led to more
books being created. He took great pride in showing these to his class and teacher. They were amused to
hear that he said he was going to be a palaeontologist when he grew up.

 QUESTIONS FOR DISCUSSION AND REFLECTION

1. What was the issue with reading for Liam?

2. Why did this approach trigger such an enthusiastic response?

3. What does this tell you that could be applied to other children who are reluctant readers?

See p195 for some suggested answers to these questions.

 **RESEARCH/EVIDENCE FOCUS**

Long-lasting effects of early phonics teaching

While there is considerable research into teaching phonics and its impact on children's reading skills, long-term follow-up studies are not so common. Vadasy and Sanders (2013) noted benefits that persisted for over two years as a result of an intervention programme given to at-risk children. These included instruction in phonemic awareness, letter knowledge, word recognition, practice to gain fluency with connected texts and comprehension strategies. Follow-up studies after one year and two years showed that those pupils who had taken part in the intervention programme significantly outperformed their peers on oral language, letter-word identification, word attack, passage comprehension and oral reading fluency.

Much of the focus on phonics in the UK has stemmed from a research study carried out in Clackmannanshire, Scotland. Rhona Johnston and Joyce Watson (2005) looked at 300 children in the first year of the Scottish primary school system. They compared three different teaching methods: synthetic phonics, analytic phonics and an analytic phonics method that included systematic phonemic awareness teaching. At the end of the programme, those children who had been taught by synthetic phonics were found to be seven months ahead of the other two groups in reading. While this research was criticised for not providing sufficient evidence for synthetic phonics (Wyse and Goswami, 2008) there has been further research on the long-term impact of this study on these children at ten years old (Johnston et al., 2012), which found that the group taught by synthetic phonics had better word reading, spelling and reading comprehension skills, and therefore the impact was sustained.

Classroom focus

Diagnosing difficulties

For children who demonstrate a lack of progress in reading, the key is to diagnose what particular difficulties they are having. Ongoing formative assessment as children are taught phonics and developing reading skills is a first step and having an effective tracking system, related to the stage of phonics being taught, is important. The Phonics Screening Check (DfE, 2012), used nationally at the end of year 1, assesses children's phonic knowledge and uses non-words such as 'mirst', 'jigh' and 'pune'. This has received some criticism, as children should, of course, be reading for meaning. However, the test is merely a check on phonic knowledge and such 'alien' words are useful for assessment purposes, as long as children are introduced to them appropriately.

Common issues that children have are summarised below.

- *Issues with phonological awareness – the ability to hear and discriminate phonemes correctly.* Individual assessment will be needed and it may be important to suggest that a child has a hearing check. Studies (Castles and Coltheart, 2004; Hatcher et al., 2004) have shown that additional phonological awareness training can be very successful with children who demonstrate difficulties with phonological awareness.

- *Difficulty learning and recalling some grapheme/phoneme correspondences, most commonly the long vowel phonemes and the different grapheme choices.* Additional individual or small group work using visual aids and mnemonics, as cited earlier, can help, together with opportunities to apply these grapheme/phoneme correspondences in reading and writing.

- *Issues with blending phonemes into words, which indicates they need more practice at blending.* Reading phonically decodable books can support this. For young children reading 'like a robot' can also help so that they talk in a staccato way, speaking the individual phonemes in words – e.g. for 'playtime' the child says: /p/ /l/ /ay/ /t/ /i-e/m/ and also practises hearing words sounded out in phonemes and then blends them into words. This is often done by using a puppet that can only 'talk' in phonemes.

- *Issues with comprehension stemming from a limited vocabulary have been shown by studies* (Perfetti et al., 2005) *to have a significant impact.* Therefore, provide both implicit vocabulary teaching through a rich experience of listening to stories and texts, and explicit teaching of vocabulary, such as identifying unfamiliar words prior to reading a text, followed by activities such as creating what are often called 'meaningful sentences' with a specific word. For more guidance on teaching vocabulary, see 'Teaching Effective Vocabulary' (DCSF, 2008).

Intervention programmes

There are many intervention programmes available and a useful summary of these and their effectiveness can be found in a report by Brooks (2013). He reiterates the effectiveness of what has been termed a 'three-wave' approach to support devised by the National Strategies. These waves consist of the following.

Wave 1: Quality first teaching – high-quality teaching that targets all learners. Brooks (2013, p13) notes:

> *When applied to early reading, this means the provision of a rich language curriculum that fosters all four interdependent strands of language – speaking, listening, reading and writing – while providing access for all children to high-quality phonic work as part of Quality first teaching.*

Wave 2: Quality first teaching plus additional time-limited tailored intervention programmes. This is usually a structured programme of small group support that occurs outside a whole-class lesson.

Wave 3: Quality first teaching plus individualised programmes. This usually involves support from a specialist teacher either one-to-one or in small groups.

For many children who are struggling with reading, additional support with word recognition (phonics and recognition of high-frequency words) is the key. Torgesen et al. (2001, p35) argue that:

> *for children with reading disabilities to achieve adequate reading skills, they must receive more intensive, explicit, and systematic instruction in word-level skills than is typically provided in schools.*

Another successful approach is the use of peer tutoring. This is usually done with older children acting as tutors to support younger ones in cross-ability tutoring sessions. Topping et al. (2016) cite the many advantages for this way of working with a range of empirical studies to validate it across primary and secondary school ages (Topping, 1996; Roscoe and Chi, 2008; Leung, 2014). Interestingly, not only does this process aid the child being tutored, but it also impacts on the tutor through having to consider the material in more depth and engage in questioning and explaining the text to others, thus increasing their own learning.

Supporting children with specific difficulties including dyslexia

Children who have specific learning difficulties such as dyslexia require specialist support, but it is also important for teachers to know what to look for that might suggest a child shows signs of dyslexia together with supporting strategies. The Rose Report (2009, p10) on dyslexia made the following points to aid understanding of the term.

- *Dyslexia is a learning difficulty that primarily affects the skills involved in accurate and fluent word reading and spelling.*

- *Characteristic features of dyslexia are difficulties in phonological awareness, verbal memory and verbal processing speed.*

- *Dyslexia occurs across the range of intellectual abilities.*

- *It is best thought of as a continuum, not a distinct category, and there are no clear cut-off points.*

Stuart and Stainthorp (2016) provide a helpful summary of signs of dyslexia at different developmental stages which include the following.

Early Years	Poor letter-sound knowledge
	Poor phoneme awareness
	Poor word attack skills
	Bizarre spelling attempts
	Problems copying text
Middle school years	Slow reading
	Poor decoding skills with new words
	Both phonetic and non-phonetic spelling attempts
Adolescence and adulthood	Poor reading fluency
	Slow speed of writing
	Poor organisation and expression in written work

One of the most important aspects is to build a child's confidence, which may have suffered from struggling to learn to read. Building on a child's strengths – for example, in oral contributions – will help. Children should receive specialist support and this intervention will usually focus on improving phonological awareness and knowledge of the alphabetic code. Singleton (2009) found that programmes which teach phonological skills systematically and thoroughly have been shown to be effective. Rose notes *that children with dyslexic difficulties particularly benefit from teaching that adheres to the following principles: highly structured, systematic, 'little and often', using graphic representation, allowing time for reinforcement and encouraging generalisation.*

(2009, p14)

Conclusion

This chapter has provided a summary of essential subject knowledge for all teachers in teaching reading. This is based on theoretical models which help to explain the complex process involved in learning to read. All these have one thing in common: they are dual route models that involve two sets of processes: language comprehension and word recognition. The role of phonics in teaching reading is to provide the key to help unlock the alphabetic code and word recognition. Phonics on its own is not sufficient and while many difficulties that struggling readers encounter are related to word recognition, it is also important to ensure that language comprehension is developing effectively, underpinned by a developing vocabulary. To support struggling readers, the importance of early diagnosis and intervention has been emphasised, together with discussion of a number of intervention programmes.

QUESTIONS FOR DISCUSSION AND REFLECTION

1. Consider why is it important to unpick the elements within the two strands in the teaching of reading.
2. How can teaching phonics be made interactive and engaging?
3. Name one or more effective intervention strategies for struggling readers

CHAPTER SUMMARY

You should now know:

- different theoretical models to explain how children learn to read, including the Simple View of Reading;
- the role of phonics to support decoding with a particular focus on the teaching of the complex alphabetical code;
- effective interactive teaching methods for phonics;
- methods of support for struggling readers.

Answers to activities

1. Using models to support practice

Harry

1. The main difficulty for Harry is with language comprehension.

2. Strategies that might help include reading simple texts that enable him to focus on the meaning as well as reading together with a older reading partner or an adult where the partner starts the reading and then Harry joins in with sections or repeated phrases. He would also benefit from reading about particular areas of interest, using different media.

3. Advice to parents would be to try and write some books together, using pictures from magazines or catalogues or images downloaded from the internet to create books he wants to read.

Ella

1. Ella is having particular difficulty with the vocabulary knowledge strand which is key to developing comprehension skills.

2. Strategies to support her would include using props to bring stories alive such as Storysacks. This should encourage her to talk about the books and help develop her vocabulary. She would benefit from listening to stories being read, followed by talking about what happened.

3. Particular intervention programmes that support oral language would help her. There is a range of useful resources and advice available from the Communication Trust at: www.the communicationtrust.org.uk/

Archie

1. Archie is struggling with word recognition.

2. There could be underlying issues which may include hearing difficulties and possibly dyslexia.

3. Archie would need to be assessed by a doctor for hearing and a Special Needs Coordinator or dyslexia specialist to see if he requires a diagnosis and intervention programme.

Answers – long vowel phonemes

1. These words contain a long vowel phoneme – rain, stern, toil, house, me.

2. Alternative spellings for the long vowel phoneme /əʊ/ – 'oa' as in boat, 'ow' as in flow, 'o-e' as in stone, 'o' as in nose.

3. How many ways can you find to spell the phoneme /ɔ/ as in 'horn'? At least six possible ways: 'au' as in sauce, 'or' as in 'short', 'oor' as in floor, 'ar' as in warn, 'aw' as in 'paw, 'a' as in ball.

Answers – making books

1. What was the issue with reading for Liam?

   The issue was that he was a child who liked to be active and sitting and reading he found boring.

2. Why did this approach trigger such an enthusiastic response?

   It triggered an enthusiastic response because it tapped into a particular interest he had in dinosaurs and it gave him ownership over the creation of his own books.

3. What does this tell you that could be applied to other children who are reluctant readers?

   It illustrates that for reluctant readers finding something that is a current interest and relevant for them can give them a real incentive to read.

Glossary

Blend   A combination of letters where individual letters retain their sounds.

Blending   To draw individual sounds together to pronounce a word – e.g. /c/l/a/p/, blended together reads 'clap'.

Decoding   The act of translating graphemes into phonemes – i.e. reading.

Digraph   Two letters which combine to make a new sound.

Diphthong vowel   A diphthong vowel sound where the vowel that glides from one quality to another as in the /oy/ sound in 'boy'.

Encoding   The act of transcribing units of sound or phonemes into graphemes – i.e. spelling.

Grapheme   A letter, or combinations of letters that represent a phoneme.

Initial consonant blend   The consonants retain their original sounds but are blended together as in 'slip'.

Long vowel phonemes   The long vowel sounds as in 'feel' or 'cold'.

Mnemonic   A device for remembering something, such as 'ee/ee/ feel the tree' for the spelling 'ee'.

Monophthong vowels   A monophthong vowel is a vowel sound that does not change as it is pronounced – e.g. the /i/ in 'hit'.

Morpheme   The smallest grammatical unit of language that has meaning. Each morpheme constitutes either a word or a meaningful part of a word.

Orthography   Standardised spelling (not spelling rules).

Phoneme   The smallest unit of speech sound in a word that changes the meaning – e.g. the letters 'ch' representing one sound.

Phonetics   The articulation and acoustic features of speech sounds. It explains the distinction between consonants and vowels and can help listeners identify the phonemic pattern of words.

Segmenting   Splitting up a word into its individual phonemes in order to spell it – i.e. the word 'pat' has three phonemes: /p/a/t/.

Split digraph   Two letters, making one sound, separated usually by a single consonant – e.g. a-e as in 'cake'.

Syllable   A unit of pronunciation having one vowel sound. This can be taught by identifying 'beats' in a word. Putting a hand flat underneath your chin and then saying a word can help, as every time the hand moves, it represents another syllable.

Trigraph   Three letters which combine to make a new sound.

FURTHER READING

DCSF (2009) Phonics intervention programme KS2. Available from: http://webarchive.national archives.gov.uk/20110809091832/teachingandlearningresources.org.uk/collection/34987

DfES (2007) Letters and sounds notes of guidance for practitioners and teachers. Available from: http://webarchive.nationalarchives.gov.uk/20110202093118/http:/nationalstrategies.standards.dcsf. gov.uk/node/84969

Jolliffe, W, Waugh, D with Carss, A (2015) (2nd edn) *Teaching Systematic Synthetic Phonics in Primary Schools*. London: Sage/Learning Matters.

Read Chapter 5 for more detailed guidance on the complex alphabetic code and Chapter 11 for detail on tracking and assessing pupils' learning.

Stuart, M and Stainthorp, R (2016) *Reading Development and Teaching*. London: Sage.

See Part 1 for essential subject knowledge on language.

Topping, K, Duran, D and Van Keer, H (2016) *Using Peer Tutoring to Improve Reading Skills*. Abingdon: Routledge.

This provides detailed guidance on the research into peer tutoring and strategies to implement this.

REFERENCES

Brooks, G (2013) What works for struggling readers: the effectiveness of intervention schemes (4th edn). The Dyslexia-SpLD Trust. Available at: www.interventionsforliteracy.org.uk (accessed 18 October 2016).

Castles, A and Coltheart, M (2004) Is there a causal link from phonological awareness to success in learning to read? *Cognition*, 9(1): 77–111.

DCSF (2008) Teaching effective vocabulary: what can teachers do to increase the vocabulary of children who start education with a limited vocabulary? Nottingham: DCSF.

DCSF (2009) The National Strategies KS2 Phonics Intervention Programme (ref: 01058-2009DOC-EN-01). London: DCSF. Available at: http://webarchive.nationalarchives.gov.uk/20110809091832/teaching andlearningresources.org.uk/collection/34987 (accessed 22 October 2016).

DfE (2012) Year one phonics screening check framework. London: DfE. Available at: www.gov.uk/government/collections/phonics-screening-check-administration (accessed 19 December 2016).

DfES (2006) Rose, J: Independent review of the teaching of early reading: final report, March (ref: 0201-2006DOC-EN).

DfES (2007) Letters and sounds: notes of guidance for practitioners and teachers. Norwich: DfES.

Geva, E and Siegel, LS (2000) Orthographic and cognitive factors in the concurrent development of basic reading skills in two languages. *Reading and Writing: An Interdisciplinary Journal*, 12: 1–30.

Goodman, KS (1998) *In Defence of Good Teaching: What Teachers Need to Know about Reading Wars*. York, MA: Stenhouse.

Gough, PB and Tunmer, WE (1986) Decoding, reading and reading disability. *Remedial and Special Education*, 7: 6–10.

Hatcher, PJ, Hulme, C and Snowling, MJ (2004) Explicit phoneme training combined with phonic reading instruction helps young children at risk of reading failure. *Journal of Child Psychology and Psychiatry,* 45: 338–58.

Johnston, R and Watson, J (2005) The effects of synthetic phonics teaching on reading and spelling attainment: a seven year longitudinal study. Edinburgh: Scottish Executive, February.

Johnston, RS, McGeown, S and Watson, JE (2012) Long-term effects of synthetic versus analytic phonics teaching on the reading and spelling ability of 10 year old boys and girls. *Reading and Writing*, 25(6): 1365–84.

Jolliffe, W (2012) *Quick Fix Phonics*. Witney: Scholastic.

Jolliffe, W and Waugh, D with Carss, A (2015) (2nd edn) *Teaching Systematic Synthetic Phonics in Primary Schools*. London: Sage/Learning Matters.

Jolly Learning (1992) Jolly phonics. Available at: http://jollylearning.co.uk/overview-about-jolly-phonics/ (accessed 19 December 2016).

Leung, KC (2014) Preliminary empirical model of crucial determinants of best practice for peer tutoring on academic achievement. *Journal of Educational Psychology*, 107(2): 558-79.

Miskin, R (2011) *Read Write Inc.: Phonics Handbook*. Oxford: Oxford University Press.

Perfetti, CA, Wlotko, EW and Hart, L (2005) Word learning and individual differences in word learning reflected in event-related potential. *Journal of Experimental Psychology: Learning Memory and Cognition*, 31: 1281–92.

Roscoe, RD and Chi, M (2008). Tutor learning: knowledge-building and knowledge-telling in peer tutors' explanations and questions. *Review of Educational Research*, 77(4): 334–74.

Rose, J (2009) *Identifying and Teaching Children and Young People with Dyslexia and Literacy Difficulties*. London: DCSF.

Scarborough, HS (2009: 24) Connecting early language and literacy to later reading (dis)abilities: evidence, theory and practice. In Fletcher-Campbell, F, Soler, J and Reid, G (eds) *Approaching Difficulties in Literacy Development: Assessment, Pedagogy and Programmes*. Los Angeles, CA: Sage, pp23–38.

Seymour, PHK, Aro, M and Erskine, JM (2003) Foundation literacy acquisition in European orthographies. *British Journal of Psychology,* 94: 143–74.

Singleton, C (2009) *Intervention for Dyslexia.* Bracknell: The Dyslexia-Specific Learning Difficulties Trust.

Stuart, M and Stainthorp, R (2016) *Reading Development and Teaching.* London: Sage.

Topping, K (1996) Effective peer tutoring in further and higher education: a typology and review of the literature. *Higher Education,* 32: 321–45.

Topping, K, Duran, D and Van Keer, H (2016) *Using Peer Tutoring to Improve Reading Skills.* Abingdon: Routledge.

Torgesen, JK, Alexander, AW, Wagner, RK, Rashotte, CA, Voeller, KS and Conway, T (2001) Intensive remedial instruction for children with severe reading disabilities: immediate and long-term outcomes from two instructional approaches. *Journal of Learning Disabilities,* 34(1): 33–58.

Vadasy, PF and Sanders, EA (2013) Two-year follow-up of a code orientated intervention for lower-skilled first-graders: the influence of language status and word reading skills on third grade literacy outcomes. *Reading and Writing, 26*: 821–43.

Venezky, RL (1973) Letter-sound generalisations of first, second and third-grade Finnish children. *Journal of Educational Psychology,* 64: 288–92.

Wren, S (2001) *The Cognitive Foundations of Learning to Read: A Framework.* Austin, TX: Southwest Educational Development Laboratory.

Wyse, D and Goswami, U (2008) Synthetic phonics and the teaching of reading. *British Educational Research Journal,* 34(6): 691–710.

12

THE WIDER ROLE OF THE TEACHER

JONATHAN DOHERTY AND DAVID WAUGH

 THIS CHAPTER

By reading this chapter you will develop your understanding of the following.

- The wider professional responsibilities of Standard 8.
- What it means to be a 'professional'.
- Being proactive in making a positive contribution to the wider life of a school.

Introduction

As a Newly Qualified Teacher, the standards will help you identify your professional capabilities, what you have already accomplished as a teacher and the aspirations you have for yourself for the future. By now, you will recognise how much more there is to the job of teaching than planning and delivering lessons. Being able to consistently deliver outstanding teaching is, of course, an ultimate goal, but reflect on how much of a teacher's job is outside this. As a trainee, you will have been encouraged to think about your involvement in the school more generally, how you interact with parents, other teachers and non-teaching staff, and how you begin to take responsibility for improving your teaching through continued professional learning. Teacher Standard 8 is concerned with the wider professional responsibilities of being a teacher. This standard seeks to develop you as a lifelong professional, prompting you to reflect on your practice in the classroom and your involvement in the wider life of the school.

Being a professional

Schools are dynamic places to work. There are exciting things happening all the time. Like wells that are constantly being refreshed, schools thrive on new ideas and talents that complement and enhance their existing workforce. In this chapter we suggest ways in which you, through your skills, knowledge and professionalism, can make a valuable contribution to school life, and to pupils, teachers, support staff and parents.

Professionalism is based on critical self-reflection, autonomy and respect for the role. It recognises and requires you as a teacher to be accountable. It has an ethical dimension, in so far as you have ethical responsibilities to yourself, to pupils, other teachers and to the wider community that you come into contact with both inside and outside the school itself. Glazzard (2016) cautions that being treated as a professional is not an automatic right, as the right to be viewed as a professional by colleagues and by parents and pupils has to be earned. He advises that if you wish to be respected as a teacher and have the recognition that goes with that, then your behaviour, your attitudes, the personal values and beliefs you bring to the school are critical.

Teaching is a profession that attracts well-qualified individuals. We all want teaching to have the status that other professions such as Medicine and Law enjoy. This means acting as a professional and being mindful of this in your appearance, in your behaviour and your social media activity. Grigg (2015) discusses teachers joining a community of professionals who contribute to discussions on teaching and learning, and whose business it is to refine their practice in the light of research, individual and collective experience and government policy. To achieve this requires an engagement with academic knowledge and the practical application that is associated with a profession. Standard 8 helpfully breaks down these professional responsibilities into five clear parts which we will now explore, and which will set you on that path to being a true professional and meeting your wider professional responsibilities.

Make a positive contribution to the wider life and ethos of the school

Your school placements as a trainee teacher will have been very different from each other, but will have given you a sense of each school's uniqueness. You will have been able to make a small contribution to the wider school life in the short time at each school. Now, you can really begin to make this contribution more impactful.

Parents' evenings or consultations (they have a variety of names) are important events in a school's calendar and are opportunities for you to demonstrate support for your school. They are a chance to meet parents, quite formally, and for parents to meet you and to discuss each child's progress in learning. Parents will ask you about how their child is settling in, their sociability, behaviour and the progress they are making. You should see these meetings as a time to represent the school. You are the class teacher and it is you who has the responsibility for that class, so you will need to prepare for the event and present yourself in a professional manner. Be punctual, keep to time. Listen, talk only about the child you are discussing and be positive about the quality of education each child receives in the school.

By this stage in your career you will have developed your curriculum knowledge considerably. Your curriculum interests are also developing and you may well be asked to contribute to a staff meeting, or even lead on a particular curriculum area. This will involve not only teachers but also non-teaching staff and so offer a good opportunity to broaden your sphere of influence and get to know colleagues from other key stages and in other roles in the school. As your curriculum knowledge increases, you may be able to contribute to teaching and learning policies. This might be in a curriculum area or be related to assessment, behaviour, health, working with parents, and so on. This is excellent experience and if there is a writing team involved, offers you superb professional development. Consider becoming involved in mentoring trainees in your school. Murray described this as *the deliberate pairing of a more skilled or experienced person* with someone with less skill or experience *with a mutually agreed goal of having the less skilled person grow and develop specific competencies* (Murray, 2001, pxiii). By doing this, you are directly helping the next generation of teachers and sharing the knowledge and skills you have gained with them.

Children love school trips, which have many benefits, both socially and academically. They are a great opportunity for you to be involved in their planning and organisation. Often they involve several classes and here too you get a chance to work with children in another class and with other teachers and support staff. Volunteer to go on residential trips. These are milestone events for children and their benefits are far-reaching. One piece of advice: get plenty of sleep beforehand – you will need it.

Many teachers have interests outside of teaching that they bring to the job to the benefit of their class or the whole school. Music, art, technology and sport are common examples where you could volunteer to set up an after-school club and offer this across the school. Look at the example below of Thomas.

 **CASE STUDY**

NQT Thomas, teaching in Year 1, was a keen and accomplished musician. He enjoyed playing the clarinet and friends suggested he use his interest in school. He agreed and talked with the headteacher and other members of staff. He learned that a number of parents had musical interests too and they had hoped that one day the school might be able to form a small band of school staff, parents and pupils. When Thomas was appointed to the school he knew this and was excited at the possibility, but was slightly concerned about how he should progress this idea. He was anxious that he had not taught in Key Stage 2 in the school, but knew that pupils who would want to play would mostly come from this key stage. He had had some involvement with parents but only those of pupils in his own class.

 QUESTIONS FOR DISCUSSION AND REFLECTION

1. What should Thomas's first step be?
2. Who should he approach first?
3. How should he begin to make the idea of a band known in school?
4. How should he begin to make the ideas known outside school?
5. What advice would you give Thomas to address his anxieties?

Book fairs, community events in the local community and religious festivals are all useful ways to contribute to the broader school life. Become involved in as much as you can. Run a stall at the Christmas fair. Consider taking on a project in the school grounds or local environment. You may enjoy being part of committees. Being part of the parent–teacher association or becoming a teacher governor are valuable ways of immersing yourself in the wider life of the school.

Develop effective professional relationships with colleagues, knowing how and when to draw on advice and specialist support

Schools in recent years have seen significant increases in the personnel who work in them and the roles they fulfil. These now include business managers, learning mentors, cover supervisors, parent support advisers, extended schools co-ordinators, etc. Each is important. Schools will have a designated member of staff for child protection who has a key responsibility for safeguarding. You will know who is the Foundation Stage co-ordinator, the Special Educational Needs co-ordinator (SENCO), who the Senior Leadership Team are and what they do. Phase leaders, subject leaders and co-ordinators have particular expertise and specialist knowledge to bring to these roles of additional responsibility outside the normal 'day job' of being a class teacher. You may well see yourself in such a role in a few years' time. Your role is likely to involve you in liaison with outside agencies such as speech therapists, educational psychologists, Social Services, the Police and support teams from the local authority, such as family support and behaviour support. All are specialists in their field with expert skills and knowledge. Your challenge is to know where this expert knowledge is and how best you can use it to benefit your job and the pupils you teach.

There is an old African proverb which says, *If you want to go quickly, go alone; if you want to go far, go together.* Collaboration is the new watchword for schools. Increasingly, teachers are working closely with other teachers and other professionals, creating new synergies in a school or across several schools such as in academy chains. Sparks (2013) comments that strong teams make strong schools and teamwork can create the time for collaboration that enables teachers to thrive and be better able to address the challenges of their work. Team working is essential in schools today, and it is vital that you are a good colleague and a good team player. It takes good relationship skills to work well with different people. It requires patience and excellent communication. Relationships that are based on trust and respect and sensitivity form the basis for good team-working. Teams provide an excellent source of experience and wisdom that you should draw on. So many of the great things that schools achieve would not be possible without good teams. The National College for School Leadership (2012) described five characteristics of effective teams.

1. They are held together by a common purpose and have a shared vison.

2. They are made up of high-performing individuals.

3. The team wish for team glory as opposed to individual acclaim

4. They have inspiring leaders among them.

5. The group see themselves as a professional learning community.

RESEARCH/EVIDENCE

As you extend your contribution across the school, you will become part of different teams, made up of different personalities, each with valuable skills and experiences. Belbin's research into teams (1981, 2010) is still fundamental to the ways businesses everywhere organise their approach to working in teams. The research found that teams made up of similar people underperform. Top-performing teams, he discovered, have a balance of nine basic roles, with each team member performing a role that reflects their strengths.

Team role	Skills
1. Resource investigator	Brings resources and information from outside to the team
2. Team worker	Co-operates with others. Listens. Avoids conflict. Stays calm
3. Co-ordinator	Often the leader. Sets clear goals. Is decisive. Delegates
4. Shaper	Thrives on pressure. Uses energy to overcome barriers
5. Implementer	Turns ideas into practical action
6. Completer-finisher	Finishes the task. Delivers on time
7. Plant	Very creative. Solves complex problems with imagination
8. Specialist	Brings expert knowledge to a group
9. Monitor-evaluator	Takes an objective approach. Evaluative. Judges accurately.

The staff at Barnfield Primary wanted to introduce a new phonics scheme. School data had highlighted that results in reading were low and the senior leadership team were keen to improve the situation quickly. There were several commercial schemes available, but the challenge was choosing one that fitted best with the pupils in the school and that the teachers would work well with. The headteacher decided to use an away-day to resolve the issue and he planned to use Belbin's work to put together the team of teachers and non-teaching staff to decide on the best scheme for the school.

 QUESTIONS FOR DISCUSSION AND REFLECTION

Use the different roles described by Belbin to answer the questions below.

- Why are shapers and co-ordinators vital for this project?
- Who would be best able to generate ideas for the project?
- What might be the contribution of the monitor-evaluators?

- What role would the resource investigator play here?

- How would the completer-finisher contribute?

- Put yourself into one of the roles above. What contribution could you make if this was a real situation in your school?

Deploying support staff effectively

One of the many changes in schools over the last decade has been the increase in the number of adults other than teachers working in schools. Teachers rarely work alone nowadays. They typically are part of various teams and they are assisted in the classroom by parents and increasingly by support staff including teaching assistants (TAs), learning mentors and higher level teaching assistants (HLTAs). Their roles vary considerably from school to school, but their support is invaluable to you as a class teacher. Most schools have clear policies that outline the roles and responsibilities of support staff. Hancock and Colloby (2013) found their main duties (their list also included nursery assistants, nursery nurses, behaviour support teaching assistants, bilingual assistants and parent helpers) involved the following.

- Clerical and administrative (e.g. checking stock, filing, photocopying).

- Out-of-class involvement (e.g. liaising with parents, clubs, supporting school trips).

- Setting up and maintaining equipment (e.g. IT support, classroom resources).

- Health and safety (e.g. first aid; overseeing children's snack time).

- Supporting the curriculum (e.g. literacy and numeracy, art, encouraging children's good behaviour).

- Releasing teachers from classroom teaching.

- Management of others (e.g. deploying other TAs).

- Service (e.g. staffroom maintenance, tidying the classroom).

Using TAs in the classroom

Since 2000, the number of full-time teaching assistants has trebled. The figure rose from 79,000 to 243,700 in 2015. Schools will spend approximately £4.4bn on support staff, equating to 13 per cent of the education budget (Weale, 2016). The impact of the classroom assistant workforce on pupil learning can be considerable. A research study by Snowling et al. (2016) found that pupils made an additional two to four months' progress when TAs were used to support small groups or individual children in a language intervention. It is, however, variable. Correlational studies looking at the impact of TAs providing general classroom support suggest that on average low-attaining pupils do less well in a class with a TA present, compared to a class where only a teacher is present. Where teaching assistants provide one-to-one or small group support, the impact can make a difference of between three and five additional months on average (EEF, 2011).

 **RESEARCH/EVIDENCE FOCUS**

Nuffield early language intervention

In the first trial of this study researchers from the University of York gave teaching assistants three days of training to lead structured sessions with small groups of nursery and reception pupils. The programme lasted 30 weeks and involved 34 schools and nurseries. Findings were that this intervention improved the vocabulary, grammar and listening skills of 4- and 5-year-olds by up to four months. A shorter 20-week version in the first two terms of primary school resulted in pupils making two months' additional progress.

In the second trial, a targeted reading support programme called Reach, TAs were used to improve the reading skills of struggling readers in Y7 and Y8 in secondary schools. One-to-one sessions focused on reading aloud three times a week for 20 weeks. Pupils made the equivalent of four months' additional progress, but for those who took part in a version which had a greater focus on language comprehension, pupils made six months' progress.

While this study had important gains for children's early language development, it also showed how, when TAs are used, to support learning in a well-structured way, their impact is considerable.

A Unison survey (2013) reported that senior leaders suggested that a reduction in TAs would have an impact on children with special education and health needs, teachers and the running of the school. The survey found a complex mix of TA responsibilities, both contrasting roles and overlaps between pastoral, pedagogic and administrative duties. As a teacher, you have overall responsibility for learning in your classroom. Typically, TAs work with low-attaining pupils or those with special needs, but when they carry out their roles with insightful questions, assisting with formative assessment and not focusing on low-level tasks in the classroom, they can complement your role and add enormous value to teaching and learning in the classroom. Practical ways to do this are through their involvement in collaborative group work and encouraging children's self-help skills. The work of Blatchford et al. (2013) provides two effective strategies for effective deployment of TAs we would encourage you to consider.

1. Change the interactions TAs have with pupils. Talking less encourages more pupil thinking and response time. Introduce questioning frameworks for TAs to scaffold pupil thinking more deeply.

2. Adopt strategies to help pupils become more in control of their own learning and better independent learners.

As a teacher, you deploy your support staff to maximise learning in the class, not just to carry out administrative roles. The value they can add to learning is potentially huge but this needs careful managing and planning, otherwise this frontline pedagogical role becomes ineffective. Problems occur when the role of the TA is ill-defined and remedial. The role is most effective when guidance is given and roles are clearly understood by everyone as in the case study. Perhaps surprisingly, the level of evidence related to teaching assistants is quite limited. The Education Endowment Foundation Toolkit (EEF, 2011 – see www. educationendowmentfoundation.org.uk/resources/

teaching-learning-toolkit) produces very readable summaries of educational research on a number of topics and provides guidance for teachers on how to use their resources to improve the attainment of disadvantaged pupils. What we know from their summary on TAs is that teaching assistants tend not to be as effective in terms of raising attainment compared with teachers (they achieve on average about half of the gains), but there are benefits across subjects at both primary and secondary levels. There is also evidence that working with TAs can lead to improvements in pupils' attitudes, and positive effects on teacher morale and reduced stress (EEF, 2011). When roles are very clear, and what has the most impact on pupil learning, is when teachers and TAs work together as a team. We see an example of this in the case study that follows.

 **CASE STUDY**

Teaching assistant Lois

Ravinda, an NQT in Year 6, wished to introduce a unit of work to her class on data handling. Before the unit started, she met with Lois, a very experienced teaching assistant, to plan together. They shared knowledge of the pupils and identified pupil strengths and gaps in knowledge in this area of maths. They agreed on the support that Lois would provide. In the first lesson, Ravinda outlined the unit and how the class would work in groups to collect different kinds of data. She introduced key words, including 'reasoning', 'calibration', 'prediction', and communicated clear learning objectives at the start of the lesson.

As agreed beforehand, Lois worked closely with a small group of children. She used skilful questions to expand their thinking. She facilitated a useful discussion among the children, listening to their ideas and scaffolding their learning. She provided feedback to encourage the children. She and Ravinda had agreed to focus on assessment for learning (AfL) as the class were familiar with peer assessment strategies, but both felt they could develop this work further. In the group Lois was able to gauge the children's understanding of data generally and had already picked up several misconceptions. Using this information, she provided clarification, ensuring that each child had grasped the concept before moving on. At the plenary at end of the lesson, Lois was pleased with the comments of several children in her group, which showed how the children's thinking had progressed. Afterwards, Ravinda and Lois met to review the lesson and plan the next one. They were both clear on Lois's role for the lesson and how their expertise complemented each other's.

The impact of the HLTA role

The higher level teaching assistant role was introduced in 2003 to raise standards and help reduce teachers' workload. It was a bridge between the role of teacher and that of teaching assistant, and was created so that HLTAs could take classes without the teacher needing to be present. They do everything that other assistants do, but with added responsibilities. For instance, they can teach classes on their own and cover teacher absences. Accreditation to become an HLTA is rigorous. Here is what Mandy, a recently qualified HLTA, had to say.

I love being an HLTA in my school. My job is to work alongside the teachers and I work across the whole school from Year 1 up. I lead lessons if a teacher is off and I organise the interventions. That means booking out the rooms and timetabling the other TAs. We work so well together. It's a responsible job and when I teach I have to make sure that my subject knowledge is good in maths and English. One day I hope to train as a teacher.

HLTAs can be instrumental in the curriculum support they can provide in the classroom. A six-step approach for working with HLTAs was provided by Wilson (2007), which was seen as effective as an 'enhancement role' for the impact it had on pupils, teachers and the whole school.

Step 1: Take a whole-school view of staffing.

Step 2: Consult with HLTAs about specialist areas.

Step 3: Allocate HLTAs to staff teams and develop teamwork.

Step 4: Define role requirements and responsibilities.

Step 5: Raise awareness of the HLTA role among staff, parents and governors.

Step 6: Support and develop HLTAs in their role.

QUESTIONS FOR DISCUSSION AND REFLECTION

1. What are the benefits of having an HLTA in your school?

2. How is the school using their expertise? How are you?

3. What impact have they had on learning?

4. Describe their impact on the learning environment in your classroom.

Take responsibility for improving teaching through appropriate professional development, responding to advice and feedback from colleagues

At the heart of your continued professional development is reflection. Good teachers never stop learning. Great teachers reflect on their work. As a trainee, you may have been introduced to reflection. An early definition saw it as the process through which teachers become aware of the motives behind their own teaching and take some deliberate steps to develop it (Gibbs, 1988). Engaging in reflection involves you moving from a semi-conscious, informal approach to a more explicit, intentional approach and is applicable to any aspect of your teaching. For Ewans (2014), there are four types of reflection that teachers commonly use.

1. Reflecting on their own school days.

2. Reflecting on episodes of teaching either observed in others or delivered by them.

3. Reflecting on other people's viewpoints and their judgement on outcomes.

4. Reflecting on what they have read.

Some of the many benefits of reflection include the following.

- Improving your teaching.

- Enquiring deeper into your own practice.

- Helping you to solve problems.

- Thinking critically.

- Managing change better.

- Making informed decisions.

- Taking your own advice.

Reflecting on your practice can take a variety of forms: reflective journals and diaries are common ways to record your thinking. (For a detailed discussion of reflective practice, see Chapter 5.)

As you become involved in events or projects in school, you will be in a position to take on board feedback from others. Accept this in the spirit it is given – i.e. helpful and constructive. Your training provider will have set you targets going into your NQT year and these will form the basis of your Induction Action Plan. A key person you will receive feedback from this year is your induction mentor. Their role is to advise and guide you in your NQT year, assisting you to make the transition from initial teacher to NQT. He or she is your first point of contact. Your induction mentor is critical to your CPD this year. They will help guide you through performance management. They will draw on other members of staff to assist them with the formal assessment meetings, of which there is one each term, and completing a formal assessment record at the end of the year. They will observe your teaching, give you feedback, and monitor and review your progress through regular meetings (Robinson et al., 2016). Consider the conversation below between an induction mentor and an NQT. Notice how the mentor, Joanne, provides constructive feedback on the teaching session she has just observed led by Della. She makes helpful positive points and gives specific targets for Della to work on. Della shows professionalism and responds positively to this feedback.

Classroom focus

Feedback from an induction mentor

Joanne: Thank you for your lesson, Della, which I enjoyed. Tell me how you think it went.

Della: Overall, quite well really. I was pleased with some of the work.

Joanne: Yes, I agree. What parts did you think went particularly well?

Della: Well, I made the objectives clear. The children seemed to get these straight away. I liked some of the questions at the start. Ben's answers were really good. He's doing so well. When they were working independently, I thought they were on task. I thought the quality of their writing was good on the whole too.

Joanne: That's true. As we agreed, you have been working on extending children's thinking through your questions. Let's talk about that for a moment.

Della: OK. It was better than before, I thought.

Joanne: It was indeed. Can you tell me what the difference was?

Della: I think I used more questions – open rather than closed, as you said.

Joanne: Correct. In the introduction to the lesson I counted nine questions, so that is an increase. Good.

          Did you notice anything about who you asked the questions to and who answered them?

Della: I hadn't thought of that. I don't know.

Joanne: You directed questions to the higher ability children and only to girls.

Della: I didn't know that.

Joanne: True. What I want you to focus on in your next lesson are two things. First, direct questions to all abilities in the class, but of course these will have to be differentiated, and second, direct your questions to both boys and girls.

          I thought the lesson went well and I can see you are taking on previous advice. These, then, are the targets for next time. Good work, Della.

Della: Thank you, Joanne. I found that really helpful.

You will be developing at pace during your NQT year. Many of the elements you were required to do as a trainee should remain as good practice and will be extended. Lesson observations, moderation and learning walks are all examples of such activities and provide opportunities to receive feedback on your performance as a teacher.

You need to continue with your professional development. Do not leave this to chance. A programme of professional development, integrated with a system of evaluating teachers' strengths and areas for improvement, can provide a boost to a teacher's performance and to student outcomes (Jayaram et al., 2012). Establish a CPD action plan early on to map your plans for further professional learning. Keep up to date with pedagogy and practice through reading. Take responsibility for your own CPD. Evidence suggests this can be patchy (Cordingley, 2005). Traditional CPD has frequently been one-off external events after school with limited impact on practice. This is changing with the shift to greater school-to-school support and collaborative working. Take advantage of the expertise in your school and listen to and act on the advice you hear.

Communicate effectively with parents with regard to pupils' achievements and well-being

It has been called 'the missing link in school achievement' (LaRocque et al., 2011) and a hallmark for good practice in schools. Primary-aged children spend at most about 15 per cent of their time in school, which means the majority of time is spent at home with their parents. Parents are the child's first educators. When parents are involved in their child's education from an early age, the effects are sustained through the primary years and into adulthood (Sylva et al., 2004). Attitudes and aspirations held by parents have a major influence on school achievement (Gutman and Akerman, 2008). A study found that for boys, family relationships have a significant influence on attainment in all subjects at Key Stage 2, and for girls, parents' education and background influenced attainment in maths and English in the same key stage (Duckworth, 2008). The current SEND Code of Practice (2015) emphasises parental involvement and aligns closely with a 'parents as partners' approach to learning for all children.

While the benefits of parental involvement in their child's learning are well documented, making it happen more consistently and sustaining it presents a challenge to most schools. It is welcomed that, increasingly, parents are now more visible in schools, whether helping with practical activities in classrooms, supporting through the PTA or involvement with governance. As a teacher, your role here is one of listener and diplomat. They have important knowledge to contribute and skills you can use to enhance your teaching. You must avoid at all costs appearing judgemental. Appear open-minded and supportive, welcoming of their involvement and understanding.

The key to working effectively with parents is communication. Establish open communication early with parents and let them know you welcome them in your classroom. Create an open dialogue by using a variety of ways to reach even those whom we call 'hard to reach parents and families'. Here are some suggestions.

- Regular face-face meetings.

- Telephone calls.

- A section on the school website devoted to parents (most schools have this already).

- Home-school diaries.

- Regularly send pupils' work home: work sent home opens up a dialogue with parents (reading diaries are a good example here).

- Email.

- Mobile phone apps that showcase pupil achievement.

- Half-term newsletters.

- Special invitations to school or class events, such as assemblies.

- Involve parents in visits and class trips.

- Family group meetings.

- E-letters or sending text messages to let parents know about a special event happening in your class.

There is a statutory right for schools to formally report to parents about their child's progress and this involves a formal report on the child's achievement each year, access to records on written request and access to the school's curriculum. This last one provides a fine opportunity for you to be proactive. Schedule an open meeting with parents in the first week or so of the first term. Here you can outline the year ahead, your curriculum coverage and the ways in which you will deliver stimulating episodes of outstanding teaching. Inevitably, there will be times when you will have to display diplomacy and professionalism, and parents' evenings are a good example of this. Read the case study below of Jillie and her experiences at a parents' evening.

 **CASE STUDY**

Parents' evening

It was NQT Jillie's first parents' evening. The first appointment was with the Downeys whose daughter Sophie was a conscientious, hard-working pupil in her Year 4 class. Jillie had already noticed that Sophie had a good attitude to work but suffered from a lack of confidence in her own abilities. Jillie knew that Sophie's parents had very high expectations of their only daughter. They employed a tutor to work with her in maths and English two afternoons each week after school. Sophie would often come into school looking tired. She looked stressed a lot of the time and over the last few weeks her work had deteriorated. Jillie suspected pressure from home was the cause.

 QUESTIONS FOR DISCUSSION AND REFLECTION

1. Was Jillie right to make the connection between Sophie's work and pressure from home?

2. How would you approach this situation?

3. What advice do you have for Jillie?

Homework

One area that has traditionally involved parents is homework. Why do parents believe in it so much and why do they want to become so involved in it? Many parents believe that homework is essential for children early on and it is instrumental for academic success. Research by Hoover-Dempsey et al. (2010) suggests they involve themselves in homework because they believe that they should be involved. Most believe that by doing so they will make a positive difference, and they also believe that their child and their child's teacher want this too.

You might be surprised that homework (certainly in the context of primary schools) does not have the impact you might think. In a review commissioned by Ofsted, Sharp et al. (2001) found a link between homework and school performance at secondary school level, but the evidence was inconclusive for primary schools. You will need to know what your school policy on homework is, as this will guide you in what to set and how much, and how you will feedback on the homework. Certainly involve parents in homework, but keep this in line with the age of the child. Younger children should do less. Homework that extends learning in the classroom is preferable. Tasks that engage children are critical, encouraging them to want to continue learning.

QUESTIONS FOR DISCUSSION AND REFLECTION

1. How do you involve parents collaboratively in homework?

2. In what ways do you think homework motivates children to engage in extra-curricular learning?

3. What ways have you seen to involve children in recording such learning? For example, learning journals and homework diaries.

4. How can you more effectively encourage parents to be involved in homework without placing additional pressure on children?

Conclusion

Standard 8 requires you to expand your role as a teacher and make a contribution to the wider aspect of school life and the ethos. By being proactive in this endeavour, you are laying firm foundations for your continued professional development as a teacher. It will demand many skills of you, including communication, diplomacy, team working and leadership as you extend your impact on the school community, inside with colleagues and outside with parents and other specialists. You will learn much more about your school and the community it serves, and your contribution will be impactful and enjoyable.

CHAPTER SUMMARY

You should now know the following.

- What is meant by teacher professionalism.

- How to make positive contributions to the wider life of the school.

- How to draw on advice from colleagues and other specialists.

- The importance of deploying support staff effectively.

- The importance of responding positively and professionally to advice from others.

- Ways of communicating effectively with parents.

▬▬ FURTHER READING ▬▬

Glazzard, J (2016) *Learning to be a Primary Teacher: Core Knowledge and Understanding.* Northwich: Critical Publishing.

A very accessible and up-to-date read. Chapter 10 is a very good chapter on professionalism.

Robinson, C, Bingle, B and Howard, C (2016*) Surviving and Thriving as a Primary NQT.* Northwich: Critical Publishing.

A useful book to read since it covers most elements of the NQT year. The sections on mentoring are very good and relevant to this chapter.

▬▬ REFERENCES ▬▬

Belbin, RM (1981, 2010) *Management Teams: Why They Succeed or Fail* (3rd edn). Burlington, MA: Elsevier.

Blatchford, P, Webster, R and Russell, A (2012) Challenging the role and deployment of teaching assistants in mainstream schools: the impact on schools. Final report of the Effective Deployment of Teaching Assistants (EDTA) project. London: IoE, University of London.

Cordingley, P (2005) *Sauce for the Goose: Learning Entitlements that Work for Teachers as well as Pupils.* Coventry: CUREE.

DfE (2015) Special educational needs and disability code of practice: 0 to 25 years. Statutory guidance for organisations which work with and support children and young people who have special educational needs or disabilities. London: DfE/DoH.

Duckworth, K (2008) Influences on attainment in primary school interactions between child, family and school contexts. Research brief RB 04. London: DCSF.

Education Endowment Foundation (EEF) Toolkit (2011) Teaching assistants. Available at: https://educationendowmentfoundation.org.uk/resources/teaching-learning-toolkit/teaching-assistants (accessed 20 November 2016).

Ewans, T (2014) *Reflective Primary Teaching.* Northwich: Critical Publishing.

Gibbs, G (1988) *Learning by Doing: A Guide to Teaching and Learning Methods.* Oxford: Oxford Further Education Unit.

Glazzard, J (2016) *Learning to be a Primary Teacher: Core Knowledge and Understanding.* Northwich: Critical Publishing.

Grigg, R (2015*) Becoming an Outstanding Primary School Teacher* (2nd edn). Abingdon: Routledge.

Gutman, LM and Akerman, R (2008) Determinants of aspirations. Centre for Research on the Wider Benefits of Learning Research, Report 27. London: Institute of Education.

Hancock, R and Colloby, J (2013) Ten titles and roles. Teaching assistants: support in action. OpenLearn. Available at: www.open.edu/openlearn/education/educational-technology-and-practice/educational-practice/teaching-assistants-support-action/content-section-0 (accessed 25 September 2016).

Hoover-Dempsey, KV, Green, CG and Whitaker, MW (2010) Motivation and commitment to partnerships for families and schools. In Christenson, SL and Reschly, AL (eds) *Handbook of School–Family Partnerships*. New York: Routledge/Taylor & Francis Group, pp30–60.

Jayaram, K, Moffit, A and Scott, D (2012) *Breaking the Habit of Ineffective Professional Development for Teachers*. Chicago, IL: McKinsey & Co.

LaRocque, M, Kleiman, I and Darling, SM (2011) Parental involvement: the missing link in school achievement. *Preventing School Failure*, 55(3):115–22.

Murray, M (2001) *Beyond the Myths and Magic of Mentoring: How to Facilitate an Effective Mentoring Process*. San Francisco, CA: Jossey-Bass.

National College of School Leadership (2012) Leading staff and effective teams. Thinkpiece. Nottingham: NCTL.

Robinson, C, Bingle, B and Howard, C (2016) *Surviving and Thriving as a Primary NQT*. Northwich: Critical Publishing.

Sharp, C, Keys, W and Benefield, P (2001) Homework: a review of recent research. Slough: NFER.

Snowling, M, Bower-Crane, C and Hulme, C (2016) Nuffield early language intervention. London: Nufffield Foundation.

Sparks, D (2013) Strong teams, strong schools, 34(2). April. Available at: www.learningforward.org (accessed 15 September 2016).

Sylva, K, Melhuish, E, Sammons, P, Siraj-Blatchford, I and Taggart, B (2004) The Effective Provision of Pre-school Education (EPPE) project: final report. London: SureStart DfES Publications. Ref SSu/FR/2004/01.

Unison (2013) The evident value of teaching assistants. Report of survey, January. London: Unison Education Services.

Weale, S. (2016) Teaching assistants improve pupils' results, studies show. *The Guardian*, 26 February (accessed 1 October 2016).

Wilson, R (2007) Scaling new heights: a six-step guide for HLTA deployment. *Practical Research for Education*, 38: 37–43, October. NFER.

13

BEING MINDFUL OF TEACHER WELL-BEING

ALISON MCMANUS

THIS CHAPTER

By reading this chapter you will develop your understanding of the following.

- Stress: a brief definition and how it affects teachers in particular.
- How to manage self-defeating behaviours.
- The relationship between self-efficacy and resilience for teachers.
- What strategies and behaviours teachers can use to combat stress and boost resilience.
- Mindfulness and its applications for the classroom as well as for individual teachers.

LINK TO THE TEACHER'S STANDARDS

This chapter will help you with the following Teachers' Standards.

Personal and Professional Conduct

- Teachers uphold public trust in the profession and maintain high standards of ethics and behaviour, within and outside school.

- Teachers must have proper and professional regard for the ethos, policies and practices of the school in which they teach, and maintain high standards in their own attendance and punctuality.

- Teachers must have an understanding of, and always act within, the statutory frameworks which set out their professional duties and responsibilities.

Introduction

Throughout this book, trainee teachers have been encouraged to take a reflective approach to their teaching practice. This chapter will encourage readers to take the same reflective approach to understand their own health and welfare in order to avoid illness and reduce stress.

When considering stress levels in education, it would be easy to create a pessimistic picture. Features such as *The Guardian's* 'Secret Teacher' blog regularly describe the anonymous experience of overworked, frustrated, stressed-out teachers. Media reports add to the sense of crisis, including a recent BBC headline which claimed that stress levels for teachers are *soaring* and that *stress is the biggest cause of staff absence save for maternity* (Precey, 2015). Kyriacou notes in his book *Stress-Busting for Teachers* (2000) that as far back as 1879, articles in *The Schoolmaster* were raising concerns about *temporary insanity* in teachers which could even lead to suicide. In Cosgrove's book *Breakdown: The Facts about Stress in Teaching* (2000), the experiences of a number of teachers who suffered stress are recounted. Although this is not necessarily a new phenomenon, it is reasonable to suggest that the pressures facing teachers have arguably never been higher.

Current concerns about teacher well-being are compounded by an increase in the number of cases of mental health issues reported in the wider population, with World Health Organization estimates suggesting that as many as one in four people are expected to encounter some form of mental health difficulty in their lifetime. Moreover, these issues are being reported at an earlier and earlier age, which has an entirely different but equally concerning impact on life in the classroom. Thus, the experience of stress in education, whether among pupils or staff, has gained increasing attention both in academic as well as popular circles, and as reflective practitioners, we must ask ourselves what teachers can do to protect themselves against the harmful effects of stress, as well as to promote well-being and resilience among their pupils.

This chapter aims to provide NQTs with ways of coping with these pressures, as well as strategies to support the well-being of their learners. A general discussion about stress and wellness will lead on to examining techniques that teachers may use to cope with stress (e.g. mindfulness) as well as case studies highlighting experiences of classroom practice, before considering the research base which supports these strategies. Finally, the chapter will conclude with an examination of how the techniques of mindfulness can be employed with children in the classroom.

Shock at the chalk-face

A well-planned lesson has gone awry: an unruly class; an unexpected observation; a fight in the playground; a steady stream of emails and text messages. Each of these may seem very far away indeed from the idealised image of teaching which many who start out in the profession may have had, and any illusions one may have harboured about day-to-day life at the chalk-face are quickly dispelled during one's teaching practice. Of course, not every day is a bad one and the rewards of teaching are high, but there are certain factors which make teaching particularly stressful.

At its most basic, 'stress' is defined as a feeling of the inability to meet expectations in the time allotted, but for teachers the demands of the workload represent only one part of the picture. There is an element of performance to teaching which is often experienced – somewhat akin to stage fright – and a feeling of unease or anxiety can suddenly overcome even the most seasoned of teachers. Panic may be all the more acute during observed lessons where the stakes are even higher. Newly qualified or trainee staff may feel especially vulnerable to criticism and may place undue pressure on themselves to meet unachievable standards of perfection.

Furthermore, there is an emotional burden to teaching, particularly in more challenging contexts. Children are more vulnerable, need more attention and are less emotionally restrained than adults, even at the best of times. It can be difficult to switch off the care or concern one feels for one's pupils, magnified during periods of difficulty for the child – for example, after a bereavement or during a family breakdown. In addition to comforting students, teachers are regularly called on to provide support to their colleagues, which can also be emotionally draining. Conflict, whether it is encountered on the playground or in the staffroom, is yet another source of tension. Finally, the unexpected and unpredictable nature of each day being different from the one before can give rise to feelings of 'firefighting' or doing battle. Thus, teaching is *uncertain, emotional and attentionally demanding work* (Roeser et al., 2012, p168). Ignoring these aspects of teaching, like ignoring the physical symptoms of stress, can lead to a more pronounced and serious burn-out, a significant and overwhelming sense of inadequacy, depression, exhaustion and lack of care for one's work.

Theory focus: Maslow's Hierarchy of Needs

An interest in motivation led psychologist Abraham Maslow (1943) to model human needs in the shape of a triangle, with one's most basic, physiological requirements at the bottom, relationship needs towards the centre, and more complex requirements, such as achieving goals, towards the top. The idea is that someone who is hungry, tired, cold, unwell or unsafe is likewise unable to give their full attention to problem-solving or logic, let alone becoming the best version of themself they can be (Maslow called this 'self-actualising'). Anyone who has ever struggled to concentrate on a lecture while needing the loo can almost certainly relate, and the intrusion of a personal problem on one's performance is similarly obvious. Why, then, do so many people behave as if their physiological and community needs are unimportant?

We live in a culture where one's work, and being busy, are given greater status than looking after one's self properly, but as Maslow was wise to note, we ignore our basic needs such as getting enough sleep, drinking plenty of water or taking healthy meals at our peril. And yet often we push our physical needs to one side, particularly throughout the course of a busy teaching day, which only leaves us feeling more depleted or making poor choices as a result. Is it wise, for example, if you are already feeling anxious and tired, to skip lunch and then reach for caffeine or sugar? Do you really need that rowdy after-work drink in the pub, or would you be better served by a hot bath followed by a nice evening in front of the telly perhaps? An old adage puts it thus: you can't pour from an empty cup, and nowhere does this apply more than to managing stress.

Wellness, resilience and teaching

Originating in the West Coast of the US, it is easy to characterise the Wellness Movement with the same whiff of pseudo-science as other alternative forms of medicine. However, just as some complementary therapies are gaining increased recognition in the scientific community, there is increased interest in wellness, especially in the academic community, and a sound scientific basis for the movement. In essence, the term 'wellness' is generally used to mean a healthy balance of the mind, body and spirit that results in an overall feeling of well-being. According to founder Halbert L Dunn, MD (1896–1975), a biostatistician at the prestigious Mayo clinic in the US, wellness is

an integrated method of functioning which is oriented toward maximizing the potential of which the individual is capable. It requires that the individual maintain a continuum of balance and purposeful direction within the environment where he is functioning

(Dunn, 1961, pp4–5)

Conceived of in this way, one's health is more than just the absence of disease, but also incorporates a healthy balance of physical, psychological, spiritual, professional and community domains.

There are obvious benefits to paying attention to one's overall well-being and making sure one's physical and psychological health are maintained. One reason a growing number of employers are taking an interest in programmes which promote wellness could be due to the clear implications this may have for employee productivity. What are the implications in a high-stress, high-attrition rate profession like teaching?

According to humanistic psychologists such as Maslow (see Theory focus, above) and others, it is imperative to prioritise one's basic needs before considering additional factors such as achieving goals. On the other hand, the reality of daily life for many teachers means that something must be sacrificed, whether that is in the workplace or at home. Here is where a discussion of resilience – another concept gaining increasing popular and research attention in the academic community – becomes important.

Resilience can be defined as one's ability to recover quickly in the face of adversity. In the first comprehensive review of the literature surrounding teacher resilience, Beltman et al. (2011) note that relatively few studies surrounding this topic have been conducted, with a wide variation of both theoretical applications and methods. However, there is general agreement that interest in resilience for teaching professionals can complement research into teacher stress and attrition. *Teacher resilience is a dynamic process or outcome that is the result of interaction over time between a person and the environment* (Beltman et al., p188). As has been discussed above, the classroom context is challenging for teachers, and it is important to be aware of potential risk factors. The review found that the biggest individual risk factors for teacher resilience are negative self-beliefs or low self-confidence, and difficulty asking for help, while contextual risk factors in the classroom were also significant.

Given this is the case, what can teachers do to increase their resilience? The research points to some interesting protective features, examining both teacher self-efficacy and one's motivation for teaching. Those teachers who felt confident and competent, alongside having a personal inner satisfaction with teaching, were those most likely to thrive in the complex and challenging work environment of a school. Going one step further, a large-scale quantitative study in Germany (Klusman et al., 2008) identified four different types of teachers, with those who were considered 'type H', or 'healthy and ambitious', reporting higher levels of job satisfaction and demonstrating the lowest ratings on exhaustion. Meanwhile, their students reported a significantly more positive experience. Conversely, those teachers who strove for perfection ('type A'), but were less clear with emotional boundaries, were seen to be at risk of both career and personal issues.

Finally, it is important to recognise that resilience is not innate but rather a skill that can be acquired and refined over one's career. Consider the following questions.

 QUESTIONS FOR DISCUSSION AND REFLECTION

1. What is your overall level of wellness?

2. How would you rate your ability to be resilient in adversity?

3. Consider Maslow's Hierarchy of Needs. Do you regularly ignore any of your basic needs? What impact might this have on your overall well-being? Or on your ability to teach?

4. What can you do to increase your wellness? What steps can you take to improve resilience?

Go to the spa

 RESEARCH/EVIDENCE FOCUS

Research/evidence focus: resilience, self-efficacy and observing experienced teachers

Self-efficacy, the belief in one's own capacity to resolve a situation or master a task, was first identified by psychologist Alfred Bandura. The implications of his theories to learning and teaching are obvious, but Bandura and other social learning theorists propose that it is equally important is to consider the impact of *teacher self-efficacy*, and its relationship to performance, resilience, job satisfaction and retention.

Recent research confirms this view. In a survey of over 250 teachers ranging from newly qualified to more experienced career teachers, educational researchers Tschannen-Moran and Hoy (2007) investigated the relationship between self-efficacy and resilience.

Simply put, if a teacher believes in his or her competency to teach, then he or she is also likely to hold confidence in future performance and classroom situations, leading to an overall increase in resilience (Tschannen-Moran and Hoy, 2007). Likewise, the researchers note that a lower sense of self-efficacy leads to an overall perception of inadequacy, which can have future expectation of failure as a consequence. Meanwhile, the experience of teacher self-efficacy can be affected by external factors. An example of one factor could be the reinforcement that a teacher receives about his or her performance and prospects for success from important others in the teaching context, such as administrators, colleagues, parents or members of the community. Another influence may come from what the researchers call 'vicarious experiences' – that is, observing the target activity being modelled by someone else, for example, by another, more experienced, teacher.

> The impact of the modelled performance on the observer's efficacy beliefs depends on the degree to which the observer identifies with the model. When a model with whom the observer closely identifies performs well, the self-efficacy of the observer is enhanced.
>
> (Tschannen-Moran and Hoy, 2007, pp945)

Conversely, if the model differs noticeably from the observer – for example,

> in terms of the level of experience, training, gender, or race, then even witnessing a very competent performance may not enhance the self-efficacy beliefs of the observer
>
> (ibid., pp945)

Thus, trainee teachers are wise to monitor their emotional reactions to those they observe, and to be aware of any unconscious biases in their reactions.

Tschannen-Moran and Hoy (2007) go on to point out that positive emotional states play a role in the perception of competency.

> The feelings of joy or pleasure a teacher experiences from teaching a successful lesson may increase her sense of efficacy, yet high levels of stress or anxiety associated with a fear of losing control may result in lower self-efficacy beliefs.
>
> (pp945)

Finally, perhaps unsurprisingly, there was a difference in the study between the levels of reported self-efficacy of experienced versus newer teaching staff, with those newly qualified reporting lower levels than their more experienced peers. One possible explanation is that self-efficacy increases with mastery and successful practice. However, it is equally possible that teachers who begin their careers with lower levels of confidence in their abilities are among those most likely to leave the profession, and only those with higher levels of self-efficacy, or those who find means of increasing their level, remain. Tschannen-Moran and Hoy conclude that

> If future research confirms that teachers' self-efficacy beliefs are most malleable early in learning and are resistant to change once set, then it would behove teacher educators and school leaders to provide pre-service and novice teachers the kinds of supports that would lead to the development of strong, resilient self-efficacy beliefs.
>
> (Tschannen-Moran and Hoy, 2007, p955)

 **CASE STUDY 1: ROSE**

Rose has taught Reception in a small primary school in a rural village near a larger town in the North-East for nearly twenty years. Although her headteacher is very supportive, she has often found herself on the brink of a breakdown in recent years as a result of stress. 'It's not the workload,' she says, 'although that is part of it, obviously. But it's all the other stuff that gets on top of me.'

Throughout our interview, Rose refers again and again to a series of self-defeating behaviours which hold her back and increase her sense of being overwhelmed. 'I can't stand being criticised, so I find observations really difficult.' She describes staying up all night in order to plan lessons or create elaborate classroom resources. 'I convince myself that I enjoy it, but in the end I just feel exhausted all the time.' She recognises that this level of perfectionism is unhealthy, but she places pressure on herself to provide picture-perfect lessons in order to avoid negative comments. 'I'll just think and think about it from every angle, trying to predict what they might say, and trying to think up a strategy or a comeback.' When asked if this type of 'overthinking' things (or rumination) is helpful, Rose admits it is not. 'I've finally had to learn that giving critical feedback is their job, and there's no such thing as a perfect lesson. I even realised that doing things that way was causing me to avoid other tasks which were equally important. By spending hour after hour working on resources, I was putting off marking, which I find less enjoyable.'

 QUESTIONS FOR DISCUSSION AND REFLECTION

1. What are the particular situations which are likely to trigger anxiety for you?

2. How do the physical symptoms of stress manifest themselves in your body?

3. Which self-defeating behaviours do you exhibit? Examples include procrastination, perfectionism, people-pleasing, rumination, and/or a lack of healthy boundaries.

4. What can you do to develop greater self-awareness of these?

5. What can you do to encourage healthier habits instead?

Mindfulness in schools

So prevalent has the problem of stress, anxiety and other mental health issues become, whether it is in classrooms or in the wider population, that an entire industry is emerging in order to help both teachers as well as students learn to cope. Mindfulness-based Stress Reduction (MBSR) is one such strategy, a technique which originated in the US for the treatment of chronic pain or other issues difficult to treat in a hospital context.

Although MBSR is relatively new, it has its origins in Eastern philosophies and practices dating back centuries but which now have new uses in contemporary Western societies. John Kabat-Zin, founder of the technique, describes the practice of mindfulness as a way of paying attention to the present, usually by focusing on the breath. He and others have developed a range of courses, usually delivered over eight weeks, and currently available through a number of nationally recognised centres in the UK and beyond.

There is a strong evidence-base for MBSR, with a range of applications including mental health issues. Meta-analysis conducted by Gu et al. (2015) evaluates evidence from a research base that is both robust and growing in size. Their research shows that in a number of randomised trials there is a demonstrated improvement for a range of clinical and non-clinical psychological outcomes in comparison to control conditions, including for anxiety, risk of relapse for depression, current depressive symptoms, stress, chronic pain, and other physical and psychological symptoms (Gu et al., 2015).

 CASE STUDY 2: ALAN

Having always wanted to be a teacher, Alan was delighted to find a permanent post and settle into teaching his Year 3 class after completing his PGCE. However, after less than a year in post, he began seriously thinking of leaving the profession. 'I just felt I had no life at all outside of work. My partner was threatening to leave because of the all the long hours, and I was experiencing some really unusual symptoms. I'd always seen myself as really sorted, so it was difficult to admit I needed help. I just put a brave face on things and worked harder in the hopes that it would all be all right.'

It wasn't until he experienced a panic attack in the classroom that he finally was ready to admit something was wrong and sought advice. 'I went to see my GP and was given a prescription for anti-depressants, and they helped take the edge off. But I still felt like I needed some new strategies, a new way of being really. My partner bought me a book on mindfulness. It included some CDs; I still remember falling asleep the first few times I listened to them. But it helped. It definitely helped. Eventually, I also changed my approach to work altogether and tried to make sure there was a clear boundary between the end of the working day and the start of my evening. I became better at saying "no" to things, and to accepting when something was good enough rather than perfect.'

 QUESTIONS FOR DISCUSSION AND REFLECTION

1. Much has been written recently about the difference between stress management versus resilience promotion in the workplace; the latter involves a more pro-active, community-based approach. Without adding to your to-do list, what can you do to promote well-being in your workplace? What about in your classroom?

2. What are the physical symptoms that you exhibit when you are experiencing stress? How can you monitor these?

3. Exercise: consider your typical day. Write down 10-20 activities that you do across the course of a normal day, and then consider which of these deplete your energy levels.

4. Consider ways in which you can practise self-care. What are some low- cost mood boosters that you can build in to the rest of your day? Some examples might be having a cup of tea or ringing up a friend.

Mindful teacher, mindful class

As has been discussed, mindfulness may well have some benefits for teacher well-being, and there are a number of resources listed at the end of this chapter. Next to be considered is whether or not mindfulness may have a practical application in the classroom.

First, though, it is important to note that mindfulness has to start with the teacher. It is no good teaching young children how to meditate if the teacher herself is anxious. Stress is infectious, and if the teacher is being affected, students sense this and may react accordingly. To illustrate this, researchers examining the impact of teacher stress on a Head Start programme in the USA found that increased levels of stress were directly associated with an increase in conflict between children and teachers (Whitaker et al., 2015), whereas when the teacher is calmer, students tend to be calmer as well. It is worthwhile observing the impact one's own attitudes and behaviour have in the classroom, as well as trying out some of the mindfulness techniques in order to become more centred and calm, before considering implementing any of the strategies with a class.

Having said that, children are naturally mindful and are remarkably receptive to the concept. One of the principles of mindfulness is to adopt a 'beginner's mind' to even the most routine or mundane tasks, similar to a child experiencing something for the first time. A well-known example of this is the 'chocolate test'. See http://psychcentral.com/blog/archives/2016/01/23/practicing-mindfulness-with-chocolate/ for a short explanation of an entertaining introductory exercise to use with children.

Mindful Schools (www.mindfulschools.org/) and Youth Mindfulness (http://youthmindfulness.org/) are just two examples of successful programmes to incorporate mindfulness techniques in classroom settings, but there are a number of ideas that can be easily incorporated into the teaching day, such as setting intentions before beginning an activity, or asking pupils to close their eyes and focus on their breathing for a few moments when moving from one activity to another.

 CASE STUDY 3: GEORGINA

Georgina's interest in mindfulness was sparked during her gap year, where she spent time on an ashram in India. 'I was really into yoga at the time, but the meditation we did was really intense,' she recalls. 'In fact, I think it made me feel more depressed and down rather than anything else.' As a result, she avoided anything to do with meditation practice for several years, until a friend convinced her to go on an eight-week mindfulness course. 'I didn't really have high expectations and thought it might all be a bit of hippy-dippy nonsense, but over time I changed my mind. I really felt more focused and clear-headed, and my sleep pattern improved as well.' Having experienced these benefits herself, she decided to try out some of the techniques with her Year 5 class.

Concerned that her students, a rowdy group, many of whom came from a range of ethnic and religious backgrounds, might balk at the idea of meditating, she took a more discrete approach. 'I found loads of support and ideas on-line, and I decided to sneak it in somewhat at first, not telling the students what we were doing or mentioning mindfulness at all. Instead, I changed the structure of our day somewhat to allow for a short period of intention-setting at the start of our activities, and thought more carefully about building in transitions to the rest of the day. So when we were doing something more excitable or active, I would ask the students to close their eyes and slow their breathing for three minutes before we moved on to the next task. I noticed the benefits almost immediately, and gradually we built up to more prolonged periods and other exercises as well.'

 QUESTIONS FOR DISCUSSION AND REFLECTION

1. Consider the contexts where you have been teaching. Could mindfulness be a useful strategy for students?

2. Are there any particular times of the day when it might be useful to encourage a more mindful approach?

3. What obstacles might there be to conducting mindfulness in the classroom?

4. What other benefits might there be to using mindfulness in classrooms?

Conclusion

Although there are many rewards associated with teaching, there are certain pressures associated with the job which are quite specific. A heavy workload coupled with the emotional and performative nature of the profession are likely to be of particular concern to teaching staff. New teachers would do well to consider ways they can protect themselves from the harmful impacts of stress. Likewise, it is essential to develop good coping mechanisms for those times when the challenges become overwhelming. An awareness of one's overall level of wellness, building resilience and self-efficacy, and practising mindfulness are all examples of helpful coping strategies teachers can use. Finally, mindfulness may also have practical applications in the classroom, with noticeable benefits for students as well as teachers.

 QUESTIONS FOR DISCUSSION AND REFLECTION

1. Conduct some further research on mindfulness and try out some of the practices. Keep a record of this and evaluate whether or not it has been of benefit to you. Consider also keeping a daily journal to record your overall level of health and well-being.

2. Discuss with colleagues how they manage their stress levels.

CHAPTER SUMMARY

You should now know the following.

- Why stress and mental health are of particular concern to teachers.
- What strategies can be used to cope with stress.
- How an awareness of self-efficacy and self-defeating behaviours can help you.
- The evidence base for mindfulness.

FURTHER READING

Brown, B (2010) *The Gifts of Imperfection: Let Go of who You Think You're Supposed To Be and Embrace Who You Are*. Minnesota, MN: Hazelden.

In 2010, US-based researcher and academic Brené Brown gave one of the most-often watched TED talks on vulnerability (www.ted.com/talks/brene_brown_on_vulnerability). Her style is popular and her books read more like self-help tomes, but her themes are supported with research and are incredibly insightful.

Williams, N and Penman, D (2011) *Mindfulness: A Practical Guide to Finding Peace in a Frenetic World*. London: Hatchette.

Probably the most popular book on mindfulness, it follows the same eight-week structure as many courses and provides an easy-to-follow pattern for the MBSR techniques. It also includes a CD with guided meditations.

REFERENCES

Beltman, S, Mansfield, C and Price, A (2011) Thriving not just surviving: a review of research on teacher resilience. *Educational Research Review*, 6: 185–207.

Cosgrove, J (2002) *Breakdown: The Facts About Stress in Teaching*. London: Taylor & Francis.

Dunn, HL (1961) *High Level Wellness*. RW Beatty Company.

Gu, J, Strauss, C, Bond, R and Cavanagh, K (2015) How do mindfulness-based cognitive therapy and mindfulness-based stress reduction improve mental health and wellbeing? A systematic review and meta-analysis of mediation studies. *Clinical Psychology Review*, 37.

Klusman, U, Kunter, M, Trautwein, U, Ludtke, O and Baumert, J (2008) Teachers' occupational well-being and quality of instruction: the important role of self-regulatory patterns. *Journal of Educational Psychology*,100(3): 702–5.

Kyriacou, C (2000) *Stress-busting for Teachers*. Cheltenham: Stanley Thornes.

Maslow, AH (1943) A Theory of Human Motivation. *Psychological Review*, July, 50(4): 370–96.

Precey, M (2015) Teacher stress levels in England 'soaring' data shows. *BBC News*, 17 March. Available at: www.bbc.co.uk/news/education-31921457 (accessed 16 December 2016).

Roeser, RW, Skinner, E, Beers, J and Jennings, PA (2012) Mindfulness training and teachers' professional development: an emerging area of research and practice. *Child Development Perspectives*, 6(2): pp167–73.

Tschannen-Moran, M and Hoy, AW (2007) The differential antecedents of self-efficacy beliefs of novice and experienced teachers. *Teaching and Teacher Education*, 23(6): 944–56.

Whitaker, RC, Dearth-Wesley, T and Gooze, RA (2015) Workplace stress and the quality of teacher–children relationships in Head Start. *Early Childhood Research Quarterly*, 30: 57–69.

CONCLUSION

Teaching is both a demanding and highly rewarding profession. Too often, teachers who have the potential to make a positive difference to children's lives are lost to the profession because they become overwhelmed by the challenges they face in their early careers. We hope the ideas and guidance provided in this book offer solutions to some of the problems new teachers face. If our attempts to show strategies for overcoming challenges help you to develop as a confident and competent educator, our efforts will have been worthwhile.

Wendy Jolliffe
David Waugh
May 2017

INDEX

Index

Index

Index